Exploring Time as a Resource for Wellness in Higher Education

Bringing together international perspectives, this book demonstrates the importance of reframing time in higher education and how we can view it as a resource to support wellbeing and self-care.

Time is a central part of our lives and structures our days, and yet often we don't think about the socially constructed nature of time or how we might reframe our relationship with time and our work in ways that support our self-care and wellbeing. *Exploring Time as a Resource for Wellness in Higher Education* suggests an alternative way to look at how we structure our time to better support our wellbeing. Drawing on a range of theoretical and personal perspectives, the authors advocate for a reconsideration and reconceptualization of our relationship with time. By sharing their experiences, the authors encourage readers to notice how they spend their time and offer strategies for an intentional focus on the relationship between time, self-care, and wellbeing. Whether it's making time, having time, or investing in time, this book explores strategies and reflections necessary to grow, maintain, and protect wellbeing.

This book is a valuable resource for those working in higher education, offering individual, collective, and systemic suggestions and strategies for navigating the ways we see time and wellbeing.

Sharon McDonough is an Associate Professor in Teacher Education at Federation University Australia in Ballarat, Australia. Sharon is a qualitative and creative methods specialist, and her research expertise focuses on the field of wellbeing and resilience in teacher education, higher education, and community settings.

Narelle Lemon, Vice Chancellor Professoriate Research Fellow at Edith Cowan University in Perth, Australia, is an interdisciplinary scholar specializing in arts, education, and positive psychology. Her research focuses on enhancing wellbeing literacy in K-12 schools, teacher education, higher education, and community settings, emphasizing evidence-based practices for proactive flourishing.

Wellbeing and Self-care in Higher Education
Editor: Narelle Lemon

Women Practicing Resilience, Self-care and Wellbeing in Academia
International Stories from Lived Experience
Edited by Ida Fatimawati Adi Badiozaman, Voon Mung Ling and Kiran Sandhu

Writing Well and Being Well for Your PhD and Beyond
How to Cultivate a Strong and Sustainable Writing Practice for Life
Katherine Firth

Prioritising Wellbeing and Self-Care in Higher Education
How We Can Do Things Differently to Disrupt Silence
Edited by Narelle Lemon

Navigating Tensions and Transitions in Higher Education
Effective Skills for Maintaining Wellbeing and Self-care
Edited by Kay Hammond and Narelle Lemon

Exploring Time as a Resource for Wellness in Higher Education
Identity, Self-care and Wellbeing at Work
Edited by Sharon McDonough and Narelle Lemon

Passion and Purpose in the Humanities
Exploring the Worlds of Early Career Researchers
Edited by Marcus Bussey, Camila Mozzini-Alister, Bingxin Wang and Samantha Willcocks

Sustaining Your Wellbeing in Higher Education
Values-based Self-Care for Work and Life
Jorden A. Cummings

For more information about this series, please visit: www.routledge.com/Wellbeing-and-Self-care-in-Higher-Education/book-series/WSCHE

Exploring Time as a Resource for Wellness in Higher Education

Identity, Self-care and Wellbeing at Work

**Edited by
Sharon McDonough and Narelle Lemon**

LONDON AND NEW YORK

Designed cover image: © Getty Images

First edition published 2025
by Routledge
4 Park Square, Milton Park, Abingdon, Oxon, OX14 4RN

and by Routledge
605 Third Avenue, New York, NY 10158

Routledge is an imprint of the Taylor & Francis Group, an informa business

© 2025 selection and editorial matter, Sharon McDonough and
Narelle Lemon; individual chapters, the contributors

The right of Sharon McDonough and Narelle Lemon to be identified as
the authors of the editorial material, and of the authors for their individual
chapters, has been asserted in accordance with sections 77 and 78 of the
Copyright, Designs and Patents Act 1988.

All rights reserved. No part of this book may be reprinted or reproduced or
utilised in any form or by any electronic, mechanical, or other means, now
known or hereafter invented, including photocopying and recording, or in
any information storage or retrieval system, without permission in writing
from the publishers.

Trademark notice: Product or corporate names may be trademarks or
registered trademarks, and are used only for identification and explanation
without intent to infringe.

British Library Cataloguing-in-Publication Data
A catalogue record for this book is available from the British Library

ISBN: 978-1-032-68862-6 (hbk)
ISBN: 978-1-032-68861-9 (pbk)
ISBN: 978-1-032-68863-3 (ebk)

DOI: 10.4324/9781032688633

Typeset in Times New Roman
by codeMantra

Contents

List of Figures	*ix*
List of Tables	*xi*
Notes on Contributors	*xiii*
International Reviewers	*xvii*
Series Preface	*xix*

1 Reconceptualising Our Relationship with Time to Enhance Self-care and Wellbeing in Higher Education — 1

SHARON McDONOUGH AND NARELLE LEMON

PART 1
Identity Takes Time to Rethink — 13

Opening poem: Navigating Academia's Labyrinth: Time, Identity, and Wellbeing — 14

NARELLE LEMON

2 Reclaiming Embodiment of My Academic Time through Yoga Practice — 15

AMY WALKER

3 Moving Abroad to Work in Higher Education, in a Different Language, as a Constructive Disruption — 25

ÉRIC BEL AND JOHANNA TOMCZAK

4 Time Keeps on Slippin', Slipping: Oldlings Holding on, and onto the Embodied Self — 34

FELICITY MOLLOY

5 Not Quite a Professor: Professional Identity, Self-care, and Time Management as an Atypical Academic — 46

CAROL-ANNE GAUTHIER

vi *Contents*

PART 2
Intensification and Care 57

Opening poem: Echoes of Academia: Time, Care, and
Collective Wellbeing 58
NARELLE LEMON

6 The Work of Wellbeing: Making Time and Creating Space in
Academia 59
ANGELA W. WEBB AND MELANIE SHOFFNER

7 Fire and Focus: The Decision of Which Flames to Fan in
Higher Education 68
DESTINI BRAXTON

8 Fighting Dragons with Contemplative Practices: A Hero's
Journey in Higher Education through Time and Self-Care 77
MELANIE REAVES

9 Time Allocation and Job Satisfaction for Women Academics:
Lessons Learned from the Pandemic 89
ASLI ERMIŞ MERT AND ELIF YILMAZ

10 Interstate Dialogues: Chronicles of Rhythms of Time and the
Art of Self-care of a Mobile Academic 102
NARELLE LEMON AND SHARON McDONOUGH

PART 3
Time Investing in Self 115

Opening poem: Embracing Balance: Nurturing Academia's Soul 116
NARELLE LEMON

11 In and out of Time: Practising Self-care When Leaving and
Re-entering Higher Education 117
CHARLOTTE BILBY

12 Overwork Is Not Evidence of Passion 128
NICOLE MELZACK

Contents vii

13 Deep Dive on Boundary Setting: Time for Maintaining and Thriving 138

MANDY DHAHAN

14 Self-care: A Guilty Pleasure or Required Academic Work? 149

DANGENI

Appendix: Titles in the Wellbeing and Self-care in Higher Education series *159*
Index *163*

Figures

2.1	My yoga mat as a space to challenge narratives of time	15
3.1	Timeline of wellbeing and alignment when moving from one part of the world to another, to work in Higher Education	26
4.1	The Borromean rings: Academic women's experience shifting in their transitional time	37
5.1	Piecing together multiple identities, statuses, and workplaces as an atypical academic is a challenge, but through job crafting, I've managed to make it work	46
6.1	An office respite	61
7.1	A mother balancing her many roles and practicing self-care	69
8.1	My hero's journey (adapted from Herosjourney.svg)	79
9.1	Reflections on wellbeing, self-care, work-life balance, and job satisfaction during the pandemic	89
10.1	Instagram post juxtaposed with a poetic response from Narelle	107
11.1	Three mixed-media, hand-crafted items: two envelopes and a badge. Made with hand and machine embroidery	118
12.1	Non-exhaustive examples of practical, personal, contractual, and cultural overwork	129
13.1	Flourishing Tucson Saguaros, as photographed by M. Dhahan	138
14.1	Rivers of wellbeing	155

Tables

7.1	Individual and collective strategies to promote focus and balance	74
9.1	Multiple regression model predicting women's job satisfaction levels based on components related to workload and other relevant components (for all women academics in the dataset)	94
9.2	Multiple regression model predicting women's job satisfaction levels based on components related to workload and other relevant components (for those who reported increased time spent on housework and/or care responsibilities in relation to the pandemic)	95
12.1	Reflection questions	136

Notes on Contributors

Dr Éric Bel is a principal lecturer in Education and associate professor in Learning and Teaching at Teesside University (United Kingdom) and a fellow of Advance HE. Having moved to the United Kingdom in the mid-1980s, Éric joined the then Teesside Polytechnic as a French lecturer and, a few years later, became head of the language centre in the same institution. In the past twenty years, Éric has worked in various areas of education. For example, he has held the position of Postgraduate Certificate in Learning and Teaching in Higher Education course leader, of BA in TESOL course leader, and of module leader at undergraduate and postgraduate levels. He has supervised the work of undergraduate, Master's, and PhD students. The focus of his own PhD was about language teachers and digital technology, and his main academic interests are language learning and teaching, internationalization of learning and teaching, as well as post-compulsory teacher training.

Charlotte Bilby is a transdisciplinary researcher based at Northumbria University, United Kingdom, who started her career as a criminologist evaluating the impact of cognitive behavioural programmes on offending behaviour. Her attention turned to the roles that making, creativity, and alternative activities – sewing, painting, crafting, and creative writing – have in criminal justice systems. From a criminological perspective, she considers the impact that doing something creative might have on personal identities and wellbeing, community, and family relationships, which may lead to desistance from crime. Charlotte now contributes to research in participatory craft and textile making and research-through-making methods, considering the aesthetics of harm and care in places of punishment and rehabilitation and their links to timespace. She works primarily with groups of people who experience harm.

Destini Braxton is a fifth-year K-12 special education mathematics teacher, a part-time fourth-year PhD student in the Education Psychology programme at Virginia Commonwealth University (VCU), and a full-time mother of two toddler boys. Currently, Destini serves as the lab co-manager for the Motivation in Context Lab and a graduate research assistant for the Multilingual Learners in Schools Lab. Her research examines how teacher-student relationships impact marginalized students' motivational beliefs, emotions, feedback experience, and trust in teachers within

xiv *Notes on Contributors*

STEM classrooms, while positively addressing the overrepresentation of Black and Latinx students with learning disabilities. Advocating for her students and her own children drives her passion to raise awareness for the need for equitable social and academic changes in education through her research. Teaching, raising children, and bridging the gap between research and practice forces her to constantly "fan fires," adjust her focus, and rearrange her priorities to maintain peace.

Dangeni (BA, MSc, PhD) is a professional development advisor in the Learning and Teaching Development Department at Newcastle University, UK, where her teaching and research focus broadly on teaching and learning provision in the wider context of the internationalization of higher education. She is particularly interested in research and practice relating to international student access, engagement and success in postgraduate taught (PGT), and postgraduate research (PGR) environments. Her recent projects have explored a variety of aspects of the transitions and experiences of international doctoral researchers at UK universities, including pre-application communications, setting and adjusting experiences of supervisions, conceptual enquiry into communities of practices as praxis in international doctoral education, and hidden curriculum in doctoral education.

Mandy Dhahan is a first-generation Asian Pacific Islander, American female person of colour. A deep trauma survivor, who did not give up, she transmuted her experiences to serve others, as someone who is still doing the work, who empathizes with pain and suffering while making room for joy and resilience. Honouring her intersectional identities and cultural belongingness, she had education serve as her saving grace which led her down a path in which she was the first in her family to go to college, carrying the weight of not only her dreams, but all of her ancestors behind her. Her passion for higher education helped her serve others and support many students who faced similar challenges as she has. She has a Bachelor of Arts in Communication from San Francisco State University and Master of Arts in Counselling, with an emphasis on school counselling from San Jose State University.

Aslı Ermiş Mert received her MSc and DPhil degrees in Sociology from the University of Oxford. Her research mainly focuses on gender, employment, quantitative social research methods, and happiness studies. She worked in various national and international research projects that focus on gender inequalities in society and particularly academia.

Carol-Anne Gauthier, PhD, holds a Bachelor's in psychology and a doctorate in industrial relations. She teaches and conducts research at Champlain Regional College – St. Lawrence campus and Université Laval in Québec City, Canada. Her teaching activities revolve around a variety of subfields of psychology (mental health, social psychology, positive psychology), management, work and employment, and qualitative research methods. Her research interests include meaningful work, remote work, mental health at work, mental health self-management and equality, diversity, and inclusion.

Notes on Contributors xv

Nicole Melzack graduated in 2014 with an MEng in Space Systems Engineering and spent six years working in the space industry. They began their PhD at The University of Southampton in September 2020, focussing on the development of sustainable batteries. Nicole is autistic and lives with dissociative identity disorder, along with chronic migraine and nerve damage which presents challenges in their day-to-day life. They are a strong advocate for EDI, part of the team for Disabled Empowerment in Higher Education Month, and run a mental health non-profit – blink mental health.

Dr Felicity Molloy (PhD I MEd I GDHE) is an independent scholar moving seamlessly between academia and experiential practices that extend research and teaching for somatics, dance, yoga, and bodywork and a dancer with renowned Limbs Dance Company before becoming an independent dance professional. Founding tertiary educator at Unitec, AUT, and University of Auckland, Felicity is experienced in programme development bringing practice-based movement, wellbeing approaches to a range of communities. Her doctoral thesis in Critical Education, Fit To Teach: Tracing Embodied Methodologies Of Dancers Who Come To Academia, was completed in 2017. Since 2009, Felicity has been researching benefits of older adults' dance and was Research Officer for the AUT/SPARC project, Can Dancing Improve Physical Activity Levels, Functional Ability and Reduce Falls in Older Adults? Designing Dance Mobility™, a method for teaching older adults, culminating in a co-authored international article and conference presentations, including one where Felicity presented at the World Congress of Physical Therapy (WCPT, 2019) in Geneva, Switzerland.

Melanie Reaves, after teaching in elementary settings for about 15 years, earned a doctoral degree from the University of Wyoming in Curriculum and Instruction with emphases on literacy education and qualitative research. She is a tenured associate professor of Literacy Education and Department Chair at Montana State University Billings. Her research focuses broadly on language/literacy and sociocultural processes within learning and teaching. In this line of study, she has studied affective investments as language and literacy learning scaffolds; learning as embodied social and multimodal practice; interest-based, purpose-driven learning and responsive teaching; social creed and cultural intersections within teaching and learning; and supporting critical thinking through creative reflection and talk. Methodologically her work is situated within post-qualitative approaches in which she seeks to open up the structure of qualitative inquiry while maintaining the use of vigorous research methods. Most recently, this quest has led to arts-based education research (ABER) methods in which she is exploring creative modes of reflection for personal and professional growth.

Melanie Shoffner is a professor of English education at James Madison University (Harrisonburg, Virginia, USA). She is the editor of *English Education*, the flagship journal of the professional organization English Language Arts Teacher Educators (ELATE), and a former Fulbright Scholar at Babeş-Bolyai University xvi *Notes on Contributors*

(Romania). She also serves on the advisory board for International Federation for the Teaching of English (IFTE). Dr. Shoffner's publications and presentations focus on the development of preservice ELA teachers and the use of reflective practice in teacher education, with recent work exploring care and emotion within the context of the COVID pandemic. Recent publications include the co-edited book *Reconstructing Care in Teacher Education after COVID-19: Caring Enough to Change* (Routledge), a co-written chapter in *International Perspectives on English Teacher Development: From Initial Teacher Education to Highly Accomplished Professional*, and a co-written commentary in *Teachers College Record*.

Dr Johanna Tomczak recently completed her PhD in Cognitive Psychology at the University of Leeds (United Kingdom). Interested in pedagogy, she is an associate fellow of Advance HE and she facilitated seminars for undergraduate students in Psychology for the entire duration of her PhD. Having lived in four different countries and studied in three of them, Johanna has a good understanding of different Higher Education contexts and what it means to learn and live abroad. Since finishing her PhD, she has moved on to a support role for other researchers in the behavioural sciences at Gorilla Experiment Builder.

Amy Walker is an early career researcher currently employed as a lecturer in Secondary Education at Federation University Australia. Prior to taking on this role, Amy worked as a sessional lecturer while completing her PhD. Amy has also lectured in the English for Academic Purposes (EAP) programme. Prior to her roles at Federation University, Amy taught English in secondary school. She also has previous working experience as a community journalist and technical writer.

Angela W. Webb is an associate professor of Science Education at James Madison University (Harrisonburg, VA, USA). Her scholarship focuses on the education and early career development of science teachers, with specific attention to science teacher identity; her recent work additionally explores care and caring practices in working with preservice and induction teachers within the context of COVID-19. Dr. Webb is the co-editor of the *Journal of Virginia Science Education*, the professional publication of the Virginia Association of Science Teachers, and an editorial review board member of the journal *Innovations in Science Teacher Education*. Her recent publications include the co-edited book *Reconstructing Care in Teacher Education after COVID-19: Caring Enough to Change* (Routledge), a co-written chapter in *Equity in STEM Education Research: Advocating for Equitable Attention*, and a co-written commentary in *Teachers College Record*.

Elif Yılmaz graduated from Istanbul Bilgi University, Sociology Department. She completed Master's degree in Comparative Studies in History and Society programme at Koç University. Her research interests include cultural anthropology, gender, and wellbeing studies. Currently, she is a people and culture professional.

International Reviewers

Ines Alves, University of Glasgow, Scotland, UK
Sarah Barradell, Swinburne University of Technology
Éric Bel, Teesside University, United Kingdom
Lauren Black, University of Auckland, New Zealand
Destini Braxton, Virginia Commonwealth University, Richmond, VA, USA
Shaun Britton, Swinburne University of Technology, Melbourne, Australia
Emily Brownell, University of Manitoba, Manitoba, Canada
Hera J. M. Casidsid, University of Manitoba, Manitoba, Canada
Urmee Chakma, La Trobe University, Melbourne, Australia
Bertha Chin, Swinburne University of Technology, Sarawak
Timothy Clark, University of the West of England, Bristol, United Kingdom
Nyla Comeau, University of Manitoba, Manitoba, Canada
Catelijne Coopmans, Independent scholar, Girona, Spain
Dangeni, Newcastle University, UK
Mandy Dhahan, University of Arizona, Tucson, Arizona
Aine Dolin, University of Saskatchewan, CA
Anita Durksen, University of Manitoba, Manitoba, Canada
Bronwyn Eager, The University of Tasmania, Australia
Dely Lazarte Elliot, University of Glasgow, Scotland, UK
Jennifer E Enns, University of Manitoba, Manitoba, Canada
Aslı Ermiş-Mert, Koç University, Turkey
Zyra Evangelista, University of Glasgow, Scotland, UK
Tracy Fortune, La Trobe University
Akiko Fujii, International Christian University, Tokyo, Japan
Jeanette Fyffe, La Trobe University and Deakin University
Louise Grimmer, University of Tasmania, Tasmania, Australia
Kay Hammond, Auckland University of Technology, New Zealand
Lauren Hansen, Deakin University, Burwood, Australia
Chiyo Hayashi, International Christian University, Tokyo, Japan
Catherine Hill, Te Herenga Waka Victoria University of Wellington, New Zealand
Mikayla Hunter, University of Manitoba, Manitoba, Canada
Miriam Jaehn, Centre for Southeast Asian Studies, Kyoto University, Japan
Imene Zoulikha Kassous, University of Glasgow, Scotland, UK

xviii *International Reviewers*

Yoko Kobayashi, International Christian University, Tokyo, Japan
Narelle Lemon, Edith Cowan University, Perth Australia
Catherine Lido, University of Glasgow, Scotland, UK
Yuqi Lin, The University of Melbourne, Australia
Chris Little, Manchester Metropolitan University, Manchester, United Kingdom
Kirsten Locke, University of Auckland, New Zealand
Patricia Lucas, Auckland University of Technology, Auckland, New Zealand
Danni McCarthy, Deakin University, Burwood, Australia
Katrina McChesney, University of Waikato, Tauranga, New Zealand
Sharon McDonough, Federation University, Ballarat, Victoria, Australia
Megan McPherson, The University of Melbourne, Australia
Nicole Melzack, University of Southampton, United Kingdom
Felicity Molloy, Independent Scholar, New Zealand
Rahmila Murtiana, Swinburne University of Technology, Melbourne, Australia
Alla Al Najim, University of Glasgow, Scotland, UK
Linda Noble, Brooklyn College, New York, United States of America
Julia Ouzia, King's College London, London, United Kingdom
Stephaney Patrick, University of Manitoba, Manitoba, Canada
Thinh Ngoc Pham· Solent University, UK
Jamie Pfau, University of Manitoba, Manitoba, Canada
Malgorzata Powietrzynska, Brooklyn College, New York, United States of America
Meenal Rai, Auckland University of Technology, Auckland, New Zealand
Melanie Reaves, Montana State University Billings in Billings, Montana
Raine Melissa Riman, Swinburne University of Technology, Sarawak, Malaysia
  Borneo
Iona Burnell Reilly, University of East London, UK
Emily Rooney, University of Toledo, Toledo, Ohio, United States of America
Estrella Sendra, King's College London, London, United Kingdom
Melanie Shoffner, James Madison University (Harrisonburg, VA, USA)
Linus Tan, Swinburne University of Technology, Melbourne, Australia
Johanna Tomczak, Independent Scholar, United Kingdom
Yao Wang, Newcastle University, UK
Izumi Watenabe-Kim, International Christian University, Tokyo, Japan
Angela W. Webb, James Madison University (Harrisonburg, VA, USA)
Minoli Wijetunga, Monash University, Melbourne, Australia
Yue Xu, Monash University, Australia
Sunyee Yip, La Trobe University, Melbourne, Australia
Sharon Zumbrunn, Virginia Commonwealth University, Richmond, VA, USA

Series Preface

As academics, scholars, staff, and colleagues working in the context of universities in the contemporary climate, we are often challenged with where we place our own wellbeing. It is not uncommon to hear about burnout, stress, anxiety, pressures with workload, having too many balls in the air, toxic cultures, increasing demands, isolation, and feeling distressed (Berg and Seeber, 2016; Lemon & McDonough, 2018; Mountz et al., 2015). The reality is that universities are stressful places (Beer et al., 2015; Cranton & Taylor, 2012; Kasworm & Bowles, 2012; Mountz et al., 2015; Ryan, 2013; Sullivan & Weissner, 2010; Wang & Cranton, 2012). McNaughton and Billot (2016) argue that the "deeply personal effects of changing roles, expectations and demands" (p. 646) have been downplayed and that academics and staff engage in constant reconstruction of their identities and work practices. It is important to acknowledge this, as much as it is to acknowledge the need to place wellbeing and self-care at the forefront of these lived experiences and situations.

Wellbeing can be approached at multiple levels, including micro and macro. In placing wellbeing at the heart of the higher education workplace, self-care becomes an imperative both individually and systemically (Berg & Seeber, 2016; Lemon & McDonough, 2018). Self-care is most commonly oriented towards individual action to monitor and ensure personal wellbeing; however, it is also a collective act. There is a plethora of different terms that are in action to describe how one approaches their wellbeing holistically (Godfrey et al., 2011). With different terminology comes different ways self-care is understood. For this collection, self-care is understood as "the actions that individuals take for themselves, on behalf of and with others in order to develop, protect, maintain and improve their health, wellbeing or wellness" (Self Care Forum, 2019, para. 1). It covers a spectrum of health-related (emotional, physical, and/or spiritual) actions, including prevention, promotion, and treatment, while aiming to encourage individuals to take personal responsibility for their health and to advocate for themselves and others in accessing resources and care (Knapik & Laverty, 2018). Self-love, -compassion, -awareness, and - regulation are significant elements of self-care. But what does this look like for those working in higher education? In this book series, authors respond to the questions: *What do you do for self-care? How do you position wellbeing as part of your role in academia?*

xx *Series Preface*

In thinking about these questions, authors are invited to critically discuss and respond to inspiration sparked by one or more of the questions of:

- How do we bring self-regulation to how we approach our work?
- How do we create a compassionate workplace in academia?
- What does it mean for our work when we are aware and enact self-compassion?
- What awareness has occurred that has disrupted the way we approach work?
- Where do mindful intentions sit?
- How do we shift the rhetoric of "this is how it has always been" in relation to over working, and indiscretions between workload and approaches to workload?
- How do we counteract the traditional narrative of over work?
- How do we create and sustain a healthier approach?
- How can we empower the "I" and "we" as we navigate self-care as a part of who we are as academics?
- How can we promote a curiosity about how we approach self-care?
- What changes do we need to make?
- How can we approach self-care with energy and promote shifts in how we work individually, collectively, and systemically?

The purpose of this book series is to:

- Place academic wellbeing and self-care at the heart of discussions around working in higher education.
- Provide a diverse range of strategies for how to put in place wellbeing and self-care approaches as an academic.
- Provide a narrative connection point for readers from a variety of backgrounds in academia.
- Highlight lived experiences and honour the voice of those working in higher education.
- Provide a visual narrative that supports connection to authors' lived experience(s).
- Contribute to the conversation on ways that wellbeing and self-care can be positioned in the work that those working in higher education do.
- Highlight new ways of working in higher education that disrupt current tensions that neglect wellbeing.

References

Beer, L.E., Rodriguez, K., Taylor, C., Martinez-Jones, N., Griffin, J., Smith, T.R., Lamar, M., & Anaya, R. (2015). Awareness, integration and interconnectedness. *Journal of Transformative Education, 13*(2), 161–185.

Berg, M., & Seeber, B.K. (2016). *The slow professor: Challenging the culture of speed in the academy.* University of Toronto Press.

Cranton, P., & Taylor, E.W. (2012). Transformative learning theory: Seeking a more unified theory. In E. W. Taylor & P. Cranton (Eds.), *The handbook of transformative learning* (pp. 3–20). Jossey-Bass.

Godfrey, C.M., Harrison, M.B., Lysaght, R., Lamb, M., Graham, I.D., & Oakley, P. (2011). The experience of self-care: A systematic review. *JBI Library of Systematic Reviews, 8*(34), 1351–1460. Retrieved from http://www.ncbi.nlm.nih.gov/pubmed/27819888

Lemon, N., & McDonough, S. (Eds.). (2018). *Mindfulness in the academy: Practices and perspectives from scholars*. Springer.

Kasworm, C., & Bowles, T. (2012). Fostering transformative learning in higher education settings. In E. Taylor & P. Cranton (Eds.), *The handbook of transformative learning* (pp. 388–407). Sage.

Knapik, K., & Laverty, A. (2018). Self-care Individual, relational, and political sensibilities. In M. A. Henning, C. U. Krägeloh, R. Dryer, F. Moir, D. R. Billington, & A. G. Hill (Eds.), *Wellbeing in higher education: Cultivating a healthy lifestyle among faculty and students* (pp. 113–118). Routledge.

McNaughton, S. M., & Billot, J. (2016). Negotiating academic teacher identity shifts during higher education contextual change. *Teaching in Higher Education, 21*(6), 644–658.

Mountz, A., Bonds, A., Mansfield, B., Loyd, J., Hyndman, J., & Watton-Roberts, M. (2015). For slow scholarship: A feminist politics of resistance through collective action in the neoliberal university. *ACME: An International E-Journal of Critical Geographies, 14*(4), 1235–1259.

Ryan, M. (2013). The pedagogical balancing act: Teaching reflection in higher education. *Teaching in Higher Education, 18*, 144–155.

Self Care Forum. (2019). Self care forum: Home. Retrieved July 27, 2019, from http://www.selfcareforum.org/

Sullivan, L. G., & Weissner, C. A. (2010). Learning to be reflective leaders: A case study from the NCCHC Hispanic leadership fellows program. In D. L. Wallin (Ed.), Special issue: *Leadership in an era of change. New directions for community colleges*, No. 149 (pp. 41–50). Jossey-Bass.

Wang, V. C., & Cranton, P. (2012). Promoting and implementing self-directed learning (SDL): An effective adult education model. *International Journal of Adult Vocational Education and Technology, 3*, 16–25.

1 Reconceptualising Our Relationship with Time to Enhance Self-care and Wellbeing in Higher Education

Sharon McDonough and Narelle Lemon

Introduction

As academics, we have both faced the challenge of how to think and work with time in relation to our academic work and in ways that will support our wellbeing. We know all too well the pressure of deadlines, of juggling multiple roles and responsibilities, and this has prompted us to think mindfully about our own self-care and wellbeing practices. This feeling of there *never being enough time* seems pervasive for colleagues in higher education and in society more broadly. Being busy and having a lack of time appear as the markers of normality for what it means to be living and working in contemporary society. By bemoaning our lack of time, by living our life by clocks and calendars, and by always considering our relationship with time as a deficit, what are we missing though? What other ways are there to consider our relationship with time, with our selves, and our wellbeing? In addressing time as an under-examined concept in higher education (Bennett & Burke, 2018; Gibbs et al., 2014), this volume *Exploring Time as a Resource for Wellness in Higher Education: Identity, Self-care and Wellbeing at Wor*k explores the ways that those working in higher education understand and enact notions of time in ways that support their self-care and wellbeing. In doing so, it enables us to reconsider our relationship and practices with time and provides the opportunity to develop a conversation about how these reconceptualisations might support our individual and collective wellbeing and self-care practices. Through considering how traditional framings of time may exacerbate injustice and oppression within systems such as higher education, it seeks to provide both an opportunity to reflect on how time impacts self-care and wellbeing, and a set of practical strategies for those working in higher education to enact. It is worth noting that while we refer to time as a resource in the title of this volume we do so in order to provoke conversation about the nature of time and our relationship to it. Rather than viewing time as a resource that we might use or 'hack' in order to become more productive, we position it as a resource that enables us to reconsider and reframe our understanding of it as a concept, and our relationship with it. In this way, we see it functioning as a resource for us to contemplate different ways to approach time in relation to our self-care and wellbeing.

DOI: 10.4324/9781032688633-1

Visual Narratives and This Volume

This volume is part of an ongoing series titled *Wellbeing and Self-Care in Higher Education: Embracing Positive Solutions*. Each volume includes chapters that incorporate a visual narrative which may be in the form of photo, sketch, illustration, artwork and which is accompanied by narrative text that invites you into the authors' experiences and understandings of self-care and wellbeing in association to time. We invite you to connect with the visual narratives, the exploration of time, and the strategies and provocations that authors have included to consider self-care and wellbeing.

One of the features of this volume is also the inclusion of a poem to introduce each section of the text. Narelle Lemon has crafted a series of poems that connect to the chapters and to our questions about time, academic work, and wellbeing. Each section commences with one of Narelle's poems, with the poem acting as an invitation to the work that is to follow.

Considering Time: What Are We Missing?

When we consider our relationship with time, it is easy to forget that time has a philosophical, cultural, economic, and social basis, with Oddell (2023) arguing that we rarely consider these elements, commenting that "Ironically, there never seems to be enough time to do something as idle as contemplate the very nature of time" (p. xiii). Rather, and particularly in the Western world, our language and approach to time is framed by conceptions of time "that arose with industrialism and colonialism" (Oddell, 2023, p. xvii). These linear and sequential conceptions of time are associated with the notion of time as money and with a requirement for time to be spent 'productively'. The proliferation of understandings of time as linear that are framed by the language of economics silences the fact that time is "contextual, subjective and relational and tied to value judgements and power relations" (Bennett & Burke, 2018, p. 920). They also silence the rich, deep understandings of Indigenous and First Nations peoples who understand time as cyclical and non-linear. It is beyond the scope of this chapter to explore these understandings, and as white cis women who are still engaging in our own process of learning about these perspectives, we encourage readers to engage with works and explorations on time by Indigenous and First Nations writers to gain a deeper appreciation of these understandings.

As academics working within the higher education context, we focus our discussion on conceptualisations of time primarily within the higher education landscape and examine the ways that understandings of time manifest in the structures and systems of higher education. Bennett and Burke (2018) describe higher education as a 'timescape', "in which participants manage their own and others' time according to normative frameworks" (p. 914). Through conceptualising time in this way they see time as being structured by institutions and subject to power relations and social and cultural constructions. They argue that not being able to meet deadlines within a dominant timescape does not mean that people are lacking ability or commitment but rather they should be "understood as occupying a different 'space-time' or 'timescape' that is tied to socio-cultural positioning and context" (p. 914). Based on this notion Bennett and Burke (2016) highlight the way that time management strategies cannot remove the power relations and social-cultural contexts that exist. We see this as vital, and while those working in higher education might exist in the same institutional timescape, our experiences of that timescape are vastly different, something which is highlighted within the chapters in this volume.

Academic workers describe experiencing a lack of time (Berg & Seeber, 2016; Davies & Bansel, 2005; O'Dwyer et al., 2018; Osbaldiston et al., 2019, Ylijoki & Mäntylä, 2003), with Osbaldiston et al. (2019) arguing that time pressure on academics is a consequence of ongoing neoliberal policies and practices, that are then internalised and carried out by academics themselves. They describe two characteristics of time use by academics, the first is that of instrumental time where academics engage in activities that are required by their roles – work such as teaching, administration, service, and grant writing (Osbaldiston et al., 2019). In contrast is the concept of substantive time, which is framed as a more enjoyable way to spend academic time by engaging in practices such as writing, reading, and time for thinking. The distinction between having time to think and that which is blocked with obligations is also reflected in Ylijoki and Mäntylä's (2003) characterisation of scheduled and timeless time. As the nomenclature suggests, scheduled time is that which consists of the obligations associated with academic work, where 'timeless' time is an "internally motivated use of time in which clock time loses its significance" (Ylijoki & Mäntylä, 2003, p. 62). In their study, academics described timeless time as being associated with research, writing, reading, and thinking. Having time for thinking and contemplation can seem like a luxury however, with Lash (2001) arguing there is "no time for reflection, and scarce dedicated space as we compose messages in trains, on planes and read our email on mobile phones" (p. 111). As we consider the nature of time and the ways that neoliberal systems and structures in higher education frame much of academic time into scheduled blocks with accompanying outcomes, we wonder about what we are missing in having time for thinking, for contemplation, and for reflection. When we sacrifice 'non-productive' time, we also sacrifice the opportunity for serendipitous ideas and conversations, for communication, and for connection, for all the things that make us more fully human. We become agents of the neoliberal agenda rather than our own agentic selves. As noted by Bennett and Burke (2018), we also risk replicating dominant understandings of time that can marginalise those from diverse social, cultural, and educational backgrounds, and those with caring and personal responsibilities. When we consider the literature on time, we see the acknowledgement of the ways that academics characterise their time, the pressures they feel in relation to time, the way that institutions can perpetuate injustices, and we aim in this volume to provide a contribution to the existing literature by highlighting the ways that academics intentionally conceptualise, use, and enact time as a resource to support self-care and wellbeing.

In recognition of these aspects and of the complexity of ways that experiences of time manifest for individuals across their academic lifespan, we have curated

4 *Sharon McDonough and Narelle Lemon*

this volume into three sections: (1) identity takes time to rethink, (2) intensification and care, (3) time investing in self. Throughout the volume, our authors share their experiences with time in a variety of ways, and as you read, we encourage you to think about how these resonate or differ from your own experiences.

Identity Takes Time to Rethink

The concept of identity in academia has been the subject of much research and discussion in recent years. It is widely accepted that identity formation is a complex process that takes time and is dynamic as individuals engage in a variety of experiences and interactions that shape their understanding of themselves and their place within the academic community (McDonough & Lemon, 2018; Pinnegar, 2005). The process of developing an academic identity and understanding the labour of being an academic is influenced by a range of factors, including personal values and beliefs, social norms, cultural and institutional contexts, and historical and structural inequalities (Cannizzo, 2017; McNaughton & Billot, 2016). The intersection of time with all of these elements is framed by the ways that we consider the notion of time by notions of how long it *should* take to develop one's identity as an academic.

In academia, identity formation often begins with the choice of a field or discipline, which can reflect an individual's interests, values, and experiences. Furthermore, identity formation is closely tied to issues of diversity, equity, and inclusion in higher education. Individuals who belong to marginalised or underrepresented groups may face unique challenges in developing a strong sense of academic identity, due to systemic barriers and biases that limit their opportunities and access to resources (Mountz et al., 2015). Understanding and addressing these issues is critical to promoting the wellbeing of all members of the academic community. Narelle Lemon's poem "Navigating Academia's Labyrinth: Time, Identity and Wellbeing" introduces this section by inviting us to see the ways that our sense of self is shaped by our values and by the experiences we have upon entry to the academy. She highlights the barriers that can exist and which can impact on identity and work before encouraging us to explore our self-care and to share collective actions and solutions moving forward.

In "Reclaiming Embodiment of my Academic Time through Yoga Practice", Amy Walker explores the complex relationship between academic time and the practice of yoga, particularly for early career researchers (ECRs). Walker reflects on her transition from a PhD candidate to a full-time academic and how the rushed notions of academic time contrast with the slower, embodied experiences of yoga. Drawing on her experiences as both an academic and a yoga practitioner, Walker challenges conventional narratives of academic time and emphasises the importance of presence, observation, and community. Through her narrative, she illustrates how embracing yoga principles can help ECRs navigate the pressures of academia, redefine success, and find balance amidst the frenetic pace of academic life. Walker encourages ECRs to view time spent as practice, discover the freedom in failing, attune to the present moment, and seek out supportive communities to navigate the challenges of academic time more effectively.

Identity formation in academia is not a one-time event, but rather a continuous, dynamic process that evolves over time. As individuals move through different stages of their academic careers, they may encounter new challenges and opportunities that require them to adapt and reevaluate their sense of identity. In Carol-Anne Gauther's chapter, the journey of an "atypical academic" is highlighted through a nuanced exploration of professional identity, self-care, and time management within the dynamic realm of academia. Despite possessing a PhD and engaging in research and teaching akin to a professor, Gauthier finds herself navigating the complexities of being "not quite" one. In her reflective narrative, she delves into the challenges of defining her role amidst varying professional identities within the Quebec educational system. Balancing multiple statuses – college teacher, university lecturer, and research professional – she grapples with the ambiguity of her position at academic conferences and in collaborative projects. Yet, amidst the turbulence, she finds solace and resilience through job crafting, self-care practices, and mindful time management. Drawing from her experiences, Gauthier emphasises the importance of prioritising meaningful contributions, protecting one's wellbeing, and advocating for structural changes within academia to foster collective wellbeing. Through her narrative, she invites readers to contemplate their own professional identities and to embrace strategies for navigating the intricate landscape of academic life with grace and resilience.

Often unheard are discussions of transitions, opportunities, or career trajectories in relation to identity and time. In "Time keeps on slippin', slipping: Oldlings holding on, and onto the embodied self", Felicity Molloy explores the overlooked wisdom and wellbeing concerns of ageing women in academia as they transition into retirement. Molloy challenges institutional culture's neglect of embodied experiences, advocating for holistic self-awareness and self-care practices. Highlighting the need for a reflexive methodology, Molloy introduces "Somathodology", drawing from somatic practices like dance, yoga, and massage to integrate embodied experience with wellbeing. Emphasising the importance of time, Molloy urges individuals to navigate transition with resilience and perseverance, engaging in self-reflection and developing a toolkit for self-care. Through embodied practices and self-awareness, Molloy suggests that academic women can reclaim agency and redefine their identities beyond the confines of institutional expectations.

In their chapter, "Moving abroad to work in Higher Education, in a different language, as a constructive disruption", Éric Bel and Johanna Tomczak explore the ways that identity takes time to develop, particularly when one is living and working abroad. They explore their experiences as internationally mobile staff and they argue that there is a paucity of research examining transitions to working in higher education abroad from a wellbeing perspective. They argue that working in higher education abroad, immersed in a new culture and language can be challenging but can also be a constructive disruption that shapes identity in new ways. They advocate for the centring of the emotional, self-care, and wellbeing aspects of such a shift, and for an understanding of the role of time in such identity transitions. Bel and Tomczak contend that planning a self-care strategy is a useful action, and they

6 Sharon McDonough and Narelle Lemon

demonstrate the importance of self-compassion as they give themselves time to the shift. They argue that self-care is associated with controlling pace and time and embracing a slower pace was necessary.

Intensification and Care

The intensification of work practices and care are two interconnected issues in higher education that impact academic work and wellbeing. On one hand, there is an increasing demand on time for productivity, scholarship, teaching, and service within academic institutions, which can lead to a culture of overwork and burnout (Mountz et al., 2015). On the other hand, care of self, others, community, and wellbeing are essential for academic success and happiness, and for the collective wellbeing of higher education communities (Eager, 2021; Lemon, 2023, 2024; Lemon et al., 2023). In the poem that opens this section of the volume "Echoes of Academia: Time, Care and Collective Wellbeing", Narelle Lemon juxtaposes the relentless drumbeat calling for productivity, with a more gentler melody calling for self-care. Her poem describes the ways that we can all break the 'silence' surrounding the intensification of academic work and that by working collectively we can find a path towards individual and collective wellbeing. In this section of the volume, our authors explore the ways that time and care relate to academic work and wellbeing, and they offer thoughtful suggestions and strategies to centre the place of care in our work in academia.

This path towards individual and collective wellbeing seems even more pertinent as the impact of the COVID-19 pandemic and other global events have intensified the emotional work of care placed on and expected of faculty (Shoffner & Webb, 2023). This work remains largely unacknowledged and unvalued by university administration, leading to additional work layered on what is already expected. As a result, there is a need for faculty to attend to their own wellbeing in intentional and deliberate ways. This silencing of the relationship between intensification, care, and wellbeing requires the creation of space and time, and as Webb and Shoffner explore in their chapter "The work of wellbeing: making time and creating space in academia", for holding each other accountable. They argue that time for a caring space is limited in higher education, yet despite this they prioritise making time for personal interactions as a means of making space for their wellbeing. They focus on intentionally engaging in practices that support both their own and their colleagues' wellbeing, and in their chapter, they describe the valuable strategies they employ to create moments and time for reflection and rest that push back against the culture of overwork and productivity.

In their chapter "Time allocation and job satisfaction for women academics: lessons learned from the pandemic", Aslı Ermiş Mert, and Elif Yilmaz consider the impact of the pandemic on time allocation and job satisfaction for women academics in Türkiye. They situate their chapter by describing the impact of the pandemic on their own self-care and drawing on data from 328 women academics they examine the changes in time allocation habits and patterns that emerged during the

Reconceptualising Our Relationship with Time 7

pandemic. They argue that the dynamics of time allocation patterns and academics' level of satisfaction with their job might impact on self-care and they offer a number of recommendations for both personal and structural considerations that might support self-care.

Empirical research reveals that the arduous nature of academic work, which encompasses heavy workloads, prolonged working hours, and an unrelenting need to deliver results, can contribute to a plethora of physiological and psychological challenges (Mountz et al., 2015). In particular, scholarly inquiry has established that academic professionals are prone to elevated levels of stress, anxiety, and burnout, which can have profound effects on their personal and occupational lives. The prevalence of these issues highlights the need for a better understanding of the complexities surrounding the wellbeing of academics. Destini Braxton's chapter "Fire and Focus: The decision of which flames to fan in higher education" explores the way Braxton has mindfully navigated academia as a mother and a scholar in ways that support self-care and wellbeing. Braxton highlights the way that 'intentional attention' has provided a way to align time with needs, values, and commitments in ways that support wellbeing. By sharing the narrative of the multiple roles she has as a mother, researcher, and educator, Braxton highlights the strategies that enable a prioritising of time, tasks, and roles. For those with caring responsibilities, balancing academic work and life can be challenging, but Braxton provides a set of individual and collective strategies that can be used to promote focus and balance in order to avoid negative impacts of burnout and isolation.

In Melanie Reaves' chapter, "Fighting Dragons with contemplative practices – a hero's journey in higher education through time and self-care", Reaves questions what happens when as academics, we do not have the time or the capacity to care. Identifying the toll that caring for students and carrying out service work can take on individual wellbeing, Reaves highlights the turning points that can prompt us to take action to care for self. Reaves describes a set of contemplative practices such as quieting the mind, mindful breathing, mindful walking, and mindful art journaling that function as self-care practices, and concludes the chapter by offering readers two activities to foster time to care for self. Considering the role of time, Reaves, like Braxton and Webb and Shoffner, makes intentional time for self-care using these contemplative practices. This focus and attention on self and wellbeing is not left to chance, it is an intentional act that recognises that without care of self, we cannot extend or foster care of others and care of community.

Care of self and connection to others is at the heart of our chapter "Interstate Dialogues: Chronicles of Rhythms of Time and the Art of Self-Care of a Mobile Academic". As a dialogic exploration of Narelle's shift to a new job in a new state, we explore the way that moving to different timezone and a new role requires shifts in the way we see, understand, and make use of our time. We explore the connection of time to our rhythms and daily habits and through a series of dialogical journal entries, examine how this impacts on self-care and wellbeing. We question what it might be to intentionally give ourselves margin (Bloomfield, 2020) to think, reflect, and be and how we might incorporate this into our calendars and collaborations.

Time Investing in Self

The impact of academia on the wellbeing of individuals has become a growing concern in recent years. This section is introduced by Narelle Lemon's poem "Embracing balance: Nurturing academia's soul" and the poem highlights the ways that heavy academic workloads and job demands can have deleterious impacts on the health and wellbeing of academics. In her poem, Lemon challenges us to see that self-care, respire, nurturing of the soul are not luxuries but rather the necessities needed for wellbeing.

It is evident from the literature that academic work can pose significant challenges to the physical and mental health of individuals in this profession (Mountz et al., 2015). The burden of heavy workloads and the pressure to deliver results can lead to feelings of exhaustion, frustration, and disillusionment. The chapter "Overwork is not evidence of passion" by Nicole Melzack explores the intersection of time management and self-care within the context of higher education, particularly focusing on academia in the UK. Melzack argues that while passion is often touted as a driving force in academia, it is frequently weaponised to justify overwork and exploitation, especially among PhD students and those on casual contracts. The chapter delves into practical and personal manifestations of overwork, highlighting how the culture of academia perpetuates unrealistic expectations and power dynamics that lead to burnout and mental health issues. Through personal anecdotes and research findings, Melzack underscores the importance of reevaluating the role of passion in academia and advocating for systemic changes to support the wellbeing of all individuals within the academic community. The chapter concludes with reflection questions aimed at fostering dialogue and action towards creating a healthier work environment in higher education.

Given the significant impact that academic work can have on individual wellbeing, it is crucial to develop a more comprehensive understanding of the mechanisms that underpin the relationship between the two. The chapter "In and out of time: practising self-care when leaving and re-entering higher education" by Charlotte Bilby explores her journey of leaving a secure lecturing role in academia for a series of part-time jobs, which led to a re-engineering of her sense of identity and relationships with wellbeing and work. Prompted by a question about self-care during a job interview outside academia, Bilby reflects on her past distorted working practices, particularly in relation to her research on working with people in the criminal justice system. The chapter delves into her decision to return to academia in middle age, highlighting the challenges and reflections that led to this choice. Bilby intertwines personal experiences with discussions on time, creativity, imprisonment, transdisciplinary approaches, and self-care, ultimately offering insights into managing boundaries, navigating career transitions, and fostering intellectual joy in research. Through her narrative, Bilby encourages readers to reflect on their own self-care practices and consider the intersection of personal and professional identities in academic settings.

In exploring the often overlooked realm of self-care within academia, Dangeni in this chapter delves into the question of whether self-care should be considered

Reconceptualising Our Relationship with Time 9

a guilty pleasure or a necessary academic practice. Drawing from personal experiences as an international PhD graduate and early career scholar, the chapter highlights the challenges faced by international scholars in developing self-care habits and the benefits of prioritising such habits for overall wellbeing. It emphasises the importance of informal, non-academic habits in nurturing self-care and navigating the demands of academic life. Through reflection on the transformative power of self-care habits, the chapter encourages scholars to embark on their unique self-care journey, prioritising their wellbeing alongside their academic pursuits. It suggests various self-reflection tools, such as visual methods and solicited diaries, to aid individuals in exploring and cultivating their own self-care practices within the academic context.

The chapter "Deep drive on boundary setting: time for maintaining, and thriving" by Mandy K. Dhahan, highlights the relationship between time, self-care, and boundary setting and how strategies can be used to honour and sustain boundaries, particularly for doctoral students of colour in higher education. Dhahan advocates for the ways that boundaries can be used in a higher education context through a lens of intersectionality that centres compassion. She argues that the use of Relational-Cultural Theory can support the building of safe spaces and address feelings of isolation. Dhahan offers a framework of collaboration and of community healing and care through mentorship and advocates for the practice of daily self-care. While arguing that time management is common block for many doctoral students, Dhahan shares how she uses Cameron's (2017) notion of sacred time as a means of self-care, development, and strengthening of boundaries.

Across this section of the volume, what is clear is the ways authors intentionally centre the role of self-care in order to support their development and wellbeing, and in sharing their strategies, they offer us the opportunity to develop our own understanding of approaches that can foster and support both individual and collective wellbeing.

Conclusion

As we have seen in this chapter, the nature of time and our relationship with it is socially and culturally constructed, subject to power relations and institutional structures. Being aware of these constructions of time is vital as we consider our work and wellbeing in relation to time. Rather than seeing our feelings of overwhelm, or of a lack of time as personal failings, we can see these as products of the industrialised and neoliberal approaches to time that exist in the higher education landscape. What we see from the chapters in this volume is a set of authors examining their own relationship and experiences with time and a sharing of strategies for considering time in new ways. In particular, we see an intentionality of making time for self-care and wellbeing, a centring of time for strategies, actions, and connections that foster wellbeing at both an individual and a collective level. What is also clear across the volume is that individual actions are not enough and that collectively we all have a responsibility to advocate for structures and systems that support wellbeing for our colleagues, our students, and our communities. As you engage with this book and read the chapters, we encourage you to think about your own experiences and approaches. We hope that this collection might provide you with an enhanced understanding of self-care and wellbeing approaches that you may be able to incorporate and enact into your day. It is our hope that ultimately, such approaches will raise wellbeing literacy in higher education and may help to identify new strategies for supporting the wellbeing of individuals within academia, which could have profound implications for the wider academic community. For, as we see in these chapters, our relationship with time and with our own self-care and wellbeing can be rewritten. We need to challenge existing neoliberal meta-narratives about time and begin rewriting them in ways that support us all.

References

Bennett, A., & Burke, P.J. (2018). Re/conceptualising time and temporality: An exploration of time in higher education. *Discourse: Studies in the Cultural Politics of Education*, *39*(6), 913–925. https://doi.org/10.1080/01596306.2017.1312285

Berg, M., & Seeber, B.K. (2016). *The slow professor: Challenging the culture of speed in the academy*. University of Toronto Press.

Bloomfield, S. (2020). *Give yourself margin: A guide to rediscovering and reconnecting with your creative self*. Andrews McNeel Publishing.

Cameron, J. (2017). *The Artist's way: A spiritual path to higher creativity: 30th Anniversary Edition*. Tarcher.

Cannizzo, F. (2017). 'You've got to love what you do': Academic labour in a culture of authenticity. *The Sociological Review, 66*(1), 91–106. https://doi.org/10.1177/0038026116681439

Davies, B., & Bansel, P. (2005). The time of their lives? Academic workers in neoliberal time(s). *Health Sociology Review*, *14*(9), 47–58. https://doi.org/10.5172/hesr.14.1.47

Eager, B. (2021). Juggling the triad: Caring for yourself with a block-mode approach to research, teaching, and service. In N. Lemon (Ed.), *Creating a place for self-care and wellbeing in higher education: Finding meaning across academia* (pp. 35–46). Routledge. https://doi.org/10.4324/9781003144397-4

Gibbs, P., Ylijoki, O-H., Guzmán-Valenzuela, C., & Barnett, R. (Eds.). (2014). *Universities in the flux of time: An exploration of time and temporality in university life*. Routledge.

Lash, S. (2001). Technological forms of life. *Theory, Culture & Society*, *18*(1), 105–120. https://doi.org/10.1177/02632760122051661

Lemon, N. (2023). Pedagogy of belonging: Pausing to be human in higher education. *International Health Trends and Perspectives*, *3*(3), Article 3. https://doi.org/10.32920/ihtp.v3i3.1845

Lemon, N. (2024). Unmasking wellbeing: Voices redefining self-care and wellbeing in higher education. In N. Lemon (Ed.), *Prioritising wellbeing and self-care in higher education: How we can do things differently to disrupt silence* (pp. 1–14). Routledge.

Lemon, N., Higgins, J., Noble, L., & Powietrzynska, M. (2023). Gently riding waves in the ocean of our humanity: Embodying contemplative practices. *Holistic Education Review*, *3*(2), Article 2. https://her.journals.publicknowledgeproject.org/index.php/her/article/view/2770

McDonough, S., & Lemon, N. (2018). Mindfulness in the academy: An examination of mindfulness perspectives. In N. Lemon & S. McDonough (Eds.), *Mindfulness in the academy* (pp. 1–21). Springer.

McNaughton, S.M. & Billot, J. (2016). Negotiating academic teacher identity shifts during higher education contextual change. *Teaching in Higher Education, 21*(6), 644–658. https://doi.org/10.1080/13562517.2016.1163669

Mountz, A., Bonds, A., Mansfield, B., Loyd, J., Hyndman, J., Walton-Roberts, M., ... Curran, W. (2015). For slow scholarship: A feminist politics of resistance through collective action in the Neoliberal University. *ACME: An International Journal for Critical Geographies, 14*(4), 1235–1259. Retrieved from https://acme-journal.org/index.php/acme/article/view/1058

Oddell, J. (2023). *Saving time: Discovering a life beyond the clock*. Random House.

O'Dwyer, S., Pinto, S., & McDonough, S. (2018). Self-care for academics: A poetic invitation to reflect and resist. *Reflective Practice, 19*(2), 243–249.

Osbaldiston, N., Cannizzo, F., & Mauri, C. (2019). 'I love my work but I hate my job' – Early career academic perspectives on academic time in Australia. *Time & Society, 28*(2), 743–762. http://doi.org/10.1177/0961463X16682516

Pinnegar, S. (2005). Identity development, moral authority and the teacher educator. In G. Hoban (Ed.), *The missing links in teacher education design* (pp. 257–279). Springer.

Shoffner, M., & Webb, A.W. (Eds.). (2023). *Reconstructing care in teacher education after COVID-19: Caring enough to change*. Routledge.

Ylijoki, O., & Mäntylä, H. (2003). Conflicting time perspectives in academic work. *Time & Society, 12*(1), 55–68. https://doi.org/10.1177/0961463X03012001364

Part 1

Identity Takes Time to Rethink

14 *Identity Takes Time to Rethink*

Navigating Academia's Labyrinth: Time, Identity, and Wellbeing

Narelle Lemon

In the depths of academia's halls,
Identity's echo softly calls,
A journey vast, a path untrod,
Where time and self converge and nod.

Within this realm of scholarly might,
Our sense of self takes shape and flight,
Guided by values, beliefs profound,
Amidst the swirls of sights and sound.

From field to field, we find our way,
Amidst challenges that come to play,
Mentors guide, peers collaborate,
As we navigate our scholarly time.

Yet for those of marginalized voice,
Identity's path is not by choice,
Barriers rise, opportunities few,
In the face of challenges, resilience grows, hopes for change burn.

But identity's tale is not confined,
To a single moment, a frozen mind,
It evolves, it shifts, over time it bends,
As new beginnings and journeys blend.

And in the dance of time's swift flow,
Boundaries blur, but we must know,
That self-care lies in balance found,
In collective actions, solutions sound.

DOI: 10.4324/9781032688633-2

2 Reclaiming Embodiment of My Academic Time through Yoga Practice

Amy Walker

Figure 2.1 My yoga mat as a space to challenge narratives of time

16 *Amy Walker*

Introduction

Building a healthy narrative around time is increasingly complicated for an early career researcher (ECR) (Figure 2.1). There is a luxury to the role of a lecturer in that, other than lectures, student conferences or scheduled meetings, you have the freedom to decide when to complete endless tasks on your to-do list. Writing that may seem like a boring, laborious chore one day might can give you a sense of enjoyment the next day when you write outside in the sunshine and words float down like butterflies. This experience, although not free time, gives a sense of freedom around time and cultivates enjoyment of the writing or experience of a task. Yet, a stronger counterpoint to the unfolding identity as an ECR, however, is how time often becomes the prison-like reality of marking 60, 1800-word inquiry proposals with three days turnaround at the close of the semester due to university deadlines. Or, sitting, while striving for the flow-like state of writing when you are on a second revision, knowing it is unlikely this version will be accepted anyway (and it is raining outside). Time takes on a trickster-like quality as it changes shape or form, depending on the tasks ahead and what narratives sit close to the surface that day. The endless tasks ahead of academics can make time feel burdensome and "scheduled" (Ylijoki & Mäntylä, 2003, p. 60) while finding a sense of enjoyment in writing might feel "timeless" (Ylijoki & Mäntylä, 2003, p. 62).

Although no-one pressures me to get my tasks done, what needs to be done by specific deadlines and my perception of what needed to be done to be successful in my role cause me to do things at a frenetic pace. It was only after finding myself overcome with stress within the first six months of a full-time academic role, I returned to a passion for yoga that had been left behind in the wake of a PhD and caring for three young children. Only months into returning to yoga, this casual practice changed into a year-long commitment to yoga teacher training certificate. It may appear counterintuitive to embark on a course when one already is a full-time ECR and mother of three young children, often complaining about lack of time. Yet, what I found was the opposite. Not only did I begin a journey that continues to open my limited understandings about yoga, but it began impacting my work as an ECR too. This intersection of my experiences has impacted on my felt sense of time, equipping me to broaden my conceptions about time while learning the importance of "presence and observation" (Quinn & Maddox, 2022, p. 1). Taming some of the unwieldly aspects of time for an ECR is an ongoing practice just like my yoga.

Conceptions of Academic Time

To achieve in academia requires an investment of time, a point noted by Bourdieu (1998) as he describes the accumulation of academic power over time (Cannizzo, 2018). Yet, while accumulating capital within their roles, the work of academics becomes "fast-paced" and "metric-oriented" (Müller, 2019). Pressure on academics to achieve is underscored by the need for universities to become efficient with their time, aligning with the trend for academic workload models where academic time is divided among types of tasks needed to be done, such as teaching, mentoring, service, and research (Kenny & Fluck, 2017). The workload model has been criticised for failing to protect staff from becoming overburdened with tasks and

Reclaiming Embodiment of My Academic Time through Yoga Practice   17

coming at the expense of a university's core goals of researching and learning (Kenny & Fluck, 2017). In fact, this need for efficiency has led for research time being squeezed so that some researchers must research on their own time (Lyons & Ingersoll, 2010). In some universities, market-oriented techniques equate to high levels of efficiency competition on all fronts, which leaves academics fragmenting time across projects, experiencing an increase in work tempo (Müller, 2019).

This pace is mirrored in the progression of research leaders in their fields from the point of receiving a PhD, as Browning et al. (2017) note in a study of Australian research leaders. They found research leaders tended to have secured their first grant in less than three years post-PhD, leading a research team in five years and were professors within 14 years of competing the PhD, suggesting that the early years post-PhD are critical if one desires to become a research leader (Browning et al., 2017). This forward-looking momentum creates "omnipresent discourse of excellence" (Vostal, 2015, p. 11), resulting in competition and a feeling of the need to speed up to keep up (Müller, 2019). Yet, within the scope of anticipation about the future, academics can overlook the present in a form of anticipatory practice about what the future might bring (Müller, 2019).

The way that academics experience time has been categorised by Ylijoki and Mäntylä (2003) in four competing ways, scheduled, timeless, contracted and personal. Briefly, scheduled, the tasks that academics must perform; timeless, moments when academics themselves within the task at hand; contracted, an awareness of how long left, generally on a funded project; and personal, which is time for self (Ylijoki & Mäntylä, 2003). They rather mournfully conclude:

> All in all, our exploration into the temporal orders of academic work has created a rather gloomy picture of the everyday realities in academia. The academics seem to be left with few options available to live a temporally balanced academic life.... Conditions like living in 'temporal prisons', experiencing work as an ever tightening 'time screw' and 'stealing time' from oneself and one's family are manifestations of the academics' everyday realities in which the temporal perspectives are seriously asynchronous.
>
> (Ylijoki & Mäntylä, 2003)

This pressure on academics to do things quickly is contested as some are taking a stand against the need to do things quickly. Advocates of 'slow science' emphasise the importance of unhurried thinking about progress and question the value of academic work done at great speed (Müller, 2019). This slowness is questioned by some, however, as it may seem to be "undesirable and regressive" (Vostal, 2015, p. 83), while complementing acceleration in academia. At risk too, within this push for efficiency is a loss around a sense of community that academics often need to explore to find their way (Nagy & Burch, 2009).

Defining Yoga and Time

Numerous interpretations of the word yoga exist, but some general conceptions are "to come together," "to unite" or "to attain what was previously unattainable"

18 *Amy Walker*

(Desikachar, 1995, p. 5). The practice of yoga is as diverse as the multitude of people that practice it, with some practitioners giving more attention to the physical elements of poses (asanas), while for others, it may be a focus on a breath practice (pranayama) or as part of a spiritual practice. Despite the different interpretations, traditions and styles, a common element is "to act and be attentive to our actions" (Desikachar, 1995, p. 5). This notion of trying to be in the present moment is difficult as the mind seeks to stray to the past or present. As evidenced in the *Yoga Sutras of Patanjali* (Stiles, 2001), and interpreted by Desikachar (1995), time is relative. The challenge is to seek clarity by distinguishing these moments, but the increments of time are so small that as humans we tend to experience it more than a flow than discreet. Through practice, however, we become better at directing our attention to what is around us at a given time without allowing the mind to drift into the past or present (Desikachar, 1995). This focus on the moment as described by Desikachar (1995) sits in some ways counter to the ways that academics experience time in their workday, described earlier by Ylijoki and Mäntylä (2003), as scheduled, timeless, contracted and personal. In fact, Quinn and Maddox (2022), both academics and yoga instructors, describe the importance of "presence and observation" (p. 1) which often sits counter the hurried practices of academics.

The frenetic pace of time for an academic, countered by embracing yogic time, is explored by Shafer (2022) in sharing about her experience of 'pendulation' (p. 72). Shaffer (2021) describes the concept of pendulation as "the rhythmic ebb of being 'on' and active, to the flow of pause and rest" (p. 72). Through resting – consciously – through yoga poses, such as *viparita karani*, or legs-up-the-wall, one can focus on self, well-being and embodiment (Shaffer, 2021, p. 72). By doing this forced rest, it can give one a chance to heal, in particular form prolonged periods of stress, which can affect the way we experience what is around us (Shaffer, 2021). It has been noted that the "confidence from embodying yoga can permeate everyday occupations, influencing participants' becoming" (Brooks & Reynolds, 2023, p. 7).

For academics, this experience of embodiment has potential not just for personal benefits but in becoming a responsive practitioner. Quinn and Maddox (2022) write about the importance of bringing an embodiment to our practice as educators: "Embracing the connections between the mind and the body are crucial, now more than ever, to create healthy, nurturing, and responsive pedagogical practices" (p. 3). The practice of embodiment that one experiences through yoga can remind educators about the need for engaging with students in the moment as a way to ensure our presence allows us to see and hear students and communicate with them openly and effectively (Quinn & Maddox, 2022).

Shifting Narratives of Time

Initial Conception: Wasted Time

When accepting the role as a full-time lecturer, I naively thought that the work as a sessional lecturer would continue but in a more advanced way. Instead, in my first meeting with the dean in early January after accepting the role late in the year

Reclaiming Embodiment of My Academic Time through Yoga Practice   19

before, she explained the concept of workload, where my time would be divided across the teaching, research and service. At that stage, other than introductory training, there were no immediate jobs that needed doing. So, I went to my office and encountered a month's worth of silence as there were no students, since classes did not start for two months, and very few lecturers around, as most were on holiday. A void before me, I did not appreciate the value of this quiet time in my office where I sat from nine in the morning until five in the afternoon, writing diligently from my PhD, expecting this work to be straight-forward as I followed the models in front of me. Although unsure, I enjoyed this expanse of time and often found a sense of "timeless time" (Ylijoki & Mäntylä, 2003, p. 62) through my writing. Yet, those submitted papers did not equal publications, only the beginning of a cycle of disappointing revise and resubmits or rejections. My first response, and throughout that year, I saw that time as 'wasted' due to my 'failed' progress.

Revised Conception: Academic Time as Practice

Reflecting on this 'wasted' time now, my conception of this time is different. In yoga, your teachers often remind you that your attempts at poses, meditation or pranayama (breathing) won't be perfect the first time (never, in fact as that's not really the point). This lesson has great resonance off the mat for me. Applying this to my conception of that early academic time as being 'wasted' was linked to a sense of a fixed mindset – an expectation or desire that everything should be right the first time, or it was a failure (Dweck, 2006). This is something that I have heard countless times, have told my children and shared with the pre-service teachers in my classes, but still find it difficult to apply to my own work. Through the lens of a yoga practitioner, I have begun to see the labours of academic writing time as 'practice.' I understand this quiet, lonely month gave me an opportunity to write uninhibited, and this is precious time for building an understanding of not only the academic writing process but becoming an academic in general, as a period of practice is needed before any of the iterations of this role will begin to feel like an expression of me.

Conception: Imagined Future

My expectations of what the PhD meant pushed me to gain a sense of momentum for an imagined career (Müller, 2019). I had always conceived the PhD as a gateway that once through would open doorways. After completing the PhD, I was caught up in the notion that as it had passed the reviewers, it must be worthwhile for immediate publication. It seemed obvious to me that I could slice up the chapters of the thesis into potential articles and chapters, and then, 'poof,' publication. The repeated revisions and ultimate rejections were crushing, while still trying to speak about the importance of these findings at conferences. Over time, it became clear that this idea of 'pushing through' was not working for me, and just creating stress. As such, I had to find a similar understanding that I had on the yoga mat – where letting go of some expectations of myself is a liberating exercise. Although

20   *Amy Walker*

it's not ideal, I may not ever publish from my PhD but can see it as merely a training process for the rigours of working as an academic, as Thomson (2018) has described it.

Revision: Notice the Current Moment

Within yoga, there is also an opportunity to use props – the mat being one, along with blocks, straps, bolsters, balls, the wall. Twenty years ago, the notion of using props for some poses, specifically blocks, seemed like 'cheating' in some way, that props meant that you were unable to do the poses. Somehow, I had turned the practice of yoga into a competition with others, not about my own individual practice or what my body needed at the time. Now, in my current practice of yoga, I realise a misunderstanding. The props are used to assist one's alignment in the poses and can help your body ease in or relax in a posture that might otherwise place too much strain on the body. In a recent yoga class, a teacher emphasised that the use of props was actually 'smart,' and sometimes, it gave your body a safe way to achieve a pose depending on where your body is presently. As an academic, the lens of 'props' can be interpreted in many ways, but for me, it's about accepting where I am on the academic path without frustration. Metaphorical academic props require an ECR to forego egotistical or perfectionist thinking and accept or seek assistance with work tasks to promote ease in the mind. This may be in delegating aspects of research, teaching or marking, when possible. An academic 'prop' may also be seeking the tacit knowledge of others – particularly from those who have worked at the university for more than a decade and understand the nuances of policies or online systems. There is an opportunity for me to take time for "presence and observation" (Quinn & Maddox, 2022), appreciating the learning of my current tasks, backing away from the constant future orientation.

This slowing down allows me time to integrate my understandings. Twenty years ago, as a beginning yoga practitioner, I would join some others exiting classes before the Savasana, also known as corpse pose, at the end. Savasana would likely go for about eight to ten minutes after the movement practice where you might be led through a meditative practice, listen to a piece of music or just rest in silence. To me, at that time, this was torture. I wanted to move more or perhaps had plans for more exercise afterwards – relaxing was not moving me towards my goals. My attention was on pushing myself through yoga, and when I could not do certain poses, I was frustrated with my body. Now, however, as my understandings of yoga have moved just beyond the surface level of the poses to gain fitness and flexibility, I respect what my body is able to do in the moment. Further, I now conceive of Savasana, or poses such as *viparita karani,* or legs-up-the-wall, to be a form of constructive rest as Shaffer (2021) suggests, which enables the body to integrate the movements and any changes brought about by the practice. It also gave me a chance to let go of expectations around myself and my body that were no longer helpful. Letting go of unhelpful expectations – and the thoughts associated with them – has becomes a sort-of academic Savasana where my body and mind are given time to take stock and integrate the changes that my daily practice in this role

Reclaiming Embodiment of My Academic Time through Yoga Practice 21

affords me, enabling me time in space for my thoughts on the possibilities of new opportunities in research.

Conception: Individual Output = Success

Although my PhD had the guidance of those more experienced, I mostly spent this time in isolation, reading, researching and writing, so my expectation was that my later academic work would be similar in nature. My perception was that academic work was always something you did to showcase your individual understandings. My individual progress was pushed by this sense of what Müller (2019) describes as a forward-looking experience of self, an "entrepreneurial self," which is "always on the run, becoming what it is supposed to already be" (p. 2). My academic experiences were projected outwards for the individual successes that I wanted to achieve, such as working at a university or publishing papers. This narrative was not mine alone as Nagy and Burch (2009) argue that in the frenetic pace of efficiency that underscores modern universities, academics perceive the need to keep to yourself, get the PhD finished and focus on publications and the career ahead.

Similar to this conception that academic time needed to be isolated to be successful, my practice of yoga had a similar history. Although not like a sporting event where people are racing or competing for points, there can be a subtle competition in classes. While a younger practitioner, I engaged in a sense of competition with others around me in those early classes of yoga, wanting to be seen as progressing through basic postures or holding them for a certain length of time. Returning to yoga as a prospective teacher, although with more life experience, that sense of competition was lurking when I entered the door. I had said to myself so many times that I should have done this teacher training twenty years ago, not now with a full-time job and three young children. I worried that others would judge me and that I would not be able to do what others would do – this ego-driven sense of competition was forcing me to overlook why I was seeking out yoga and this training.

Revision: Community Is Vital to Success

Within the first few moments of entering the yoga teacher training with others, I realised that my motivations were shared by others and there were a range of people of various ages. Thus, my fears subsided, and I realised that I was at the right place, in the right time, with a group of like-minded individuals. Ironically, my sense of competition took a backseat to a sense of community that sprang forth. I was no longer an isolated practitioner. This changed conception of time about my experience of yoga – from a competition with myself or others to an understanding that I am in a community – has resonance with my work as an ECR.

In my academic work, I found little success from my writing or work in isolation. Within this self-focused sense of work, it's easy to fall into a trap of comparing yourself to others in academia, or as someone described education academics to me the other day, as 'pracademics.' You open your email and someone has secured

22 *Amy Walker*

a publication, you open another one and someone has secured a grant or a trip, while your abstract was rejected. The push for efficiency in universities can mean academics strive in isolation, as suggested by Nagy and Burch (2009), overlooking the potential to gain support through voluntarily seeking out a supportive community of practice. Just as one keeps returning to the mat in yoga to find a sense of balance, so does the academic need reminding that the sense of competition is looming all around. It was not until putting my hand up to take part in two research groups – as a learner and then as part of the research team – that I realised how my understanding around academic progress was limited. The information that was collected through one group as a self-study led to shared publications while the other group researched student work with trauma-informed practices is on the verge of one. Through investing time in these groups, I've shared in successes and found support through community.

Taming the Trickster of Time

To those further down the academic track, my observations may seem naïve, but from my positioning, this information would have helped me when beginning my full-time role as assuming the title of ECR.

View Time Spent as Practice

The need to perform on the job quickly when awarded work as an ECR overlooks the need for practice. Just as Hattie (2003) has spoken about the pressures on graduate teachers performing the same functions as those later in their careers, despite the demarcations by registering bodies, so might we argue are the pressures on teaching as an ECR. My experience as one in Education is that I made a personal assumption that having been in the classroom, lecturing would be an easy transition. To some degree, it was better than I expected as there was no classroom management (those not interested or too busy just wouldn't show up!), but in other ways, it was harder, as I was only one step ahead of some of the knowledge I was supposed to impart or trying to fix issues in the courses on the run. The other assumption is that the freshly awarded PhD automatically means that people are interested in your research and are dying to publish it. Early writing from your PhD can be looked at as practice, which may be successful, while you are working towards other opportunities.

Discover the Freedom in Failing

It's hard to communicate the amount of failure that I've experienced in my efforts to become an academic. My PhD went smoothly but I had hiccups when pursuing an MA by research in another field and more recently in my efforts to publish. Recognising my effort in those areas is not 'wasted' time is significant, but further to this is the importance in seeing that failure is okay. The ubiquitous Dweck's (2006) growth mindset is so important in helping to reframe the notion of failure as an ending. Instead, failure can lead to new discoveries as you try something again. This has happened in my writing, where one paper stemming from my PhD – although not published YET – has been rewritten so many times that it no longer resembles its original shape. Through these revisions, I've written myself into confidence about some new ideas. Despite the final resting place of this paper, I've gone from despair to hope where my future writing starts from a stronger position having learned from the review process.

Attune to the Here and Now

Academic work is stressful and this is well-documented. In many ways, it sits in opposition to being able to find time to attune to the here and now – as you are focused on the future and what must be done, as our performance expectations are allotted through a workload model. Yet, one advantage of being an ECR is that the universities aim to provide work-life balance where possible through added research time. A piece of advice that I was given in that first meeting as a full-time staff member was to use my calendar to give myself time. I was encouraged to use Fridays as a writing day at home, which I blocked off successfully for months until responsibilities like marking crept in. I also scheduled time for marking or other jobs that had to be done at certain times on my calendar. This works very well in some instances, but there will be times that no matter how much time you've managed to allot yourself for writing or marking – it is not going to happen. So, I tend to push back in the way that I can by attuning to the here and now (as long as I'm not in the marking cave). Sometimes, my later self may have to cope because my right now self needs to go walk in the sunshine or have a chat with a colleague. By listening to my body and mind in the moment, I may not be able to get everything done as I had anticipated but it gets done when my brain can handle it.

Find Community

Maybe someone told me to find a sense of community and I didn't listen, but this wasn't a point that I felt strongly about when pursuing my PhD or entering a full-time role in academia. Simultaneous to my disappointments from publishing from my PhD came my successes of working in groups. Although I was on the peripheral and still am to some degree, I see this as part of my practice at being an academic, learning from others while I gain my confidence. Finding a community where you feel supported to learn is important. It may not be the first group that lets you in, and you may need to find others. It also may not be the person who 'seems' like they would be easy to work with or is a good friend. Often, the best groups work when you put your hand up because it comes from a similar interest, or, in my experience, I had no idea what they were working on, but was curious and wanted to gain experience. In my own way, I could push back at a system that was demanding me to be competitive by finding a sense of community. Further, through researching this chapter, I found that I was not alone in my discoveries about time. I found so many more experienced researchers (as in quoted literature

24 *Amy Walker*

above) that had written about what I was experiencing, giving me a sense of shared experiences. Although I do not delight in the fact that others have been stressed by academic time, it is comforting to know that there is a community out there, ready to push for changes in the way that narratives have been told about academic time.

References

Bourdieu, P. (1988). *Homo academicus*. Stanford University Press.

Brooks, S., & Reynolds, S. (2023). The exploration of becoming as a yoga practitioner and its impact on identity formation, health, and well-being. *Journal of Occupational Science*, 1–17.

Browning, L., Thompson, K., & Dawson, D. (2017). From early career researcher to research leader: Survival of the fittest? *Journal of Higher Education Policy and Management*, *39*(4), 361–377.

Cannizzo, F. (2018). The shifting rhythms of academic work. *Journal of Research and Debate*, *1*(3), 1–4.

Desikachar, T. K. V. (1995). *The heart of yoga: Developing a personal practice.* Inner Traditions International.

Dweck, C. S. (2006). *Mindset: The new psychology of success.* Random House.

Hattie, J. (2003). Teachers make a difference: What is the research evidence? *Paper presented at the Australian Council for Educational Research Annual Conference on Building Teacher Quality*. Melbourne, Australia.

Kenny, J., & Fluck, A. E. (2017). Towards a methodology to determine standard time allocations for academic work. *Journal of Higher Education Policy and Management*, *39*(5), 503–523.

Lyons, M., & Ingersoll, L. (2010). Regulated autonomy or autonomous regulation? Collective bargaining and academic workloads in Australian universities. *Journal of Higher Education Policy and Management*, *32*(2), 137–148.

Müller, R. (2019). Racing for what? Anticipation and acceleration in the work and career practices of academic life science postdocs. In F. Cannizzo and N. Osbaldiston (eds.), *The social structures of global academia* (pp. 162–184). Routledge.

Nagy, J., & Burch, T. (2009). Communities of Practice in Academe (CoP-iA): Understanding academic work practices to enable knowledge building capacities in corporate universities. *Oxford Review of Education*, *35*(2), 227–247.

Quinn, B. P., & Maddox, C. B. (2022). The body doesn't lie: Yoga and embodiment in the higher education classroom. *Teaching in Higher Education*, 1–17.

Shaffer, D. K. (2021). Pendulation: Awakening to rest. In N. Lemon (ed.), *Creating a place for self-care and wellbeing in higher education* (pp. 72–86). Routledge.

Stiles, M. (2001). *Yoga Sutras of Patanjali: With great respect and love.* Weiser Books.

Thomson, P. (2018, May 21). Publishing from the PhD make a publication plan. *patter.* https://patthomson.net/2018/05/21/publishing-from-the-phd-make-a-publication-plan/

Vostal, F. (2015). Academic life in the fast lane: The experience of time and speed in British academia. *Time & Society*, *24*(1), 71–95.

Ylijoki, O. H., & Mäntylä, H. (2003). Conflicting time perspectives in academic work. *Time & Society*, *12*(1), 55–78.

3 Moving Abroad to Work in Higher Education, in a Different Language, as a Constructive Disruption

Éric Bel and Johanna Tomczak

Constructive Disruption?

The notion of disruption when going abroad brings to mind some challenging situations and negative experiences, for various categories of people. This is likely to be particularly true for those who move to a different part of the world to work in a university, especially when they are not native speakers of the main language used in the host institution. In this chapter, we argue that this type of disruption can be positive at different levels, without ignoring, of course, the difficulties in moving out of one's comfort zone and managing change in a constructive manner.

Indeed, etymologically, 'disrupting' refers to the idea of 'breaking up' or 'separating'. This is clearly what happens when one leaves something behind, when one severs links with a known environment. Paradoxically, the oxymoron 'constructive disruption' also emphasises the potentially positive nature of this same experience, as well as the idea that the individual is not a passive recipient of some negative external influence, but an active player in building and shaping responses and outcomes. In our discussion, we apply this optimistic concept to a specific section of the Higher Education (HE) population: those whom we will call internationally mobile staff.

In the next section, we have created a visual representation of our view that moving abroad to work in HE can be a challenging but, over time, constructive disruption. This will be followed by a brief narrative describing our own international transition to working in British HE. Then, a short review will be undertaken of key concepts related to international professional experiences, for example in terms of cultural understanding, identity, self-care, wellbeing and time, and of how these interact when trying to manage disruptions. Finally, recommendations will be made for changing often negative perceptions of international mobility into a more positive interest in this type of transition. Ultimately, we hope that readers of this chapter will want to embrace some of the rewarding opportunities that we discuss, and that they will engage in a personal and reflective voyage of self-discovery, which could very well inspire them to cross frontiers, be they physical or more subjective ones, towards constructing some new understanding of what working in HE abroad, in a different language, could offer them.

DOI: 10.4324/9781032688633-4

26 *Éric Bel and Johanna Tomczak*

Visual Narrative

Personal objectives change, often through adaptation to new situations, new environments. This is what happened to us, as we initially left two different parts of the world for the United Kingdom (UK), where we eventually gained employment in two different universities. It is worth noting that, in the places we originally come from, there is not much tradition of taking HE staff's wellbeing seriously. However, over many years spent in the UK, we have experienced, benefitted from and learnt to appreciate, the value of referring to this concept when we review the development of our personal as well as professional lives.

The visual narrative, Figure 3.1, depicts our personal journey – and perhaps yours, in the future or already experienced – from a rather stable life, through a stormy disruption, to reconstructing a more harmonious equilibrium over time, when moving geographically from one place in the world (World Place 1) to another (World Place 2), to work in HE, especially in a different language. For most people, working in a new environment will look quite daunting, anyway, a real challenge to their own fundamental, personal values and references, but for those facing a transnational cultural change, as well as, often, exposure to a language that they do not master, the disruption is even greater. It will lead to some turbulent questioning, as well as a feeling of vulnerability, as many aspects of their own identity, values and beliefs will experience a degree of imbalance that could not be anticipated, be it at an emotional, social, cultural, spiritual, physical, mental, communicative, cognitive, indeed, deeply personal or even professional level.

Therefore, in our visual narrative, this process starts with a version of one's self (Self 1), where some of the main aspects of personal and professional life may be a little precarious, bumpy at times, but show some degree of stability and alignment. Then, comes the disruption of moving abroad to work in HE institutions where,

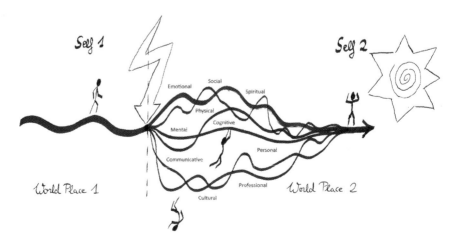

Figure 3.1 Timeline of wellbeing and alignment when moving from one part of the world to another, to work in Higher Education

often, the main language of communication is different. Finally, a new self (Self 2) appears, with realignment of some of the main constituents of one's life.

Brief Review of the Literature

This chapter on moving abroad to work in HE, in a different language, as a constructive disruption, is about transitions undertaken by people willingly, with a focus on the academic world. Therefore, it does not address the changes experienced by those who have had to move from one part of the world to another against their will, for example, for political or economic reasons.

Our review of the literature on disruptions that people experience when transitioning to HE shows that much research has been carried out on students' first year at university, which, indeed, is a crucial moment in their lives. However, there seems to have been less interest in the internationally mobile staff's transitions to working in HE abroad (Bailey et al., 2021, pp. 349–350), at least not from a well-being perspective. This is strange, because the Higher Education Statistics Agency (HESA, 2024) shows that, in British HE, more than a third of the staff originally come from outside the UK. It seems that, somehow, internationally mobile staff are expected to have enough experience of life and the personal and professional skills to adapt to new and complex situations almost naturally. For many staff, nothing could be further from reality, though. From our point of view, internationally mobile staff experience the same disruptions, in particular in terms of belonging, identity, orientation and academic traditions, as well as challenges related to language barriers and cross-cultural interactions. Indeed, transitions can take many forms (Colley, 2007, p. 428), at different stages in an individual's life, including related to language, as emphasised in this chapter. However, they have in common that one experiences them when moving from familiar to unfamiliar situations (Cheng et al., 2015).

In HE, transitions often refer to the systems which are put in place to support students, but another perspective on this notion, which we are keen to promote here, is one which concentrates on individuals and their 'becoming': they move not only from a given environment to a new one, but more interestingly, also often, from a version of themselves to a different one. Transitions are very much, as Eteläpelto et al. (2014) suggest, about 'identity and agency' (see also, Bailey et al., 2021, p. 360). In fact, according to Colley (2007, p. 432), this notion of agency is closely linked to the ability to imagine one's own future and make, and take responsibility for, significant personal life choices, and "learning about who we can become and where we can locate ourselves, socially and spatially" (Colley, 2007, p. 428). Therefore, wellbeing will depend largely on timely engagement with the idea of acknowledging present, as well as self-defining future belonging, a concept therefore 'bounded in time and space', as discussed by Ecclestone et al. (2009, p. xix).

For Jones et al. (2023), "transition is a continuum and must be embedded throughout the academic journey…" (p. 3). It is never quite a punctual, sudden change of state but rather a sometimes (very) long process. In her 1925 novel,

28 *Éric Bel and Johanna Tomczak*

'Mrs Dalloway', Woolf promoted the idea that our attitudes should internalise time as a key parameter for enjoying the now and then and learning and improving ourselves. The difference between thinking positively and negatively about disruption may be just a question of feelings (Ecclestone et al., 2009, p. 7) or perception (or lack?) of time. For Bergson (1889), time should be described as a main driver for the organisation of our lives. Indeed, in academia, we are regularly under pressure to regulate and pace our actions in, and our thinking about, the short, medium and longer terms. The consumerist approach to time prompts us always to remain busy, to hurry from one deadline to the next. No mental space to think about disruptions creatively. No time to prepare for, to anticipate, to imagine what working in HE abroad would be like. This goes against the very nature of successful transitions, which begin with individuals thinking about changing something in their lives.

In fact, the nature and extent of the disruption depends on individuals' responses to various on-going external factors and also on prior individual experiences. Internationally mobile people, who will bring to their new destination a great diversity of ethnic, cultural, religious, academic and language references (Callender et al., 2011, p. 11), will face a range of challenges, which may generate anxiety and confusion (Bailey et al., 2021, p. 351). McGarvey et al. (2021, p. 488) lists them as: 'moving away from home', 'feelings of isolation', 'cultural and religious beliefs', 'lack of knowledge of the host country' and new academic expectations. They further suggest that "discrimination" (p. 494), "slower rate of language processing", as well as broader communication issues (p. 501), often are barriers to integration.

Although the experience of moving abroad to work in HE, especially in a different language, may, for some, not be considered as a positive one, with collegial and collaborative support received from their new environment, the challenges faced by people arriving from abroad will be more manageable. Thus, a socio-cultural approach to conceptualising transitions to HE may offer a relevant framework for the development of essential 'communities of practice' (Wenger, 2011), in a compassionate university environment, in which staff can join, and collaborate with, others to reduce the risk of isolation. This will help them to overcome unexpected personal crises, and what Bailey et al. (2021, p. 351) call 'unfamiliar' paradigms, and develop some self-acceptance and enter into a conscious personal, balancing process of what Piaget, as discussed by Supratman (2013), described as 'assimilation' and 'accommodation' to new environments. This representation of how individuals can attempt to adjust and aim to achieve some form of self-equilibrium or alignment over time, as we have tried to show in our visual narrative, is definitely more satisfying than any quick integration model, which, in the literature, is still widely referred to as expected (for example, see Ammigan et al., 2023). Indeed, the idea of 'acculturation', which is defined by Sharif (2019) as a "process that individuals from different cultures undergo in their adaptation to new host cultures" (p. 1), leading to a "culturally-based change in a person's behavior or identity" [sic], would suggest that internationally mobile people need to change almost as soon as they arrive in their new environment.

In fact, what staff really need is, as for students (Callender et al., 2011, p. 11), not only self-awareness but also self-love, self-compassion and self-regulation, which will all contribute to personal (and professional!) wellbeing. This is so important in trying to make working in HE abroad, especially in a different language, a constructive experience. Through anticipating the impact of their decisions to move to another part of the world on their future lives, staff should be able to prepare themselves as early as possible and plan what is sometimes referred to as a self-care strategy. According to the Self Care Forum (2023), self-care is any "actions that individuals take for themselves on behalf of, and with, others in order to develop, protect, maintain and improve their health, well-being or wellness" [sic]. In fact, promoting self-care has become central in British universities. Thus, Owens and Loomes (2010, p. 275) explain how interactions within a HE institution, and with the wider local community, contribute to a collective sense of belonging, which is essential for mental and emotional wellbeing. The authors base their analysis of internationally mobile people's needs on Maslow's hierarchy of needs, which enables them to describe how wellbeing can be affected when facing what looks like a negative disruption. "Work, leisure, accommodation, social life, medical care" are listed by Callender et al. (2011, p. 9) as changes that will affect all students going to university for the first time. This will be true for staff moving to HE abroad, too, with the added dimension of the foreign nature of their new environment, especially when working in a different language. Staff taking employment abroad, like students (Owens & Loomes, 2010, p. 278), will initially concentrate on looking for decent accommodation, feeding themselves appropriately, which may be directed by specific dietary or religious requirements, and buying suitable clothes to cope with weather conditions that, often, they are not used to. Others, who come with children, will want to find a suitable school for them, whilst opening a bank account or registering with the police or immigration services may also be urgent. If such basic needs are not met, internationally mobile staff may never be able to develop a sense of safety and personal satisfaction that is universally sought, neither are they likely to be able to develop the stability and resilience that are essential to succeed in academia. They may even be tempted to turn their frustration against themselves. Not a constructive disruption!

Reflection

Before adding some anecdotal, but relevant, personal insights to the short review of the literature undertaken in the previous section, we would like to emphasise the fact that, whilst we have experienced more positive than negative aspects of the disruption caused by working in HE abroad, we do appreciate that not all internationally mobile people will have been so lucky. Still, we hope that the following reflective comments will exemplify what it may feel like, for internationally mobile staff, to go through potentially negative disruptions, but actually being able to transform them into positive ones over time.

Of course, the first few weeks, or even months, working abroad are not at all equivalent to going on a relaxing, sunny foreign holiday. Transitioning to a new working environment is never a simple process. For us, it was not merely about

30 *Éric Bel and Johanna Tomczak*

deciding, one day, to change, and, the next one, to adapt and adopt seamlessly new ways of thinking or doing things. However, at least initially, our attitudes and behaviours were certainly defined by our desire to fit in with the new social norms that we were discovering, to apply the following traditional British saying: 'do in Rome as the Romans do'. Later, though, instead of letting ourselves be guided by externally imposed acculturation (see above a brief reference to this controversial concept), we favoured more personal control over which aspects we wanted to accommodate in our own lives and which ones we would assimilate or just ignore. Gradually, we became more self-aware and, increasingly, we developed the confidence to protect fundamental aspects of our individual identities. At the same time, we learnt to accept feedback received from others, for example, about our English language skills, which often made us feel, explicitly or implicitly, that, somehow, we were 'different' from what was expected of us.

For example, in terms of communication, first, we did try to learn as much English as possible in the least possible time, and we were even tempted to try and lose our respective foreign accents, in order, at least, to 'sound like' native speakers, if not behave like them. However, we soon became aware of, and often reminded by others about, our poor fluency or our 'strange' choices of words or expressions. This led us, increasingly, to be quieter in English. As highlighted by Ammigan et al. (2023), receiving comments about accents can contribute to feelings of unease, uselessness and insecurity. Still, over time, we became less focused on our pronunciation. We accepted it as part of our personalities, and while language learning never stops (we still use English dictionaries to look up words occasionally, although we have lived in the UK for several years), we came to the conclusion that spontaneous, authentic and genuine interactions, even with imprecise grammar, inaccurate intonation or hesitant fluency, mattered to us more than constrained, artificial and impersonal communication. Immersing oneself completely into any given language can be a very challenging exercise but also very rewarding in terms of social gains.

Thus, we had to remind ourselves that our mental health and overall wellbeing were priceless and that we should not try too hard, too much or too fast. Indeed, it is physically demanding, quite tiring and soon overwhelming, to try and cope with rapid changes on a daily basis, especially through the medium of a language which one does not master. Self-care is about controlling pace and time, and, therefore, for our own wellbeing, we had to allow the whole process to take place as slowly as necessary.

As implied above, with time, we managed to increase our language ability, but we have never felt, even after several years of living and working in the UK, that we could master all the intricacies of the English language. However, with time came the realisation that this was not necessary, because what really matters is to enjoy communication and the human interactions that it allows. In terms of relationships, building a support network around us also took time, but it was a very rewarding process and enabled us not to be alone, for example when feeling homesick. We found it helpful early in the process to interact with a range of people, some who had experienced similar international mobility and others who had not.

While the former confirmed the importance of taking the time to find appropriate solutions in our attempts to locate ourselves in our new environment, the latter welcomed our efforts to immerse ourselves in the new culture. Indeed, we developed new ways of living, merging some of our own habits with those of our host place. At the beginning, we asked ourselves questions about who we were becoming, how our behaviours were evolving and whether we were happy with our changing personal circumstances. Sometimes, we were unsure of our decisions and that moving abroad was really worth it. However, these reflective moments prompted us to confirm to ourselves that our own international mobility, from World Place 1 to World Place 2 (see visual narrative above), had created many opportunities, professionally and in terms of personal development. We realised that these would enable us to grow and flourish, something that is unlikely to have been possible had we stayed in World Place 1, or at least not to that extent, or not in the fascinating new direction that we were taking.

Indeed, personally, we came to understand different social expectations, for example, in terms of cultural references. Having grown up in a different part of the world, our childhood memories were different but also the games we played, the books we read, the films we watched, the jokes we made. Not having the same cultural references can be interesting, though. So, instead of allowing ourselves to feel like outsiders, we used this opportunity to reflect on, and if necessary, challenge our own ways of thinking and doing things, and prompt others to try and understand them. Through reaching out proactively to the local community, we were able to make long-lasting connections with many people. Through joining established societies and enrolling on evening adult courses, or simply attending the local sports centre, we felt increasingly more part of the World Place we had moved to. Visiting our next destination, even just for a short period of time, before moving there for work, enabled us to plan our more permanent future stay.

Professionally, we sought support as soon as possible, including asking for a mentor and our respective line managers to give us regular feedback on our early progress. Enrolling early on staff development workshops, attending conferences and joining professional societies enabled us to learn about work practices that were acceptable in our new respective host institutions. While navigating new administrative processes was tedious, talking to colleagues about how things are done allowed us to unblock barriers. Such informal discussions, as well as more formal attendance at meetings, helped us develop further our English language skills, especially in terms of adjusting to the local academic language.

While some of the above-mentioned aspects of our new personal and professional lives were easier to align than others, all required time; time for our brains to process new information; time for us to make decisions about how we wanted to change; time for actually accepting the developing new Self in each of us.

Concluding Comments

We now take it as axiomatic that many of the main underpinning concepts that we have touched upon in this chapter can be applied to the majority of people who

32   *Éric Bel and Johanna Tomczak*

become willingly internationally mobile, wherever they come from, whatever their nationalities or cultures, whichever languages they speak.

Although the type of situations discussed above is likely, first, to create a number of challenges, some obvious ones, others unexpected, we are convinced that such international transitions, eventually, will appear positive for any staff moving abroad to work in HE. Indeed, far from being detrimental, such disruptions enable individuals to grow, personally and professionally. Presented with problematic choices, but with an open mind, we are prompted to try out new ways of doing things, discover unknown aspects of ourselves and accept to go beyond our comfort zone.

McGarvey et al. (2021, p. 491) note that there are three main areas that internationally mobile people, as well as host organisations, should consider carefully: 'personal and emotional adjustment', 'social adjustment' and 'attachment'; whilst Pho and Schartner (2021, p. 490) promote the idea of 'psychological and academic adaptation'. More specific examples of these principles include the following, which contribute to maintenance of, or to better, personal wellbeing, equal or increasing satisfaction, and consequently, probably more positive and happier transitions between World Place 1 and World Place 2 (see visual narrative above):

- Intentions, motivations and aspirations, as well as anticipation, expectations and preparation, for working abroad;
- Creativity and potential for imagining one's future;
- Willingness to learn about, and from, different people and cultures;
- Allowance for (slow) change in oneself and in one's choice of belonging;
- Respect for, and regular interactions with, others, in various contexts;
- Confident self-reflection and ability to seek support;
- Some foundational knowledge of the target language, or, at least, an interest in communicating and learning foreign languages.

Whilst the above is likely to benefit internationally mobile people, in this chapter, there is some emphasis, as its title indicates, on the use of a *different language*. In our own experience, working in HE abroad, in a language one is not a native speaker of, adds an extra layer of potential difficulties that native speakers are unlikely to encounter, or, at least, not to the same extent – acknowledging, though, that the academic language may feel alien to many people!

Still, in this chapter, we have tried to show that moving abroad to work in HE, in a different language, can be a positively transformative experience. An open-minded approach to change, willingness to adapt and a more self-tolerant mindset will lead to self-reflection, self-questioning, self-evaluation, a search for self-equilibrium and eventually to a paradigm shift allowing a necessary re-conceptualisation of the notion of disruption.

Thus, with relatively small individual adjustments, but constant over a sufficiently long period of time, and in ecosystems where artificial barriers to full acceptance of diversity are removed as a matter of fact, such transitions should be truly constructive disruptions.

References

Ammigan, R., Veerasamy, Y. S., & Cruz, N. I. (2023). 'Growing from an acorn to an oak tree': A thematic analysis of international students' cross-cultural adjustment in the United States. *Studies in Higher Education, 48*(4), 567–581.

Bailey, W., Bordogna, C. M., Harvey, H., Jones, G., & Walton, S. (2021). Transformational, inclusive, and multicultural or empty rhetoric? Perceptions and experiences of international academic staff. *Journal of Further and Higher Education, 45*(3), 349–362. https://doi.org/10.1080/0309877X.2020.1762848

Bergson, H. (1889). *Time and free will: An essay on the immediate data of consciousness.* Doctoral thesis.

Callender, J., Fagin, L., Jenkins, G., Lester, J., & Smith, E. (2011). *Mental health of students in Higher Education.* College report CR166, Royal College of Psychiatrists. college-report-cr166.pdf (rcpsych.ac.uk)

Cheng, M., Pringle Barnes, G., Edwards, C., Valyrakis, M., & Corduneanu, R. (2015). *Transition skills and strategies – Critical self-reflection.* Enhancement Themes. http://www.enhancementthemes.ac.uk/pages/docdetail/docs/publications/transition-skills-and-strategies---critical-self-reflection

Colley, H. (2007). Understanding time in learning transitions through the lifecourse. *International Studies in Sociology of Education, 17*(4), 427–443. https://doi.org/10.1080/09620210701667103

Ecclestone, K., Biesta, G., & Hughes, M. (2009). *Transitions and learning through the lifecourse.* Routledge.

Eteläpelto, A., Vähäsantanen, K., Hökkä, P., & Paloniemi, S. (2014). Identity and agency in professional learning. In: Billett, S., Harteis, C., & Gruber, H. (eds.) *International handbook of research in professional and practice-based learning.* Springer International Handbooks of Education. Springer. https://doi.org/10.1007/978-94-017-8902-8_24

Higher Education Statistics Agency (HESA) (2024). *Higher Education Staff Statistics: UK, 2022/23.* https://www.hesa.ac.uk/news/16-01-2024/sb267-higher-education-staff-statistics

Jones, H., Mansi, G., Molisworth, C., Monsey, H., & Orpin, H. (2023). *Transitions into Higher Education.* Critical Practice in Higher Education Series. Critical Publishing.

McGarvey, A., Karivelil, D., & Byrne, E. (2021). International students' experience of medical training in an English-speaking European country. *Journal of Studies in International Education, 25*(5), 487–504. https://doi.org/10.1177/1028315320976029

Owens, A. R., & Loomes, S. L. (2010). Managing and resourcing a program of social integration initiatives for international university students: what are the benefits? *Journal of Higher Education Policy and Management, 32*(3), 275–290.

Pho, H., & Schartner, A. (2021). Social contact patterns of international students and their impact on academic adaptation. *Journal of Multilingual and Multicultural Development, 42*(6), 489–502. https://doi.org/10.1080/01434632.2019.1707214

Self Care Forum (2023). *Support people to self care.* https://www.selfcareforum.org/

Sharif, R. (2019). The relations between acculturation and creativity and innovation in higher education: A systematic literature review. *Educational Research Review, 28.* https://doi.org/10.1016/j.edurev.2019.100287

Supratman, A. M. (2013). Piaget's theory in the development of creative thinking. *Journal of the Korean Society of Mathematical Education, 17*(4), 291–307. https://doi.org/10.7468/jksmed.2013.17.4.291

Wenger, E. (2011). *Communities of practice: A brief introduction.* STEP Leadership Workshop. University of Oregon. http://hdl.handle.net/1794/11736

Woolf, V. (1925). *Mrs Dalloway.* Penguin Classics.

4 Time Keeps on Slippin', Slipping

Oldlings Holding on, and onto the Embodied Self

Felicity Molloy

Introduction: Who Worked the People?

Working woman, wives, burdened unwell, student, sister, professional, partner, Mother, menopausal mood swinger, lecturer, leader, grandmother, granddaughter, fatigued person, employee, dreamer, daughter, colleague, blusher, and bleeder are not singular titles for women in academic workplaces. On these terms, academic women may be perceived as unlike each other in their assemblages of body, social, and work life roles subtly, inevitably shifting over time. However, awareness of the 'who' of the body is not readily taken into account in the academy and consequentially often overlooked before women leave it. Do we leave our bodies behind – or do we take them with us?

Butler (2015) writes:

> Not every discursive effort to establish who 'the people' are works. The assertion is often a wager, a bid for hegemony. So, when a group or assembly or orchestrated collectivity calls itself 'the people,' they wield discourse in a certain way, making presumptions about who is included and who is not, and so unwittingly refer to a population who is not 'the people.' ... those considered to threaten 'the people,' or to oppose the proposed version of 'the people'.
>
> (p. 4)

Individuals approaching the conclusion of their academic journey must navigate feelings imposed by retirement. Recognising possible fragmentations of professional life accrued throughout a career is critical. It may be a time to learn new strategies for self-care. Arguably, all women hold in their bodies an experiential mix, conglomerate of roles and embodied selves. While previously experienced as a collective, women transitioning out of academia may unconsciously subvert to "not the 'people'" Butler (2015, p. 4) describes. The fragmentation of bodily experience could hinder any woman's overall wellbeing.

The goal of this chapter is to explore the experience of women as they age and prepare to leave academia. At the end of the chapter, I offer doable ways to practice wellness. McNaughton and Billot (2016) highlight a tendency to downplay

DOI: 10.4324/9781032688633-5

personal effects of developed and devolving role expectations. The central question guiding this chapter is about how women recognise when their previous academic identity no longer provides a sufficient sense of self, agency or secure identity. I bring holistic self-care to the foreground of wellbeing, positing that women may experience diminished wellbeing if not familiar with these personal effects held in sensorial expressions of the working body's wellness.

Rather than separating the experiencing, lived-in body from work within the academy, I regard the body as absorptive, holistic, agentic, and rich with the creation of experiential matter over time. Yet, I use Butler's term the 'precarity of performativity' to identify vulnerabilities of the body for women living with ageing and change. 'Lived-in' means a wholeness of the agentic self (Devos & Banaji, 2003) rather than living with expectancies drawn of hegemonies in sometimes-precarious professional lives. Achieving conscious balance amidst the multiplicity of roles in (and out) of academia requires an intelligence beyond the intellect.

Ageing, Selfhood in Health, and the Absented Body

Within complex roles at the university, bodily mixtures of social and work life may have been made invisible for women who stayed for 40-plus years. Active ageing requisites and "ageistic attitudes" (Marques et al., 2020, Introduction, para 1) require time, space and place for seeing, honouring, and resolving experiences that are embodied – by the individual. My concerns are heightened by a demographic shift towards an increasingly ageing population in higher education.

There are prolific citations that earth's human population is ageing with people 60 years and over expected to more than double in numbers by 2050. In addition, we face dilemmas of life expectancy advancements that have taken place (Rudnicka et al., 2020; United Nations Department of Economic and Social Affairs (UNDESA), 2017). Marques et al. (2020) state determinants of ageism are negatively positioned for oldlings[1], citing institutional tensions over resource allocation. As shortages become pronounced and coupled with a rising number of us, challenges over how resources are distributed become susceptible to pre-eminent institutional instances of ageism (Vauclair et al., 2015).

The term wellbeing already belongs to narratives of health, ageing and self, but more often than not Western medicalised health precludes an autonomous well self. Despite discussions about fostering healthy workplaces (Stoewen, 2016; Whatu Ora, 2023), work-life balance (Gragnano et al., 2020), and workloads linked to academic outputs (Kenny & Fluck, 2022), institutions overlook embodied experiences, treating people within the organisation as a homogeneous entity. Ageing selves plus professional experience might become the 'not' of Butler's surmise, if working women's bodies are aggravated by stress, deadline pressure cookers, and chronic compulsions to succeed. If we place wellbeing at the heart of the discussion about concluding work life in higher education, healthy behaviour must be understood as present, individually agentic, and unfixed. Through wellbeing

36 *Felicity Molloy*

narratives, I am alerted to how academic women hold a reciprocating need for inclusive holistic professional resources.

Psychological or pharmaceutical interventions become less pertinent if they are maintenance measures for addressing ill-health long after cumulative bodily experiences occur. The New Zealand Ministry of Health Manatū Hauora (MoH, 2012) defined "health behaviour change for improved chronic disease self-management" as "promoting the adoption of skills, behaviours and coping strategies to enable patients to actively participate in their health care and decision-making, and to maintain health and wellbeing" (p. 6). I consider the emphasis on changing behaviour for absenting chronic disease as ubiquitous and devaluing of ageing healthily, especially for women to leave their workplace in one embodied piece. Health-related contexts may lead the individual transitioning into becoming a patient or experiencing a decreased sense of patience with themselves.

Social justice advocate and second-wave feminist bell hooks challenges assumptions that focus on ageism or disembodied bodies. hooks (2015) entreats a release from hierarchical control, whether felt as coercive or perceived as benefit from institutional privileges. She emphasises the need to reject notions that perpetuate domination by addressing these issues in a comprehensive, holistic way. Social culturalist Hall (2011) uses terms like dislocation, displacement, or detour from Gramsci (1971) who locates hierarchies fissures when "incurable structural contradictions have revealed themselves" (p. 178). That is, bodily experience may need to be at the ready, and health behavioural change in balance with roles and their privileges, if they are no longer to be controlled within the academy.

Leder's work, *The Absent Body* (1990), and recent contemporary feminists such as Simon-Kerr (2021) partially detach activism from privilege, as work life inevitably transforms action, particularly when an integration of roles results from longevity and consequently, embodied experience. Shapiro (2011) writes "cognition emerges through dynamic interaction of the brain, body and the world" (p. 119). I employ Damasio's (2010) focus on the vanishing body of amnesiacs (and consequential threats to strong physical markers of an organism), to think through threats I associate with a reduction of body awareness in academic work. I assert relationship between individual and shared experience and agency. The theorists' articulation of cognition with bodily capability is consistent with wellbeing issues produced by us not developing a scholarly dialectic of body practicing.

Through this condensed sortie of literature, I highlight an absence of practical experiences along the work, ageing, and wellbeing continuum (refer to Figure 4.1). The studies substantiate the need for allocating time, changing approaches, and deliberately slowing down the pace of transition as a proactive means for self-care. I call this a method of holding onto self, and empowering the 'I', the 'myself' from embodied, bodily perspectives.

Somatics and Salving Not Slippin' Slipping Away from a Future Self

Somatics is a term coined by Hanna in 1976 and he, amongst others, developed praxes to inform expressive, technical, and performance skills of dancers and

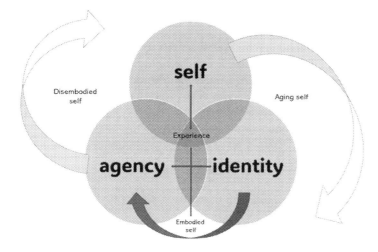

Figure 4.1 The Borromean rings: Academic women's experience shifting in their transitional time

Note: I have had to think through how to expand my working definitions of precarity, experiencing, embodiment, and 'lived-in' for use as methodological explanation, and eventually uphold somatic activities that support women transitioning out of the academy. The chart above visually depicts the interpretive shape and flow of my topic. It is a new graphic version of a hand drawing I made for the front page of my doctoral thesis. My drawing and my thesis utilised the mathematical metaphor of Borromean rings to develop a qualitative reflexive methodology named somathodology (Molloy, 2016).

bodyworkers. Somatic practices support "personal discovery and growth, including an emphasis on the development of kinaesthetic sense, a focus on the primacy of internal authority, and a fundamental belief in the wholeness of each individual" (Burnidge, 2012, p. 46). Fortin et al. (2002) state that somatic study upholds the capability to rework individual perspectives about the lived world, beginning with the most personal aspect: ourselves. Bruno and Pavani (2018) perceive the body simultaneously engaging with an internal milieu and external environments. Taken together, these perspectives show that somatics offer a grounding place for bodies in-action, presenting alternative ways for women to reset their milieu.

Body-based disciplines lead me to understand what an enduring embodiment practice might look like. Dance, yoga, and massage bask in the somatic landscape, where breath and extension become coordinates of timing, space, and pace of being in the world. In this chapter's brevity, an expansive description of each is not possible. I resort to Godard's (Godard & Bigé, 2019; Haaland, 2023) non-hierarchical movement theories to describe them as mind body disciplines: mechanics of movement (physiology), coordination (flow, effortlessness achieved within effort – practice), perception of movement (proprio- and interoception), and the libidinous (reflexive joy in moving at all, or sensing movement and stillness). These connections between physical, sensorial, spiritual, and mental wellbeing advance holistic approaches to health and wellbeing.

38   *Felicity Molloy*

I value these practices from practicing them and reflect on their principles for developing the somatic activities. Each practice promotes stress moderation as a mediated relationship with internalised context, felt from the external world. The expression of self – the 'I', the 'me' is a central ethic of mind. By cultivating conscious connections between the body made more aware, and the lived body as she is, we do mind! Or do you mind? These assertions recur with my themes. In effect, self, ageing, and agency are woven together to foster lifelong, profound comprehensions of one's owned embodied condition.

Getting from the Mind Body in Theory to Practice

A triquetra design of discursive entry points leads the chapter's trajectory. Intersections between themes of wellbeing, oldling bodies, and self-identification inspire a self-reflexive approach (Pagis, 2009; Field-Springer, 2020) to locate a methods framework that anchors our capability for articulating intuition, sensation, and insight. A deconstructive method inspired by the Borromean rings theorem (Chichak et al., 2004, p. 1308) becomes a tool to unpack a correspondingly reflexive interplay of themes, theories, and assumptions as core to the somatic activities, which are the central purpose of this chapter.

The fluid interpretive repertoire of somathodology (Figure 4.1) provides a nuanced approach for exploring ageing, transitioning, and embodiment. To start, I place the words 'experience' in the centre of the Borromean torsional form. The component rings of the Borromean structure represent theories of self, agency, and identity as dynamic and interconnected with experience. Already theories of embodied experience, now inside the interlocking circles, they instigate a confluent repertoire. I engage in somatic reflexivity, one that traverses my assumptions of what experience means to self, identity, and agency in and out of the academy.

Due to tensions implied by Borromean geometrics, the rings form an elliptical trajectory, arcing away from my central proposition – that experience is dynamic. Borromean intersections and extensions express ways women, previously settled within their time-drenched academic experience, become unsettled when transitioning out of the academy. Fragmented and wielded outwardly, themes become deconstruction of the overarching topic. In the Borromean pattern once one ring is separated, all rings fall apart. Self, agency, and identity become unsettled, or fall apart. Similarly, I am bound in thinking that these three themes are inseparable for holding onto effects of embodied experience.

Continuing to work from the centre across the interlocking themes to the expressions released out of the tension – hurled from the centre so to speak to capture ways women may be able to take from their experience to reconnect to self during transition and manage wellbeing. In brief, this ancient mathematical design in methodological form reveals how experience is a valuable resource for wellbeing. Each perspective once interwoven in Borromean style underpins how somatic principles of dance, yoga, and massage practices could be wellbeing currency for an oldling in the academy.

Time Keeps on Slippin', Slipping   39

The Somatic Activity

> To become agents of our own satisfaction, we need to approach the embodiment ... as a self-navigating meditative process to locate what may have previously escaped our attention – what can be asked of us and what can be discarded and how we become available for change.
>
> (P. Thomson, personal communication, 17 November, 2023)

An academic might fail to acknowledge the importance of cultivating a positive, resilient sense of ongoing selfhood through practices of self-care when there is imbalance. In the activities shared below and with compassionate regard for the 'myself', a somatic lens draws out how body knowing may help "locate what may have previously escaped our attention" and thereby conserve holistic identity. I make no assumption that the readers of this text are practiced in dance, yoga, or massage. I think of practice understanding as comfort and support for individuated transition purpose – the usefulness that is required of autonomous selfhood and integral to an enduring identity.

Common self-deprecating narratives can divert women from achieving meaningful transitional objectives. Baseline somatic practices of awareness and listening in reflective mode rest in self-determining motivations to change direction as in 'where to from here', and intention – willingness to see what might be around the corner. These words become practice scaffolds for experiencing adaptability. For women who become independent scholars post academia, the sequences of holistic practices may guide and nurture their embodied academic self-outside of a previous working life. The somatic activities offered below need to be approached from these points of view.

In the following sequence of activities for you to try, there are three practice prompts and eight embodiment prompts. This is not an intellectual exercise, rather stay curious and systematically seek new awareness. Above all this is an interior practice of engagement not for overly externalising gain as for example, roles and workplaces are. Upshot practice prompts to slow down change circumstances are to:

- Connect daily life aspirations for wellbeing to work life in somatic modes of reflection, awareness, and listening.
- Instantly reflect as a tool to override overwhelm, or suspend a lack of self-worth, instead highlighting our collegial potential for bodily intelligence to become tantamount with academic context.
- Set up a regular sustainable self-practice and balance embodied identities for flexible long-term experiencing.

Draw on experiences of academia and look for familiar strengths, or aspirations described previously as self-determining modes of motivation (M), direction (D), and intention (I). Use somatic modes of reflection (R), awareness (A), and listening (L) to sense body areas made more acutely aware. Be guided by your intuition,

40   *Felicity Molloy*

which might take a little time. Note that the same event or decision you bring to mind can be used in more than one activity. This repetition will create a somatic sequence and valuable insights.

The inspirational metaphors of interdisciplinary educator, Olsen (2022), articulate ways to immerse and communicate the 'myself' of the body in somatic action. I have, therefore, added body locations and her interpretive repertoires with each embodiment prompt, as bases for practicing sensorial feeling. Eventually practicing knowing the body will develop an acuity for feeling elsewhere.

Integrate reflection into your practice routine. Take time to assess your progress and identify areas for further development. Refine your approach by regularly evaluating what can be learnt from oversights. Include in your reflections distractions, fatigue, or disorganisation as they are embodied coordinates to harness progress in the making. Using the practice prompts 1–3, a 60-second writing activity becomes a summary of purpose.

As it is not possible to predict individualistic outcomes of a somatic synthesis process, this chapter leaves us without a one size fits all or generalisable conclusion, nor is it meant to. As Butler indicates in the opening reference, "Not every discursive effort to establish who 'the people' are works" (Butler, 2015, p. 4). Instead, let us have a look at an example of the somatic process and develop a distinctive self-awareness toolkit to persevere with agency in the face of ageing change, identity, or self in transition.

Example 1.

Embodiment prompt 8. Resilience and Perseverance: Develop resilience to face challenges and setbacks. Does improvement involve overcoming obstacles and is perseverance key to long-term success?

Motivation (M) – *To leave the institution but stay with scholarly work.*

Direction (D) – *I need to find out who will support me in this motivation.*

Intention (I) – *My intention is to leave at the end of 2023. I don't think I am ready to 'retire'.*

Reflection (R) – *On reflection, others have done this before me, they may know the best process; I have left a work life before and survived; I had to change departments, that felt hard, and I don't know if I have gotten over it – will this memory hold me back from moving forward?*

Awareness (A) – *I am aware of fatigue, and emotional[2] unsteadiness requires nurturing – who will do that? Can I anticipate setbacks rather than have to improvise with them?*

Listening (L) – *If I listen to myself, I know that I was not yet ready to leave. Emotional entanglement may mean I have to take more time to navigate departure (or change my remaining time).*

Body part: *"The feet are our base of support … they contain many nerve endings for sensing and responding… Shoes … encourage most of us to lose the articulate sensitivity which our feet possess. … Our feet constantly inform us of the stability of our base" (Olsen, 2020, p. 305).*

Time Keeps on Slippin', Slipping   41

Embodying the Body in Action

I am not going to be able to do all this in one go, and yes, there are disappointments. Where do I feel a) anxiety, b) possibility... ahhh, heart gets heavy when I worry; what if I breathe to melt my indecision. And my toes tingle at the thought of moving forward – go for a walk, stand and balance...

Summary of My Purpose for Navigating Transition with Resilience and Perseverance

I connect to life aspirations but less so easily on a daily wellbeing-to-work life mode. What reflective connections become the art of resilience to face transition challenges and setbacks? I see how much embodied at ground level is balanced as identity – flexible, and certain that timing and people can help me. I help 'myself' or, without a support/nurture person in mind, I have tools to notice or suspend my lack of my self-worth. I wonder if becoming embodied highlights, the collegial potential with academic others, especially if 'perseverance is key to my longer-term satisfaction'.

Now It Is Your Turn

I suggest using a maximum of three embodiment prompts in any one session. Return to them for insight, reflection, revision, or find new ones if you experience a setback.

Select an embodiment prompt from the following sequence and write a brief description of a prior experience (incident or event) from any one role felt by yourself in higher education. (Use the roles listed at the beginning of the chapter for inspiration).

Write an immediate connection you make to three synthesisers of experience:

Motivation (M)
Direction (D)
Intention (I)

Note the body part listed, and Olsen's (2020) excerpts for interpretation.

Use somatic modes to reflect on familiar strengths, aspirations, distractions, fatigue, or disorganisation as perceptual coordinates:

Reflection (R)
Awareness (A)
Listening (L)

Rewrite the embodiment prompt and develop a summary of purpose in a 60-second writing activity guided by the words of the practice prompts listed as 1–3.

And – go well.

42   *Felicity Molloy*

Embodiment Prompts

Adaptability: Cultivate adaptability in practice. Are you willing to adjust your strategies and goals based on others feedback? What would it feel like to practice witnessing changing circumstances, or new information?

Head. "The skull is the top body weight, balanced effectively on the spine. Sutures… are responsive to change, with subtle shifts in relation to inner pressures or exterior blows… changes to spinal patterns often involve work" (pp. 43–44).

Clarity of purpose and desired outcomes: Clearly define your objectives before engaging in embodiment practice. How do you recognise desired outcomes and align your efforts accordingly as in a micro-level time framing for a macro-level day-to-day potential?

Spine. "The weight transfer from the skull to the spine is crucial for … efficiency of the nervous system… brain and spinal cord are bathed in fluid for nourishment and protection" (p. 49).

Collaboration and Community: Engage with a community of practitioners. How will you share insights, learn from others, and build a network for support, inspiration, and diverse perspectives?

Shoulders. "The shoulder girdle helps us reach, hold and push away… A levering system into the centre of the body for force and shock absorption" (pp. 65–66).

Ethical Practice: What does it feel like to prioritise ethical considerations that ensure actions align with principles of integrity, honesty, and respect for self and others.

Thorax. "Assists in breathing and protects the lungs and heart…a highly mobile structure consisting of 12 ribs on each side… the bottom two are considered floating" (p. 57).

Innovation and Creativity: Foster innovation and creativity within your practice. What needs to happen to help encourage experimentation witnessing development of unique approaches that also enhance the relevance of your skills in other settings.

Gut. "The digestive system is involved with taking in, integration and letting go… Like breathing, digestion is an exchange with the environment; our inner outer dialogue affects efficient functioning" (p. 127).

Long-Term Vision: Short-term aspirations are important, but will you truly recognise how your current academic identity aligns with professional experience and contributes to your overall wellbeing?

Pelvis. "A highly mobile structure constantly responding to activity… When we work on these areas… the blocks are the places where the personal connections will come" (p. 83).

Presence: Practice with full presence. How will you focus and nurture a state of flow between body and the world around you to maximise your intention's effectiveness?

Legs. "Having a leg to stand on… I was more interested than afraid… with a sense of releasing old tensions" (p. 93).

Time Keeps on Slippin', Slipping 43

Resilience and Perseverance: Develop resilience to face challenges and setbacks. Does improvement involve overcoming obstacles, and is perseverance key to long-term success? (see Example 1).

Feet. "Our base of support… they contain many nerve endings for sensing and responding… Shoes… encourage most of us to lose the articulate sensitivity which our feet possess… Our feet constantly inform us of the stability of our base" (p. 305).

Conclusion

Physical and psychological responses manifested in the body can be a means to self-monitor positive and negative emotional states during a period of transition. Engaging with consistent practices of awareness and embodied responses is a situated means to exemplify practice-based cultures. By drawing attention to transition and process, I was able to see how an oldling academic could find their embodied space. Issues that come from thinking of the academy as hegemonic brought forward issues of when academia prescribes indelible marks on the agentic self. Prior to an academic woman becoming more or less 'patient', wellbeing identification work may connect us to aware states of experiences occurring at the coalface. Utilising embodied responses to monitor negative affective behaviours during a transition helps redefine professional identity. This redefinition is an emphasis on self, adaptation, and relationship for transitioning modes. In a nutshell, my colleagues take care with what you are doing, take ownership of your process, take time to process change in embodied roles, and find out what is significant from day-to-day self-reflexive embodying practices.

Notes

1 As I teach them dance and provide massage, I reflect on the term older adult. For this writing, I have chosen to use the word oldling, and on its definitions variously expressed here, I am reminded of the reliability of lineage, respect in engagement, and the authenticity of experience in the academy:

- Born or brought forth earlier than another or others (Webster, 2014).
- Comparative of old: seniority (English Wiktionary, n.d).
- Of longer standing or superior rank, position, validity, etc. (The American Heritage Dictionary of the English Language, 2016).

2 I differentiate emotion from feeling in this chapter. Emotion refers to a psychological state that involves complex reactions to a situation or stimuli. Feeling is more specific, a conscious awareness or subjective experience of an emotion heralding a response or the potential for adaptation (Ei4Change, 2022) (Oosterwijk, & Barrett, 2014).

References

Bruno, N., & Pavani, F. (2018). Perceiving your own body. In *Perception: A multisensory perspective*. Oxford University Press. https://doi.org/10.1093/oso/9780198725022.003.0002

Burnidge, A. (2012). Somatics in the dance studio: Embodying feminist/democratic pedagogy. *Journal of Dance Education, 12*, 37–47. https://doi.org/10.1080/15290824.2012.634283

44 Felicity Molloy

Butler, J. (2015). *Notes toward a performative theory of assembly.* Harvard University Press.

Chichak, K.S., Cantrill, S.J., Pease, A.R., Chiu, S.H., Cave, G.W., Atwood, J.L., & Stoddart, J.F. (2004). Molecular Borromean rings. *Science, 304*, 1308–1312. https://doi.org/10.1126/science.1096914

Damasio, A.R. (2010). *The feeling of what happens: Body and emotion in the making of consciousness.* Houghton Mifflin Harcourt.

Devos, T., & Banaji, M.R., (2003). Implicit self and identity. In M. R. Leary & J. P. Tangney (Eds.), *Handbook of self and identity* (pp. 153–175). Guildford Press.

Ei4Change. (2022, August, 20). *The difference between emotions and feelings* [Video]. YouTube. https://youtu.be/mUlmDSEEQq8

Field-Springer, K. (2020). Reflexive embodied ethnography with applied sensibilities: Methodological reflections on involved qualitative research. *Qualitative Research, 20*(2), 194–212. https://doi.org/10.1177/1468794119841835

Fortin, S., Long, W., & Lord, M. (2002). Three voices: Researching how somatic education informs contemporary dance technique classes. *Research in Dance Education, 3*(2), 155–179.

Godard, H., & Bigé, R. (2019). Moving-moved / A study in gravity. In S. Paxton (Ed.), *Drafting interior techniques* (pp. 89–104). Culturgest.

Gragnano, A., Simbula, S., & Miglioretti, M. (2020). Work-life balance: Weighing the importance of work-family and work-health balance. *International Journal of Environmental Research and Public Health, 1, 17*(3), 907. https://doi.org/10.3390/ijerph17030907

Gramsci, A. (1971). *Selections from the prison notebooks.* (Q. Hoare, & G. N. Smith, Eds. & Trans.). Lawrence & Wishart.

Hall, S. (2011). The neoliberal revolution. *Soundings, 48*, 9–28. https://doi.org/10.3898/136266211797146828

Haaland, P. (2023). Tonic function model: The human gravity response system. *Structure, Function, Integration. 50*(3). https://www.sfijournal.org/article/tonicfunction-model-the-human-gravity-response-system

hooks, b. (2015). *Outlaw culture: Resisting representations.* Routledge.

Kenny, J., & Fluck, A.E. (2022). Emerging principles for the allocation of academic work in universities. *Higher Education (Dordrecht), 83*(6), 1371–1388. https://doi.org10.1007/s10734-021-0747-y

Marques, S., Mariano, J., Mendonça, J., De Tavernier, W., Hess, M., Naegele, L., Peixeiro, F., & Martins, D. (2020). Determinants of ageism against older adults: A systematic review. *International Journal of Environmental Research and Public Health, 17*(7), 2560. https://doi.org10.3390/ijerph17072560.

McNaughton, S.M., & Billot, J. (2016). Negotiating academic teacher identity shifts during higher education contextual change. *Teaching in Higher Education: Critical Perspectives, 1*(6), 644–658. https://doi.org/10.1080/13562517.2016.1163669

Ministry of Health. New Zealand Guidelines Group. (2012). Effective health behaviour change in long-term conditions: A review of New Zealand and international evidence. https://www.health.govt.nz/system/files/documents/publications/effective-health-behaviour-change-long-term-conditions.pdf

Molloy, F. (2016). Fit to teach: Tracing embodied methodologies of dances who come to academia. (Doctoral thesis, University of Auckland). ResearchSpace. https://researchspace.auckland.ac.nz/handle/2292/34441

Olsen, A. (2020). *BodyStories: A guide to experiential anatomy.* University Press of New England.

Olsen, A. (2022). *Moving between worlds: A guide to embodied living and communicating.* Wesleyan University Press.

Oosterwijk, S., & Barrett, L. (2014). Embodiment in the construction of emotion experience and emotion understanding. In L. Shapiro (Ed.), *The Routledge handbook of embodied cognition* (pp. 250–260). Routledge/Taylor & Francis Group .

Pagis, M. (2009). Embodied self-reflexivity. *Social Psychology Quarterly, 72*(3), 265–283. https://doi.org/10.1177/019027250907200

Rudnicka, E., Napierała, P., Podfigurna, A., Męczekalski, B., Smolarczyk, R., & Grymowicz, M. (2020). The World Health Organization (WHO) approach to healthy ageing. *Maturitas, 139*, 6–11. https://doi.org/10.1016/j.maturitas.2020.05.018.

Seniority. (n.d.). Wiktionary. Retrieved February 23, 2024, from https://en.wiktionary.org/wiki/seniority

Shapiro, L. (2011). *Embodied cognition.* Routledge.

Simon-Kerr, J.A. (2021). Relevance through a feminist lens. In Dahlman, C., Stein, A., & Tuzet, G. (Eds.), *Philosophical foundations of evidence law.* Oxford University Press. https://doi.org/10.1093/oso/9780198859307.001.0001

Stoewen, D.L. (2016). Wellness at work: Building healthy workplaces. *Canadian Veterinary Journal = La revue veterinaire Canadienne, 57*(11), 1188–1190.

Te Whatu Ora Health New Zealand. Regional Public Health (2023). Workplace health and wellness. https://www.rph.org.nz/public-health-topics/workplace-health-and-wellness/

The American Heritage Dictionary of the English Language (5th ed.). (2016). Eds. *American Heritage dictionaries*, Houghton Mifflin Harcourt Publishing Company.

United Nations Department of Economic and Social Affairs. (2017). *World population prospects: The 2017 revision, key findings and advance tables.* United Nations.

Vauclair, C.M., Marques, S., Lima, M.L., Bratt, C., Swift, H.J., & Abrams, D. (2015). Subjective social status of older people across countries: The role of modernization and employment. *Journals of Gerontology Series B: Psychological Sciences and Social Sciences, 70*, 650–660. https://doi,org/10.1093/geronb/gbu074.

Webster's New World College Dictionary. (2014). Houghton Mifflin Harcourt.

5 Not Quite a Professor

Professional Identity, Self-care, and Time Management as an Atypical Academic

Carol-Anne Gauthier

Figure 5.1 Piecing together multiple identities, statuses, and workplaces as an atypical academic is a challenge, but through job crafting, I've managed to make it work

Introduction

Most people have a clear answer to the question "what do you do for a living?": nurse, salesperson, car mechanic... (Figure 5.1) And for a while, I had a simple answer to that too: college teacher. However, a few years after completing my PhD, I was invited back into the world of research and started combining multiple

DOI: 10.4324/9781032688633-6

statuses: college teacher, university lecturer, research professional, and eventually, college researcher. When I describe my activities to graduate students, they often respond with something like: "So... like a university professor, but not quite?" To which I laugh and say "yeah, like a university professor, but without the drama."

For context, in Québec, secondary education ends after five years, and most undergraduate degrees last three years. In between the two, students who wish to attend university generally complete a two-year pre-university program in a college. These are equivalent to the last year of high school and the first year of an undergraduate degree in the rest of North America. These colleges also offer technical degrees. To be hired, teachers must hold a bachelor's degree in the discipline to be taught. Many hold a master's degree, and a few hold a PhD. Although colleges are considered higher-education establishments, there is some debate as to whether teachers should be called professors or teachers. The English version of our collective agreement calls us professors, but the French version calls us teachers ("enseignants"). Amongst college teachers, professional identities (i.e. the meaning one attributes to one's work and one's sense of belonging to a professional group; Fray & Picouleau, 2010) can be quite varied. Indeed, a technical program teacher with a B.Sc. who also practices their profession (e.g. nursing) might not see themselves in the same light as a psychology teacher with a PhD who is still actively engaged in research.

Officially, I am a full-time, permanent college teacher with release time to participate in a university research team. This is made possible through a provincial research grant program that attributes funds to colleges to relieve teachers from part of their teaching load. I am also a university lecturer and research professional.

Many situations have made my atypical position quite salient. At academic conferences, I'm never quite sure what to respond when asked what I do or where I work. When I say, "I work with such-and-such a professor," they assume that I am a graduate student. When I teach graduate-level courses at university, I sometimes get asked by students if I can supervise their master's thesis, which I must regretfully decline despite having a PhD and being an expert in the field they are interested in. As a college teacher with a PhD, I can apply for my own research grants because certain funding bodies recognize colleges as institutions that can manage research funds. However, as a university research professional, although I can develop and coordinate research projects in collaboration with a professor who considers me a peer, I can't submit them to the university's research ethics board myself. One retired university professor bluntly told me that college teachers shouldn't be doing research. These are all little reminders that despite having the training and qualifications of a university professor, and despite doing a lot of the same work that they do, I am "not quite" what they are.

These kinds of encounters have led me to start thinking about how one defines oneself when one engages in almost all the same activities as a university professor but isn't "quite" one. My status has also led me to reflect upon my priorities and time management strategies. For example, when one is a professor, securing research grants and publishing in academic journals becomes a clear priority. At the university where I work, professors are provided with a clear set of expectations

48 *Carol-Anne Gauthier*

with regards to obtaining tenure. This, in theory, should help them establish clear priorities. But what about when one's professional identity fluctuates between teaching and research? When one has two or more employers? When the composition of one's workload can vary according to preferences and opportunities? How does one manage one's time when there are no clear, "objective" priorities?

Since both teaching and research can take up as much time as we let them, I must constantly decide how much time to devote to each type of work. I get to decide which projects to be involved in based on what I am passionate about, not what is more strategic based on my career goals. I write because I want to, not because I worry about losing my job if I don't produce enough. When I take a vacation, I don't worry about missing whatever important email that might be career changing. However, being an "outsider" also has some downsides, both materially and psychologically. There can be some psychological costs to feeling like one is "not quite…"

It certainly does not help that academia is particularly challenging for self-esteem. Egos and the importance of status are often inflated. Although "rationally" I know that my worth as an academic is not defined by my status, sometimes I feel like I am "not quite enough," or I experience different forms of cognitive dissonance (i.e. discomfort felt when one holds two opposing beliefs). I try to remind myself that *what I do* is more important than my job title, that I can contribute just as much either way, but it requires some identity work, self-care, priority-setting. and time management. These, in turn, require time, space, and energy, including time to reflect about professional identity, which can be a challenge when one is engaged in the fast-paced, intense world of academia. Nevertheless, I try to cultivate space to hold these reflections through self-care, self-management, and time management strategies. I do this by giving myself time to process, to distance myself, and to re-centre myself on my priorities and on maximizing my opportunities for contribution through job crafting (which I will define and explain later).

Professional Identity

Professional identity can be understood as being a part of a person's global identity. It involves three main aspects: the objective work situation and the meaning an individual gives it; the subjective perceptions of interpersonal relationships and the sense of belonging to an informal group; and professional trajectories and perceptions of the future (Fray & Picouleau, 2010, p. 75). Professional identity is developed through the interaction between one's self-identity – the mental representations that allow individuals to find coherence and continuity between past and present experiences (Sainsaulieu, 1985) – and others (such as peers and colleagues). Developing a strong professional identity may be conducive to perceiving meaningfulness in one's work, leading to increased wellbeing (Toubassi et al., 2023).

I find that there are many terms in English that capture my professional identity relatively well. I am an academic. A social scientist. But my university teaching and research are conducted primarily in French. In French, I have yet to find a clear label for what I *am*. So, I've been thinking about how to concisely describe what I *do*. So far, the best I've come up with is "*enseignante et chercheuse au collégial et à l'université,*" which translates to *college and university teacher and researcher*.

Although I am fairly satisfied with this professional identity, I still struggle with the "not quite" status that I have in the university setting. For example, I teach, develop courses, and conduct research with professors as an equal in their eyes, but I don't have a seat in department meetings, I am not invited to sit on committees, and I am not consulted about things such as program changes. In other words, I hold no power in important decision-making processes. It sometimes makes me feel like I don't quite belong, like I am not a "full" member of the academy. Like I don't really *matter*. Mattering is defined as "the individual's feeling that he or she counts, makes a difference" (Rosenberg, 1985, p. 215). "When we feel valued, we are appreciated, respected, and recognized. When we add value, we are able to make a contribution or make a difference" (Prilleltensky, 2019, p. 2). More specifically, mattering *at work* focusses on the relational aspects of work (Jung, 2015). It includes the perception that one's work matters to society as well as the sense that one's colleagues care about one. A sense of mattering at work has been associated with higher job satisfaction and better mental health (Jung, 2015).

Luckily, I work with amazing individuals who make me feel like I *do* matter and belong. I wouldn't still be doing university research if they didn't. The university professors I work with treat me like a peer. Some even ask me when the department will hire me as a professor, wondering why they haven't already. On one hand, it is a nice sign of recognition. On the other hand, it implies that being a university professor is a more enviable position than the one I am currently in. It reminds me that right now, I am "not quite...."

I sometimes feel like my atypical professional identity and status take a toll on my psychological wellbeing. In order to cope, I engage in self-care and self-management.

Self-care and Self-management

I would like to start by acknowledging the black feminist origins of the term *self-care*. For civil rights activists, self-care meant engaging in activities to take care of themselves to be able to sustain their activism. In recent years, self-care has also been conceptualized as a way of coping with the stress and distress associated with systemic discrimination and oppression (Wyatt & Ampadu, 2022). As someone who was active in the student and union movements for many years, I am familiar with activism burnout. I cannot begin to fathom how much heavier the burden would have been if I had also been a primary caregiver, a member of a marginalized group, or someone with a chronic illness.

Self-care has also been recommended as a set of strategies one can use to help facilitate coping and prevent and/or cope with burnout in stressful situations (Wyatt & Ampadu, 2022). When it comes to stressful situations, I think we can all agree that academia fits the bill. Nevertheless, thousands of graduate students choose this path despite most of them never landing coveted professor positions. I was once one of these graduate students.

As I was finishing my thesis, I started applying for professor positions. After a few disappointments, not wanting to remain precarious and burnt-out into my 30s, I decided to start exploring my options. Because I was social scientist who loved teaching, my partner suggested I might enjoy college teaching. Eureka! I applied on a few job postings, and I was quickly hired for a part-time position which eventually evolved into a full-time, permanent position. Stepping away from pursuing a university professor career allowed me to fully engage in a workplace that embraced me, with colleagues who appreciate my company and even throw compliments my way every once in a while. I very much enjoy college teaching, and for a while, all of my time and energy went into developing my pedagogical skills. Although the workload can get somewhat intense at times, it is relatively predictable, and I still had plenty of time for self-care as well as the occasional university lecturer contract.

When I was solicited to help develop a course with a professor at university, I was happy to help. The professor treated me like an equal, a colleague and an expert. That was a welcome change from my previous university experience. Our collaboration continued when he asked me to be a co-researcher on a project. That was a catalyst for the reframing of my professional identity to include "researcher."

Later, I was approached to coordinate a research Chair that specializes in mental health self-management. The first question I was asked was if I could take a leave of absence from my college position to work at the university full-time. My answer was a resounding "no." By this time, "college teacher" was my clear, strong professional identity. I simply could not imagine life without teaching. But I could take it on part-time to start.

This seems like a good time to introduce the concept of self-management. Self-management comes from the field of chronic illness management. It suggests that a patient is an active participant in their treatment, and that they can use strategies to manage their symptoms and/or prevent relapse (Barlow et al., 2002). Individuals can develop these strategies on their own, or they can learn them, for example through self-management education. More recently, it has been applied to mental health conditions such as mood and anxiety disorders (Lorig et al., 2014; Zoun et al., 2019). For example, self-management strategies that might be used by individuals struggling with depression include exercise and overcoming barriers to exercise adherence, building and sustaining social relationships, learning constructive communication techniques, and spirituality (Duggal, 2019).

Many self-management techniques can also be beneficial for individuals without mental illness diagnoses, but who nevertheless struggle with their mental health. Following the mental health continuum model (Keyes, 2002), we view mental health as more than the absence of mental illness. We also recognize that one can experience psychological difficulties without having symptoms severe enough to warrant a diagnosis. In this context, self-management strategies can be useful to alleviate languishing (i.e. low wellbeing) and promote flourishing. They can be particularly important for individuals who work in sometimes hostile environments (hello academia![1]).

Nevertheless, although self-care and self-management have different origins, some of the strategies they suggest are the same and can be applied by individuals who would like to minimize their languishing and maximize their flourishing. It occurred to me later that I've been practicing self-management without knowing it for twenty years, so it seems fitting that I would end up working for a research Chair on self-management!

Indeed, although for most of my life I had no diagnosis, I struggled with focus, impulse control, compulsive behaviours, and low mood/motivation. As a person who menstruates, I also struggle with hormonal cycles, which can wreak havoc on my ability to think clearly, to work productively, to take care of myself, and to manage my emotions. This is not something we talk about much in academia or in work life in general. In addition, research on the topic is scarce.

To me, self-management and self-care mean "protecting the asset" (i.e. conserving and investing in oneself, and one's creative abilities) (McKeown, 2014) whilst also reminding myself that my work (and status) does not determine my worth. "Protect the asset" is a term I like to borrow from Greg McKeown's book *Essentialism*. This book has a slightly different take than most books on productivity, as it is geared towards folks who have already had a certain level of success and are over solicited. McKeown invites the reader to reflect upon which activities and commitments truly create value and foster fulfilment, and those that don't. This, he argues, is the key to living a meaningful life.

This also happens to be the book that led me to explore stoicism. *The serenity to accept the things I cannot change, the courage to change what I can, and the wisdom to know the difference.* This mentality got me through the chaos of COVID and keeps me afloat in the complex jungle of academic life.

To me, self-care means taking care of not only my mind and body but also my spirit. Existential self-care means making sure my activities align with my values and goals for living a meaningful life. What makes my work meaningful is that it allows me to prioritize contribution while finding balance and wellbeing. Protecting the asset requires creating rules around time management. This is a skill I've been working on for years. It started when I was a PhD student trying to juggle many responsibilities. I wanted to "unlock the secrets to productivity." Below I share a few lessons I've learned on this journey.

Time Management

At its core, time management is priority and boundary management. With many competing, varying (albeit overlapping) engagements, this has become a constant theme in my life. I often take a step back, assess what I am doing, and determine what I want to do less of and what I want to do more of. In terms of priority management, the position I am in makes it complicated at times. If I was a university professor, I would focus on writing and publishing. If I was a full-time college

52   *Carol-Anne Gauthier*

teacher, I would prioritize teaching. I have chosen to prioritize knowledge transmission, through teaching and publishing.

Once my priorities became clear, I needed to start managing boundaries. For example, it can be a challenge to put up boundaries with respect to logistics related to ongoing research projects. When a project involving partners is about to launch, there are always several little strings left to attach and little fires to put out. If I let myself, I will get completely sucked into these logistics and become overwhelmed, leaving little time to reflect on my teaching and try out new pedagogical methods, let alone write meaningful articles or book chapters. I have learned to do what I can within specific time slots and tell my team members that I am unavailable at certain moments. The good news is that someone usually steps up and gets it done. But when you are a people pleaser who likes to get things done ahead of time, learning to manage the stress and guilt that comes with boundary setting can be a challenge!

I realize that my ability to set certain priorities and boundaries, thanks to my job security and high autonomy, is a privilege. In the field of organizational psychology, it is called *job crafting.* Job crafting is defined as "the physical and cognitive changes individuals make to the relational boundaries of their work." (Wrzesniewski & Dutton, 2001, p. 179). It can include modifying the form or number of activities one engages in while at work. The ability to engage in job crafting has been positively associated to wellbeing (Slemp et al., 2015). Examples of how I job craft include: blocking off time for deep work (writing, thinking, creating) almost every morning, requesting that the courses I teach be scheduled during the afternoon, and minimizing meetings and logistics-related tasks. On this topic, I highly recommend two books by Cal Newport: Deep Work (2016) and A World Without Email (Newport, 2021).

Individual Time Management Strategies

On an individual level, I highly suggest creating an individualized system that works for you. This can take a while to develop, but it beats trying to force yourself to use something that doesn't work. I use the *Getting things done* framework (Allen & Fallows, 2015) with a bullet journal (Carroll, 2018) and a productivity app like Notion. Any new task or idea that arises goes in the bullet journal. It is like an inbox. Then, a few times a week, I plug things into a master task list in Notion.

Every semester, I list my engagements in my "master task list": courses I teach, research projects I'm involved in, articles I am writing, etc. I input them into Notion by deadline. Then, I have another column for a self-determined "next time I should work on this" date. For example, if an article is due in November, I might start working on it regularly starting in September. Then, I work on it almost every morning for an hour or two and push back the "next time…" date. I do this because I find it difficult to work on a complex task for more than an hour or two at a time. I like to switch things up.

That being said, I also know that context switching can ruin my attention and dampen my creativity. To help reduce it, I use batching and time-blocking.

For example, I batch all my small teaching-related administrative tasks and do them all one after the other within a specific timeframe (for example, Monday afternoons at 3pm). When these little tasks pop up during the week, I note them in my bullet journal. Then, once a day (or once every few days), I take all these little tasks and add them to a Notion list (which has – you guessed it – a "next time" date).

Every week, I review my Notion "master task list" and plan my week accordingly. Once my weekly task list is complete, I plug the tasks into my calendar. For example: writing from 6am to 8am, marking from 1pm to 3pm, etc. This can vary quite a bit as my schedule changes, so I schedule it in my digital calendar. Every morning, I check my calendar and to-do list, and I plan my day accordingly. One of the core aspects of this system is pre-setting certain non-negotiables. For example, my yoga classes are already set in my calendar for the rest of the year. So are my deep work writing sessions and a few family events. I treat them like I would any other important appointment. They are what keep be grounded, mindful, and able to manage the stress related to being an academic. They are some of my core self-management strategies, designed to protect the asset (i.e. me!).

Of course, none of this advice is useful if you are consistently overloaded. It also doesn't help answer the core questions of what you *want* to do and *why*. I recommend taking the time to reflect upon these things at least twice a year. I like to do it during winter and summer vacations. I usually take this time to read a personal development book. I rarely learn anything new, but it always reminds me that my time on this earth is limited, and that I want to contribute as much as possible. Also, I refuse to spend most of it *languishing*. Thus, when deciding on my priorities, I try to focus on contribution. What are the things I am doing that I find most useful? What might not be, that I can let go of?

One of the biggest life changers for me was learning to say no to meetings. Or at least, saying no to meetings that occur during my peak focus hours or that don't *really* require my input. I've explicitly told my research team that I don't accept meeting invitations before 10am. That is because one of my central roles in the team is writing articles and engaging in other forms of knowledge transfer. This decision stems from my firm belief that one of the main contributions I can make in this world is sharing knowledge with a diversity of audiences in a variety of formats.

Collective Strategies

Of course, none of these tips address the core issue, which, according to me, is the organizational culture of academia. If you're reading this, chances are you know what I'm talking about. So, what can we do? I think professors can use their power and position in academia to nudge things in the right direction. For example, in Québec, most university professors are unionized. In recent years, appropriate workloads are one of the main bargaining demands. This includes recognizing all the types of work that professors do (for example, unfunded research, service to the

54 *Carol-Anne Gauthier*

community, serving on thesis juries, time spent staying abreast of advancements in their field), as well as hiring more colleagues and support staff to redistribute work to make it healthier for everyone.

In addition, professors, individually and collectively, can be role models. They can take days off, including mental health days, and discuss it openly. They can ask their students and colleagues how they are *really* doing and ask how they can support them. They can teach students how to prioritize and plan their work and teach them to work in teams to share the load. Research teams can set rules for working together sustainably. They can stop perpetuating the toxic idea that becoming a professor is somehow "better" than other research and teaching jobs such as the ones found in colleges, industry, or government, and that anyone who "settles" for these jobs has somehow "lost" at the game of academia.

Another strategy involves making more space for non-professors in universities. There are plenty of lecturers and research professionals with PhDs who could lead research projects if they had access to the funding and infrastructure necessary to do so. They could be a strong addition to research teams, including as mentors to graduate students. This could help professors lighten their loads as well, while providing alternative role models to students. However, the low status and high precariousness of these jobs make them unappealing to most graduate students, in addition to being detrimental to these workers' wellbeing. Structural changes like increasing autonomy (e.g. having the right to request research funding and to submit ethics board approval requests) and status (e.g. better representation on decisional bodies, more job security, and better pay) are central to changing this situation. For more insights on these and related topics, I recommend *Doing Academic Careers Differently* (Robinson et al., 2023) and *The Slow Professor* (Berg & Seeber, 2017).

Conclusion

In closing, although my position in the academy has its drawbacks in terms of power, autonomy, and recognition, it also provides insights and opportunities. Indeed, it has compelled me to reflect upon my professional identity, to engage in job crafting, and to develop self-management strategies – which happen to be some of my research interests. It has also forced me to set my own priorities and boundaries to ensure that I focus on what makes my work meaningful, so that it fits into my larger vision of a life well lived. Although the individual strategies discussed in this chapter might benefit other academics, they will never compensate for larger structural issues, for which I also humbly suggest collective strategies to promote wellbeing in academia.

Note

1 Funny story: I had the privilege of meeting Martin Seligman at the 2023 International Positive Psychology Association congress and asked him if he thought academia might eventually catch on to the importance of promoting wellbeing at work. He laughed.

References

Allen, D., & Fallows, J. (2015). *Getting Things Done: The Art of Stress-Free Productivity* (Revised edition). Penguin Books.

Barlow, J., Wright, C., Sheasby, J., Turner, A., & Hainsworth, J. (2002). Self-management approaches for people with chronic conditions: A review. *Patient Education and Counseling, 48*(2), 177–187.

Berg, M., & Seeber, B. K. (2017). *The Slow Professor: Challenging the Culture of Speed in the Academy* (Reprint edition). University of Toronto Press.

Carroll, R. (2018). *The Bullet Journal Method: Track the Past, Order the Present, Design the Future* (Illustrated edition). Portfolio.

Duggal, H. S. (2019). Self-Management of depression: Beyond the medical model. *The Permanente Journal, 23*, 18–295. https://doi.org/10.7812/TPP/18-295

Fray, A.-M., & Picouleau, S. (2010). Le diagnostic de l'identité professionnelle: Une dimension essentielle pour la qualité au travail. *Management & Avenir, 38*(8), 72–88. https://doi.org/10.3917/mav.038.0072

Jung, A.-K. (2015). *Development and validation of a work mattering scale* [University of Missouri-Columbia]. https://mospace.umsystem.edu/xmlui/bitstream/handle/10355/47122/research.pdf?sequence=2&isAllowed=y

Keyes, C. (2002). The Mental health continuum: From Llnguishing to flourishing in Life. *Journal of Health and Social Behavior, 43*, 207–222. https://doi.org/10.2307/3090197

Lorig, K., Ritter, P. L., Pifer, C., & Werner, P. (2014). Effectiveness of the chronic disease self-management program for persons with a serious mental illness: A translation study. *Community Mental Health Journal, 50*(1), 96–103. https://doi.org/10.1007/s10597-013-9615-5

McKeown, G. (2014). *Essentialism: The Disciplined Pursuit of Less*. Crown Currency.

Newport, C. (2016). *Deep Work: Rules for Focused Success in a Distracted World*. Grand Central Publishing.

Newport, C. (2021). *A World without Email: Reimagining Work in an Age of Communication Overload*. Portfolio.

Prilleltensky, I. (2019). Mattering at the intersection of psychology, philosophy, and politics. *American Journal of Community Psychology, 65*(1–2), 1–19. https://doi.org/10.1002/ajcp.12368

Robinson, S., Bristow, A., & Rattle, O. (Eds.). (2023). *Doing Academic Careers Differently: Portraits of Academic Life*. Routledge.

Rosenberg, M., & McCullough, B. C. (1981). Mattering: Inferred significance and mental health among adolescents. *Research in Community & Mental Health, 2*, 163–182.

Sainsaulieu, R. (1985). *L'Identité au travail. Les effets culturels de l'organisation.* Presses de Sciences Po.

Slemp, G. R., Kern, M. L., & Vella-Brodrick, D. A. (2015). Workplace well-being: The role of job crafting and autonomy support. *Psychology of Well-Being, 5*(1), 7. https://doi.org/10.1186/s13612-015-0034-y

Toubassi, D., Schenker, C., Roberts, M., & Forte, M. (2023). Professional identity formation: Linking meaning to well-being. *Advances in Health Sciences Education, 28*(1), 305. https://doi.org/10.1007/s10459-022-10146-2

Wrzesniewski, A., & Dutton, J. E. (2001). Crafting a job: Revisioning employees as active crafters of their work. *The Academy of Management Review, 26*(2), 179. https://doi.org/10.5465/amr.2001.4378011

Wyatt, J. P., & Ampadu, G. G. (2022). Reclaiming self-care: Self-care as a social justice tool for black wellness. *Community Mental Health Journal, 58*(2), 213–221. https://doi.org/10.1007/s10597-021-00884-9

Zoun, M. H. H., Koekkoek, B., Sinnema, H., Van Der Feltz-Cornelis, C. M., Van Balkom, A. J. L. M., Schene, A. H., Smit, F., & Spijker, J. (2019). Effectiveness of a self-management training for patients with chronic and treatment resistant anxiety or depressive disorders on quality of life, symptoms, and empowerment: Results of a randomized controlled trial. *BMC Psychiatry, 19*(1), 46. https://doi.org/10.1186/s12888-019-2013-y

Part 2
Intensification and Care

58 *Intensification and Care*

Echoes of Academia: Time, Care, and Collective Wellbeing

Narelle Lemon

In the corridors of academia, where time's relentless churn,
We find ourselves caught in a cycle, where work and care intertwine and yearn.
For productivity's demand grows, a relentless drumbeat,
While the call for self-care echoes, a melody sweet.

The intensification of work, a weight we bear,
Heavy burdens of scholarship, teaching, service we share.
But amidst this hustle and bustle, let us not forget,
The importance of care, a haven where we set.

The overwork culture, an added layer of strain,
Emotional labor compounded, as we strive to maintain.
Yet, in the face of adversity, let us not despair,
But instead, nurture our wellbeing with utmost care.

The silence surrounding intensification and care, we must break,
Creating space and time, our voices to awake.
For in holding each other accountable, we find strength anew,
In weaving individual and collective wellbeing, a path we pursue.

Reflection becomes our guide, a beacon in the night,
A valuing of time, where personal and academic worlds unite.
As we navigate the complexities of academia's sway,
Let us prioritize our wellbeing, day by day, moment by moment.

For in understanding the factors that shape our mental health,
We pave the way for interventions, fostering collective wealth.
So let us heed the call, with wisdom and with grace,
Navigating the currents of academia, in this sacred space.

DOI: 10.4324/9781032688633-7

6 The Work of Wellbeing

Making Time and Creating Space in Academia

Angela W. Webb and Melanie Shoffner

As teacher educators, we know that teachers must possess an integrated specificity of knowledge, skills, and dispositions in order to teach effectively; indeed, our day-to-day work is focused on developing those competencies in our preservice teachers. We also include self-care and wellbeing as part of our preservice teachers' professional competency. While in the past, we tended to address issues of care as questions arose or in tandem with other topics, we are increasingly incorporating these issues directly to intentionally develop their self-awareness and personal resilience. Developing competency with self-care offers preservice teachers additional tools to proactively support their own wellbeing and, by extension, counter whatever institutional or systemic issues that make self-care a necessary component of their professional lives.

Like our preservice teachers, we also need to approach the knowledge, skills, and dispositions necessary to our wellbeing with intentionality. Faculty wellbeing has always been a multifaceted concept (e.g., Larson et al., 2019; Sabagh et al., 2022) but, as we have written elsewhere (Shoffner & Webb, 2022), the pandemic highlighted both the need for and lack of faculty self-care. We know we must focus on our physical, mental, and emotional health, for all the reasons we convey to our preservice teachers, but the work of wellbeing requires time and space to do so.

As we have written elsewhere, "care is a complex endeavor in education, with no one standard definition and no one recognized enactment…[but]… the central element of care remains that of relationships" (Shoffner & Webb, 2022, p. 3). The time to inhabit a relational caring space is sorely lacking in higher education. As O'Dwyer et al. (2018) aptly explain, "there is never enough time, the clock is against us, we are behind schedule, tasks take too much time, time is running out" (p. 244). Acts of wellbeing take time away from the work of scholarship, teaching, and service required by our profession, generally, and our institutions, specifically – and we inhabit institutional spaces that increasingly charge us

> to produce more, to produce more that is measurable, to produce more with less; to engage, to engage with impact, to engage with more significant impact; to deliver, to deliver with efficiency, to deliver with more efficiency; to be available, to be more available, to be available without delay.
>
> (O'Dwyer et al., 2018, p. 244)

60 *Angela W. Webb and Melanie Shoffner*

With so much *more* needed from us on a daily basis, carving out space in our schedules to address our own wellbeing seems to add another facet to our workload. The constant pressure of limited time to do unlimited work makes it feel as if our colleagues are taking too much of our preciously guarded time when they stop us in the hallway with questions or drop by our office for conversations. So, we throw out a "how are you?" as we walk quickly from classroom to office; we shut our office door to focus on our computer screens; we offer a quick smile as we leave campus.

However, we believe that taking the time for personal interactions with colleagues is making space for our wellbeing. Rather than relying on serendipitous moments of interaction, we must be intentional in reaching out to others. By spending time with and creating space for colleagues on a daily basis, we are able to engage in small acts of self-care that collectively support our individual wellbeing. So, in this chapter, we two teacher educators reflect on wellbeing as intentional work, highlighting ways that we consciously oppose the culture of busyness inherent to academia to focus, however briefly, on the happiness, health, and prosperity – i.e., the wellbeing (Merriam-Webster, n.d.) – of ourselves and each other.

Visualizing Wellbeing

Never underestimate the benefits of a comfy chair, a sunny window, a piece of chocolate, or a cup of hot tea. Any one of these seemingly small things can offer a moment of respite; in combination, they describe a corner of Melanie's office (Figure 6.1).

We are professors at a recently reclassified research-intensive university located in a picturesque mountain valley in northwest Virginia (USA). Melanie is an English teacher educator, Angela a science teacher educator; we both have prior teaching experience at the secondary level. In our professional capacities, we teach multiple classes, work with preservice teachers, engage in research, and write for publication. We serve on departmental and college committees while engaging in administrative work at the university level. All of this work is influenced by several university-wide initiatives reshaping the current academic environment. Beyond the university, we serve our state and national organizations in different capacities; we also edit the professional journals *English Education* (Melanie) and *Journal of Virginia Science Education* (Angela).

Our daily work life in the college happens in a converted high school building – built originally in the 1920s – without many of the amenities of the more modern facilities on campus. Offices are a hodge-podge of shapes and sizes, with furniture scavenged from the university's surplus supplies, located in suites carved out of former classrooms.

Certain offices in the building, like Melanie's, have the saving grace of six-foot-tall windows. Melanie's love of sunlight means the blinds are always open for a view of the trees lining the parking lot and the skies above. A green and blue padded chair, liberated from an unoccupied office, sits under one of those

The Work of Wellbeing: Making Time and Creating Space in Academia 61

Figure 6.1 An office respite

windows, a small table beside it. The latest copies of the journal she edits sit on a corner of the table; a box of tissues, a stapler, and a bowl of assorted chocolates are arranged across the surface. The bookshelves above the chair hold an assortment of items – Melanie's published scholarship, recent young adult novels, a small plant – as does the window ledge: a button stating, "truth over lies," a framed print proclaiming, "Put your big girl panties on and deal with it!"

This chair is where students perch during office hours to discuss their progress, where colleagues stop to ask a question or share an update. This chair is where Angela sits with her laptop and mug of tea during our collaborative work sessions, where Melanie settles when she needs a respite from the computer. But this corner is more than a workspace: It is a small space of wellbeing.

Some may be familiar with the increasingly distant concept of *visiting*, where friends and family drop by unannounced for a brief period of socializing. Those who *came visiting* were always offered something to eat or drink; they might stand in the kitchen if there was work to do or sit on the porch if there wasn't, but they

62 *Angela W. Webb and Melanie Shoffner*

were always welcomed. This was an accepted ritual in the rural American South of our childhoods. Angela grew up in a small town in North Carolina, with Melanie's rural home just a few miles away, as we were surprised to learn when we met at our current institution. So, perhaps our familiarity with unannounced visits makes us more open to pausing the constant work when Angela plops down in the corner of Melanie's office. The pause, the checking in, the listening and conversing – all elements of moments of respite and integral to how we cultivate wellbeing for ourselves and one another amid an academic culture of busyness and productivity.

Positioning Wellbeing

Engaging in wellbeing is work – and this work is hard. We are operating within systems that benefit when faculty prioritize the work of the profession over personal care, and the ever-increasing commodification of higher education only adds to those pressures (Ball, 2004). The push to produce more scholarship, teach additional courses, and provide increasing service comes at the cost of faculty wellbeing, and the strength of that push has only increased with the fallout from the COVID-19 pandemic (Brabazon, 2021). With "the nature of academic work…inherently problematic for wellbeing and recent changes in higher education exacerbat[ing] the problem" (Rhew et al., 2021, p. 44), cultivating care and wellbeing is an act of resistance against the busyness narrative that dominates academic work.

The "complex, non-linear relationships" (Mudrak et al., 2018, p. 325) between our work environments and our wellbeing are even more so for women faculty. Although all faculty are affected by the stress and pressure of academic work, gender is an important mediating factor. Women faculty are expected by students, colleagues, and institutions to care in more and specific ways or risk being labeled as selfish, uninterested in success or advancement, or disengaged from our jobs; by taking time to care for and focus on our own wellbeing, women faculty are problematized in specific negative ways (Bellas, 1999; Elliott & Blithe, 2021).

Even when institutions address faculty wellbeing – and especially within institutions that lack such a focus – faculty bear the onus of crafting spaces and establishing time for wellbeing (Roos & Borkoski, 2021), making the relationship between the academic work environment and faculty wellbeing even more fraught (Mudrak et al., 2018). For example, university initiatives focused on participation in affinity groups or the creation of exercise regimens may benefit faculty wellbeing but they also require faculty, rather than institutions, to carve out time for these activities. As such, self-preservation becomes a factor. As Audre Lorde (2017) clarified, "caring for [ourselves] is not self-indulgence, it is self-preservation" (p. 130). It is all too easy to lose ourselves to the many demands on our time.

The ways in which universities do and do not support the health and wellbeing of their students, staff, and faculty are vitally important for mental wellness as well as academic and professional success. For faculty, "engaging in self-care is not only worthy for us as individuals, but rather, enables us to return to our work with students and colleagues with renewed energy and enthusiasm" (O'Dwyer et al., 2018, p. 244). After all, students' success and wellbeing are influenced, overtly and

The Work of Wellbeing: Making Time and Creating Space in Academia 63

covertly, by their faculty and that faculty's wellbeing (Cavanagh, 2023; Roos & Borkoski, 2021). As Cavanagh (2023) explained, students' "emotional experiences during learning mirror *our* emotional experiences during teaching" (emphasis in original, para. 7).

Daring to care about our wellbeing is a reclamation that faculty are more than our academic work, an increasingly difficult stance with institutional imperatives to deliver more. Yet, it is work – seen and unseen – to push back, to swim against the current, to create space for our wellbeing. That work is situated against the inflexible quantity of time: It does not and cannot increase. Within the time available to us, then, we must not only recognize the importance of caring for ourselves but engage in wellbeing through specific actions.

Respite as Wellbeing

The United States Surgeon General's (2023) framework for workplace mental health and wellbeing, rooted in the post-pandemic 'return' to the workplace, speaks to the intentionality required for individual wellbeing. The framework centers worker voice and equity through five essential elements: (1) protections from harm, (2) connection and community, (3) work-life harmony, (4) mattering at work, and (5) opportunity for growth. These integrated elements and practices are necessary – yet on their own insufficient – to support workplace wellbeing while acknowledging that mental health and wellbeing in the workplace are not solely the responsibility of the worker.

Although not specific to academia, this framework resonates with the issues faculty face in attending to their own wellbeing. Academia features key elements of work-life harmony – namely autonomy and flexibility (Office of the Surgeon General, 2023) – but the nature of the profession blurs boundaries between work and non-work time, as outside-of-work needs, roles, and responsibilities suffer to meet explicit and implicit work expectations (e.g., Elliott & Blithe, 2021). The intentional strategies we have adopted for our wellbeing are directly associated with the essential elements of connection, community, and work-life harmony of the workplace wellbeing framework (Office of the Surgeon General, 2023). Our working relationship has organically transcended that of co-workers to that of friends; from a place of common background and shared perspectives, we have developed a trusting relationship and created opportunities for collaboration.

The different ways in which we work intentionally to support our wellbeing may be small steps in the larger context, but this intentional work to care for ourselves keeps us human in institutional contexts that often do not uplift or celebrate our humanity. Our efforts to make time and create space for wellbeing occur across locations (e.g., on- and off-campus) and foci (e.g., work-related and non-work-related). The unifying feature, though, is respite.

The opportunities for respite we share below allow us to slow down, think, and reflect, regardless of location or activity. Our non-work strategies revolve around fellowship, celebration, and support. Even when the focus is work-related, productivity and competitiveness are not the goal. Rather, those work-related moments of respite are humanizing, helping us to keep or reclaim a sense of ourselves in the academic space.

On-campus

The comfy chair in a sunny campus office pictured in Figure 6.1 is our on-campus space of respite. It is where we've created collaborative conference presentations, co-edited our books, talked through teaching dilemmas, and asked for and shared professional advice. This chair in the corner is also the site of our work to resist busyness, take time, and care for ourselves and one another.

This chair is the space of respite in which we share celebrations, concerns, and quandaries – both personal and professional – over snacks and hot tea or while peering over our laptops in concentration. This is where we share how we successfully prioritize our own wellbeing, where we fall short, and check in on how the other is taking care of themselves. Refrains of *I'm glad you spent some time cozied up with a book!, Have you eaten?,* and *Don't stay too late* echo from this corner. Even when work is the focus of our on-campus conversations, the hurried pace of productivity is absent as we relish our collaborative thinking. The vulnerability of asking questions, constructing nascent ideas, and sharing aspirations nurtures our professional selves and helps us reclaim the humanity in our work.

Off-campus

Our off-campus sites of respite vary in location and duration but they always create the time and space to care for ourselves and each other. As the adage goes, "you can't pour from an empty cup." For us to show up in our personal and professional lives, wholly and authentically, we must take the time to focus on our own wellbeing.

Sometimes, our respite is found in 'writing' retreats during semester breaks: brief getaways to rented houses in small towns around our state where the intent is scholarly writing but the reality is doing whatever we feel is needed in the moment to care for our whole selves, free from judgment. This may be writing editorials, reviewing chapter proofs, or drafting manuscripts but it is just as likely to be enjoying a cup of coffee overlooking the soothing waters of an inlet, taking long walks, practicing yoga, cozying up with a book, or exploring local shops and restaurants. We recognize the privilege in being able to take these retreats that both restore and refocus our scholarship; we also appreciate the power in unapologetically centering ourselves within our work and our lives for a few days.

On a smaller scale, our off-campus strategies also include making time for hours-long work sessions in comfortable spaces. We find respite in the shaded calm of Angela's back porch, joined by her sleepy dogs, and the casual comfort of Melanie's home office, surrounded by her many plants. Wherever we are, salty snacks, chocolates, hot teas, and Diet Cokes are on hand, with no judgment offered on the choices we make to fuel our work sessions. In these moments, we inhabit a

The Work of Wellbeing: Making Time and Creating Space in Academia 65

caring space that comes from the acceptance of each other's idiosyncrasies and the focus of working together toward a common goal.

Sometimes, wellbeing is found in the respite of an intentional treat. 'Lovely Ladies Days' (and sometimes Nights) are the adventures we plan with another colleague-turned-friend, from lunches and manicures to winery visits and dinners. Sometimes, these are planned well in advance to celebrate career milestones, birthdays, or holidays; other times, they are in response to a group text message questioning when we last saw each other for purposes other than work. When it's the latter, dinner is immediately scheduled for the next evening when we're all available. Sometimes, work creeps into the Lovely Ladies' conversations; oftentimes not. Instead, we talk about family, hobbies, new adventures (such as Angela's adult ballet class through the city's parks and recreation department) and what we're reading and watching (Melanie consistently recommends the perfect book or TV series for any particular sort of mood). In the stretches of time between our get-togethers, we stay connected through a group text thread, sharing updates and checking in on each other even as we sit in the same meetings or pass one another in campus hallways. In the cadence of our text thread, we honor each other's rhythms of life – Angela an early bird; Melanie a night owl – while making time to celebrate, support, and care for each another one small text bubble at a time.

Fundamentally, these strategies come down to holding space and time for one another and, in doing so, resisting the pervasive academic culture of busyness and productivity. Do these strategies distract time and focus away from answering emails, grading student work, editing our respective journals, writing manuscripts, or completing committee tasks? Of course. Do they center us and refill our cups in order to do this academic work? Absolutely! However, we need to create for ourselves the spaces and opportunities for *visiting*, as described above, in support of our individual and collective wellbeing and we feel the absence of these spaces and opportunities when we lose ourselves to work demands on our time.

Conclusion

In their invitational poem to readers, O'Dwyer et al. (2018) offered these inflection points for resisting the culture of busyness and productivity inherent to academic work: "Remember this is what you do, not who you are…Remember this is your job, not your life" (pp. 246, 247). Remembering these points – and navigating our work as though we remember these points – is easier when we collaboratively and collectively make time and create space for these efforts.

In many ways, our individualized, personalized efforts to care for each other are a visible rejection of the increasing commodification of higher education and changing university priorities. We are critical of our academic environment (Shoffner & Webb, 2020, 2022) precisely because we *do* care – about our colleagues, our students, and ourselves. We care because we see them – us – as individuals, not interchangeable cogs in a machine, individuals who care for and about one another – and ourselves – through responsive relationships (Noddings, 2005).

Admittedly, the work of wellbeing is not easily replicated in the institutional context of the university. After all, we each work and live in unique contexts and our intersecting positionalities affect how we give, receive, and perceive care. There is value, however, in pulling back the curtain to share what works for us and, just as importantly, how we make it work in support of our individual and collective wellbeing: The more examples offered of making time and holding space for our wellbeing, the better able we may be to find strategies that work for us personally.

Our wellbeing, then, has immediate consequences in our work as teacher educators, creating ripples for our preservice teachers that extend to their future students. Knowing student success and wellbeing are inextricably linked to faculty wellbeing (Cavanagh, 2023; Roos & Borkoski, 2021), we see how our efforts benefit our preservice teachers. When we attend to our own health and wellbeing, we are able to show up fully in our profession, engage authentically with our students, and respond meaningfully to their learning needs. In doing so, we model various ways of supporting one's health and wellbeing, including how to be a self-advocate. A diverse range of strategies offers more and varied options to address wellbeing, increasingly necessary as today's educational contexts require teachers to care for themselves and their students differently than before.

Without being thoughtful, purposeful, and willful, self-care and wellbeing can easily become afterthoughts – casualties of academia as opposed to vital components of our satisfaction with work and life. As comedian Amy Poehler (2014) emphasized, "Do work that you are proud of with your talented friends" (p. 250). Making time and creating space across locations and foci enable us to deliberately support our wellbeing – with our talented friends – while holding each other accountable for our individual and collective self-care.

References

Ball, S. J. (2004). *Education for sale! The commodification of everything?* King's Annual Education Lecture, University of London. http://www.asu.edu/educ/epsl/CERU/articles/CERU-0410-253-OWI.pdf

Bellas, M. L. (1999). Emotional labor in academia: The case of professors. *The Annals of the American Academy of Political and Social Science*, *561*(1), 96–110.

Brabazon, H. (2021, April 22). The academy's neoliberal response to COVID-19: Why faculty should be wary and how we can push back. *Academic Matters*. https://academicmatters.ca/the-academys-neoliberal-response-to-covid-19-why-faculty-should-be-wary-and-how-we-can-push-back/

Cavanagh, S. R. (2023, May 2). *They need us to be well*. The Chronicle of Higher Education. https://www.chronicle.com/article/they-need-us-to-be-well

Elliott, M., & Blithe, S. J. (2021). Gender inequality, stress exposure, and well-being among academic faculty. *International Journal of Higher Education*, *10*(2), 240–252.

Larson, L. M., Seipel, M. T., Shelley, M. C., Gahn, S. W., Ko, S. Y., Schenkenfelder, M., Rover, D. T., Schmittmann, B., & Heitman, M. M. (2019). The academic environment and faculty well-being: The role of psychological needs. *Journal of Career Assessment*, *27*(1), 167–182. https://doi.org/10.1177/1069072717748667

The Work of Wellbeing: Making Time and Creating Space in Academia   67

Lorde, A. (2017). *A burst of light and other essays.* Ixia Press.

Merriam-Webster. (n.d.). Well-being. In Merriam-Webster.com dictionary. Retrieved October 27, 2023, from https://www.merriam-webster.com/dictionary/well-being

Mudrak, J., Zabrodska, K., Kveton, P., Jelinek, M., Blatny, M., Solcova, I., & Machovcova, K. (2018). Occupational well-being among university faculty: A job demands-resources model. *Research in Higher Education, 59*(3), 325–348. https://doi.org/10.1007/s11162-017-9467-x

Noddings, N. (2005). *The challenge to care in schools: An alternative approach to education.* Teachers College Press.

O'Dwyer, S., Pinto, S., & McDonough, S. (2018). Self-care for academics: A poetic invitation to reflect and resist. *Reflective Practice, 19*(2), 243–249.

Office of the Surgeon General. (2023). *Workplace mental health & well-being.* U.S. Department of Health & Human Services. https://www.hhs.gov/surgeongeneral/priorities/workplace-well-being/index.html

Poehler, A. (2014). *Yes please.* Dey Street Books.

Rhew, N. D., Jones, D. R., Sama, L. M., Robinson, S., Friedman, V. J., & Egan, M. (2021). Shedding light on restorative spaces and faculty well-being. *Journal of Management Education, 45*(1), 43–64. https://doi.org/10.1177/1052562920953456

Roos, B. H., & Borkoski, C. C. (2021). Attending to the teacher in the teaching: Prioritizing faculty well-being. *Perspectives of the ASHA Special Interest Groups, 6*(4), 831–840. https://doi.org/10.1044/2021_PERSP-21-00006

Sabagh, Z., Hall, N. C., Saroyan, A., & Trépanier, S.-G. (2022). Occupational factors and faculty well-being: Investigating the mediating role of need frustration. *The Journal of Higher Education, 93*(4), 559–584. https://doi.org/10.1080/00221546.2021.2004810

Shoffner, M., & Webb, A. W. (2020, Nov. 19). Commentary: Questioning care in the academic world. *Teachers College Record.* https://journals.sagepub.com/pb-assets/cmscontent/TCZ/Commentaries%20Collection/2020%20Commentaries/Questioning%20Care%20in%20the%20Academic%20World%20-1656108981.pdf

Shoffner, M., & Webb, A. W. (Eds.). (2022). *Reconstructing care in teacher education after COVID-19: Caring enough to change.* Routledge. https://doi.org/10.4324/9781003244875

7 Fire and Focus
The Decision of Which Flames to Fan in Higher Education

Destini Braxton

Introduction

fire \fī(-ə)r\ *n*, [Middle English, from Old English *fȳr*; akin to Old High German *fiur* fire, Greek *pyr*] (before the 12th century). **1 a** (1): the phenomenon of combustion manifested in light, flame, and heat (2): one of the four elements of the alchemists **1 b** (1): burning passion: ARDOR (2): liveliness of imagination: INSPIRATION **2 a**: fuel in a state of combustion (as on a hearth) **b**: *British* a small gas or electric space heater **3 a**: a destructive burning (as of a building) **b** (1): death or torture by fire (2) severe trial or ordeal **4**: BRILLIANCY, LUMINOSITY … (Merriam-Webster, n.d.)

fire Something that is really good, amazing, crazy (in a good way) *"That song is straight fire"* (Urban Dictionary, n.d.)

The varied definitions for fire seemingly parallel life for many academics. To be sure, burning passion is one of the necessary fuels that fire the persistence required on the educational journey to becoming an academic. The brilliant sparks of discovery and connections with others often continue to sustain inspiration throughout careers. And, there are few, if any, points within the semester where academics do not feel as though they are surrounded by little (and some not so little) fires everywhere, with each fire representing a key priority, and together threatening what feels like our combustion. Many – particularly women and those who exemplify sociocultural characteristics counter to the norm of the institution – experience burnout (Lawrence et al., 2022). Perhaps worse, many hide their burnout and other physical and psychological ailments in fear of professional stigma (Gaudet et al., 2022).

The literature on burnout and academia is meaningful to me – a Black woman in academia drawing from my experience as a doctoral student and mother (see Figure 7.1). Given my positionality, high demands and the importance of finding and sustaining balance and focus have been constant for me. In this chapter, I highlight how intentional attention has helped me align my time with my needs, values, and commitments, minimizing threats to my burnout and combustion. Throughout, I describe personal examples of what it can feel and look like when I am (or am not) able to mindfully choose which flames to fan when fires seemingly surround me. I also describe intentional strategies and approaches I have tried with my advisor and individually.

DOI: 10.4324/9781032688633-9

Fire and Focus 69

Figure 7.1 A mother balancing her many roles and practicing self-care

I identify as a Black woman, born and residing in the United States. With my identity comes the roles of a mother of three kids, researcher, and educator. Placing priority on the roles in which they were presented, I quickly learned that the flames of the fire were rarely going to be put out. What I did come to understand is that sacrifice always played an active role in where to place my focus, and with sacrifice and focus came balance. I was forced to learn how to prioritize tasks and roles based on deadlines, physical and emotional needs, and resources. However, this often meant that the deadline, my needs, and resources for me to thrive, almost always came last and with a mental price to pay. *What needs my immediate attention today?* That was the question I had to finally ask myself before I realized that I needed to rest, relax, and refocus on the goals of (a) being the best mother to my children, (b) achieving my goal of becoming Dr. Braxton, and (c) taking care of myself before burnout came back around. Luckily, with the right resources, strategies, and support in place, managing my roles as a mother, researcher, and educator became more bearable.

To this very day, I can remember the bittersweet feeling that I experienced as I read my acceptance letter to my doctoral program. Bittersweet because I was excited that I was on the road to becoming Dr. Braxton, but nervous because I would be eight months pregnant with my first son when the program began. As

70 *Destini Braxton*

I prepared to start my doctoral program, work full-time as a teacher, and bring a child into the world, I decided to sit down with my advisor to develop a plan for success. She shared with me the university's policy on family leave and maternity leave, along with my rights as a mother scholar. This was essential and highly appreciated because I did not know that I would be able to take maternity leave as a student. Becoming knowledgeable of the university's policies around this matter was critical in order to better advocate for my needs as a mother scholar. I want to point out that although I knew I would be allowed maternity leave from work and school, I only chose to take leave from work. This decision was due to me believing that if I took time off from the program, I would be failing myself and setting myself behind with my progress in the program. This did not sit well with my advisor (or me, as I now sit and reflect), as she was extending more grace and kindness to me and my situation than I was.

Being a mother and a scholar came with an additional challenge that was unforeseen – postpartum depression. Although postpartum depression was an unfamiliar term and diagnosis to me, it was not unknown to my advisor or the 29%–44% of Black mothers in the United States (Floyd James et al., 2023). This was not an easy decision for me to make because once again I felt as if I was letting myself down, but realized I was really letting myself and the baby down by not prioritizing my mental health in order to properly care for both of us. During this time, I also understood that if I was not mentally at my best, everything around me would suffer (e.g., how I showed up for myself and children, my coursework, my desire and endurance to complete the program). Additionally, it made a huge difference to have an advisor who shared the same mental health experience that I did as I transitioned into motherhood because it made the support and encouragement more genuine.

Once I returned from maternity leave, I had to practice being intentional about when I scheduled meetings without excessively interfering with my time with my children or for myself. An example of my intentionality was my decision to not engage in any research-related tasks on Wednesdays, so that I could mentally reset and refocus on the tasks that needed to be completed by the end of the week. To this day, I have also tried my hardest not to schedule meetings on Friday to practice being present with my children while they are awake. Another purpose for not scheduling meetings on Fridays was for me to focus solely on completing research tasks (e.g., scholarly writing, course assignments). I would work on research tasks when my children went to sleep.

When needing to decide which flames to fan, this came with a strong sense of urgency while trying to figure out what tasks and demands needed my attention the most. A perfect example of this was when I was working on my dissertation, working on a manuscript, trying to find time with my children, and needing to fulfill my duties as a special education teacher. At the time, everything needed my immediate attention and my initial response was to spend time with my children and then go to sleep because I was overwhelmed. After taking a deep breath and having a conversation with my advisor, I was able to create a backward timeline to help break down the writing tasks and create a sense of time. I also communicated with my co-authors that I needed to move to the last author based on the time commitment and writing contributions. Had I not practiced effective communication, I would have been ignoring my mental needs and letting down my co-authors when trying to meet the deadline. I was also able to work on my tasks as a special education teacher during my planning after communicating with my principal that I was overwhelmed and needed time while I was at work to complete my obligations with fidelity.

Although I was able to fan the flames and even temporarily put out the fire, I realized that I was still sacrificing my best self when it came down to me being a mother. Even though I was physically present with my children, I was not mentally present because I was constantly thinking about the other tasks that needed my attention. Balancing and focusing on all of these tasks and parenting demands forced me to put things in place so that I could keep moving forward in the doctoral program and maintain a healthy household, mentally and physically.

Literature

In this section, I briefly explore the literature on women in academia, mothers as graduate students, mothers in faculty positions, and Black women in each role. In doing so, I hope to set up the need for balance and focus while navigating graduate programs and higher education faculty positions.

Women in Academia

Being a woman, let alone a Black woman, in academia presents advantages and disadvantages. Of the many advantages is the idea that we get to show up and work hard to make a strong name for ourselves. On the contrary, it also means that we have to fight for a seat at the table, when in fact, we are more than capable and qualified to make our own table. Furthermore, we are often looking imposter syndrome in the face and constantly creating self-doubt and self-sabotaging thoughts. Let's end those negative habits and find better habits and ways to take care of ourselves mentally while we navigate and meet the demands of academia.

Having a strong sense of belonging in a space that is (a) White and male dominant and (b) forcing women to try harder to make themselves known (Walkington, 2017) requires an immense level of mental strength and constant advocating for women in academia. Ane Ogbe (2022, p. 680) said it best, "It is therefore important that someone speaks for the Black woman and advocates for her inclusion." – especially when speaking up for Black women. However, finding and maintaining the mental strength to show up in places where inequities and oppression are presented and experienced (Henderson et al., 2010) requires a strong practice of self-care.

A strong mentorship and self-care practices are two of many factors that can increase retention rates, manage roles and demands in academia, and decrease social isolation and mental health issues. In Henderson and colleagues' (2010) article, they point out that as women continue to face oppression, gender and race needs to continue to be explored when trying to better understand the intersectionality of roles and identities in academia, especially at a predominantly white institution.

72 *Destini Braxton*

Parenting

Creating and striving for a healthy work/life balance for parents is crucial in academia. Practicing various self-care strategies can promote balance, prevent burnout, and develop a sense of resilience for parents. Walkington (2017) mentioned that a healthy work/life balance and self-care practice can promote a sense of resistance for women in faculty and graduate roles. Some of the self-care strategies mentioned within her article forced women in both roles to protect their work/life and family/life. However, the findings mentioned in the article focused on Black women in faculty and graduate student roles. For example, it was reported that some Black women chose when to respond to campus communication, engaged in mental health days, and accepted tasks that resonated with their research interests and were meaningful to their professional growth (Henderson et al., 2010; Walkington, 2017).

Motherhood and Graduate Students

Shining light on mother scholars in graduate programs is of importance when recognizing that life does not stop while pursuing degrees in higher education. More specifically, it is against societal norms to have not one, but multiple children during one's academic journey. However, I experienced firsthand what it was like to expand my family three times, while being a Black doctoral student. While in both roles, the challenge of creating a work/life balance continued to be present. More specifically, some of the challenges for mother scholars are (a) supporting their family financially, (b) finding and maintaining childcare while attending classes, and (c) attending to the ongoing demands of parenting (Espiritu et al., 2023). Pursuing a graduate degree, working full-time, and meeting the needs of one's family require sacrifice, self-care, and strict scheduling. Additionally, while trying to balance both roles, mother scholars from their study reported that the following specific coping strategies helped face these challenges: multitasking, time management, and "standing up and being strong" (p. 6).

It was often perceived that motherhood affected the trajectory of academic success and completion of graduate programs. One of the many inaccurate perceptions of academic mothers, as compared to academic fathers, is the idea that mothers are less committed and lack interest in completing their graduate program (Hillier, 2023). This perception tends to force mother scholars to feel the need to work nonstop or ten times as hard compared to their graduate student peers because they constantly feel they have something to prove. Additionally, it often leaves mother scholars constantly questioning whether they are "good enough" when it comes to them being a mother and student. This is a negative perception that should be corrected as mothers continue to persevere and accomplish what others are displaying doubt about often. The lack of parental resources while pregnant on campus and navigating the graduate program plays a strong factor when examining mother scholars' sense of belonging. It is imperative for students to learn about their rights and policies at their attending university as it pertains to maternity leave and maternal accommodations. Overall, these policies and accommodations contribute to mother scholars' educational experience, emotional and mental experiences, and leave a lasting impression as they strive to accomplish their goals and meet the daily needs of their children.

Disclosing a pregnancy is ultimately based on the woman's discretion. However, it is highly recommended based on comfort to disclose their pregnancy to their academic advisor, so that support and resources can be discussed as the mother scholar continues to progress in the program. The academic advisor can assist with communicating with professors, brainstorming academic plans, and serving as their advisee's biggest advocate. This is also another factor that plays a strong role in mother scholars' academic experience (Hillier, 2023).

Motherhood and Roles in Academia

The demands of motherhood are almost, or just as, equivalent to the time and mental demands of working a full-time faculty position. They have to constantly find ways to create balance and focus on providing their best selves while at work and at home. In addition, they continue to be faced with the idea that getting pregnant is deemed as unprofessional because of the emotional, mental, and physical transformation noticed among colleagues (Huopalainen & Satama, 2019). Creating a stronger need for self-care to be present at home and work as they strive to develop a sense of belonging in the workplace.

Having children is deemed to negatively affect mothers' lives, personally and professionally, more so than fathers (Huopalainen & Satama, 2019). One factor that plays a role is the policy on maternity leave or family leave. Oftentimes, maternity leave is not offered unless the woman has been employed at the university for at least a year, forcing women to be at a disadvantage if they enter the work field while pregnant or indirectly forcing women to put their career before their life choices due to paid leave. Unfortunately, this produces feelings of guilt, lack of worth, and inadequacy. However, despite the disadvantages and negative stereotypes of becoming a mother while holding a faculty position, it is possible to be a "good" mother and academic simultaneously. Huopalainen and Satama (2019) make a strong point to acknowledge the good that is produced while encompassing both identities in academia.

Strategies to Create Focus and Balance

In this section, I provide and describe the strategies that I have implemented individually and collectively with my advisor to produce a better experience by promoting focus and creating a space that strongly prioritizes my mental health and self-care. I focus on how to manage scholarship (e.g., course work, dissertation writing, projects, etc.), motherhood, and mental health while navigating a doctoral program and academia by providing practical tips for women in faculty positions, women as graduate students, and women advising mother scholars (see Table 7.1). Drawing from the author's narrative, the table focuses on women supporting

74   *Destini Braxton*

Table 7.1 Individual and collective strategies to promote focus and balance

Priorities	Women in faculty positions	Women as graduate students	Women advising mother scholars
Managing scholarship	Learning when to say "no" Being realistic about scholarship goals (e.g., grant opportunities, writing manuscripts) and deadlines	Accept scholarship tasks that align with academic and career goals Designate days and times for writing and reading Chunk scholarship activities based on deadlines and skill enhancement	Being mindful of our thoughts about our scholarly work Being explicit about scholarly expectations
Managing motherhood	Working on lectures during 9–5 hours Answering emails after children go to sleep Understanding and familiarizing ones' self with the university's policies for family and maternity leave as a mother and faculty member	Designate a day that you do not schedule meetings. Designating a time to check emails Understanding and familiarizing ones' self with the university's policies for family and maternity leave as a student	Building a village within the department and research lab Providing a welcoming and child-friendly space during lab meetings/event
Managing mental health	Understanding, utilizing, and familiarizing ones' self with the university's wellness resources Knowing when to take a break from work tasks	Set aside time for mental health days Understanding and familiarizing ones' self with the university's wellness resources	Be explicit in communicating both party's need

women in higher education as they begin to normalize pursuing an undergraduate or graduate degree, transitioning into motherhood, and striving for a career in academia. The table is not intended to exclude or overlook the demands of fathers while navigating higher education and parenthood.

Conclusion

This article draws attention to the need for self-care practices while navigating the academic field. The literature included throughout the article demonstrates the oppression that has been brought to light, in regards to women in faculty roles and graduate student roles. Furthermore, it sheds light on the intersectionality of roles in academia and lifestyle roles (i.e., motherhood). There is a critical need to center and promote self-care practices during each role to decrease the rates of burnout, dropping out, and isolation. Henderson and colleagues (2010) said it strongly by stating, "If diversity, inclusiveness, and the successful performance and advancement of African American women are goals in higher education, we must develop effective initiatives that address the unique positioning of Black women" (p. 34).

When trying to understand the roles of intersecting identities in academia (e.g., women, Black women, mothers, faculty, graduate students), it is important to take into consideration the mental load that women carry while navigating academia. To prevent burnout and increase mental health issues, it is critical to implement a variety of self-care strategies to create and sustain work/life balance. The strategies presented within this chapter can be summarized as follows:

1. *Set intentional boundaries and scholarly expectations*
2. *Set appropriate time limits and flexible deadlines*
3. *Say "yes" to meaningful tasks that promote professional development*
4. *Say "no" when you have too many "flames to fan"*
5. *Set appropriate and clear communication expectations*
6. *Plan mental health days, as necessary*

There is a strong need for research and more emphasis on self-care for women, Black women, and mothers in academia. There have been articles that focus on individual self-care practice (Walkington, 2017), future research can focus on collective self-care practice. This article aims to provide individual and collective approaches to self-care practices while drawing from my intersectional identities. Furthermore, I provided strategies in this article with the hope that it will serve as a guide for mother scholars in faculty and graduate student roles. Additionally, because the strategies mentioned were strategies that I tried together with my advisor, I hope that they bring light to ways that advisors and academic mentors can better mentally and physically support their graduate students throughout their educational program while promoting the importance of self-care, focus, and balance.

References

Espiritu, E. J. P., Auguis, J. J. M., Phoebe Mae, C., Gedaro, M. S., Lucas, C. E. T., & Niog, S. P. C. (2023). Dual roles: Bearing the academic and parental responsibilities of being a student mother. *Science and Technology, 6*(4), 82–90.

Fire. (2024). In *Merriam-Webster Dictionary*. https://www.merriam-webster.com/dictionary/fire

Floyd James, K., Smith, B. E., Robinson, M. N., Thomas Tobin, C. S., Bulles, K. F., & Barkin, J. L. (2023). Factors associated with postpartum maternal functioning in black women: A secondary analysis. *Journal of Clinical Medicine, 12*(2), 647.

Gaudet, S., Marchand, I., Bujaki, M., & Bourgeault, I. L. (2022). Women and gender equity in academia through the conceptual lens of care. *Journal of Gender Studies, 31*(1), 74–86.

Henderson, T. L., Hunter, A. G., & Hildreth, G. J. (2010). Outsiders within the academy: Strategies for resistance and mentoring African American women. *Michigan Family Review, 14*(1), 28–41.

Hillier, K. M. (2023). Academia and motherhood: A narrative inquiry of Ontario academic mothers' experiences in university graduate programs. *Journal of Family Issues, 44*(6), 1597–1621.

Huopalainen, A. S., & Satama, S. T. (2019). Mothers and researchers in the making: Negotiating 'new'motherhood within the 'new'academia. *Human Relations, 72*(1), 98–121.

Lawrence, J. A., Davis, B. A., Corbette, T., Hill, E. V., Williams, D. R., & Reede, J. Y. (2022). Racial/ethnic differences in burnout: a systematic review. *Journal of Racial and Ethnic Health Disparities, 9*, 257–269..

Ogbe, A. (2022). A seat at the table is not enough: a perspective on Black women representation in academia. *Immunology and Cell Biology, 100*(9), 679–682.

Urban Dictionary: Fire. (n.d.). In *Urban Dictionary*. https://www.urbandictionary.com/define.php?term=Fire

Walkington, L. (2017). How far have we really come? Black women faculty and graduate students' experiences in higher education. *Humboldt Journal of Social Relations, 39*, 51–65.

8 Fighting Dragons with Contemplative Practices

A Hero's Journey in Higher Education through Time and Self-Care

Melanie Reaves

I'm in a caring profession – teaching. What happens when I don't have the capacity or time to care? In this chapter, I weave a tale of my hero's journey through the land of higher education and self-care. I tell of my adventures, precipice moments of decision, and coming home transformed to whom I want to be.

The recent pandemic and societal changes have significantly shaped the roles of women faculty in higher education. Workloads have increased (e.g., Indiana General Assembly, 2022), and we are often tasked with caring for the "university family" (Docka-Filipek & Stone, 2021, p. 2158). I feel these changes in my soul as a female senior faculty member in a college of education. Words like *overwhelmed, depleted, or drowning* are my everyday vocabulary. When I began experiencing attacks of anxiousness, I knew a journey through self-care was needed.

I'm not alone. Self-care for teacher educators has come sharply into focus (e.g., Lesh, 2020). As I embarked on my journey, I was inspired by Dutro's (2019) work in which teachers bring vulnerability to caring classrooms through reading, writing, talking, and listening. I took up Lemon and McDonough's (2021) call to "place wellbeing and wholeheartedness at the centre of the educational endeavour" (p. 317). I created safe dialogic spaces for care, for healing, for growth. In preparation, I packed my bags with self-care *contemplative practices* (e.g., quieting the mind; mindful breathing, art journaling, and walking). I honed my multimodal literacies using words, images, and creative movements (e.g., Albers & Sanders, 2010) in performative autoethnographic texts. Finally, I attended to time – the lack of it, the way I spend it, how I put it on my side. In these acts of caring, I found what Spry (2001) called "interactional textures occurring between self [and] other" (p. 708). I found a new space and a new me in and out of the academe that allowed for "expression of passion and spirit" (p. 708). This flow allowed me as human|professor to be the hero of my own story.

Connected Literature

In this tale, I take up the political and socially conscious act of doing autoethnographic research as "both process and product" (Ellis et al., 2011, p. 273). I assembled memories of past experiences that punctuated moments "after which my life

78 *Melanie Reaves*

[did not] seem quite the same" (p. 275). In my endeavour, I problematized the notion of "data" as things that can be extracted and analysed. Instead, I saw empirical materials, such as mindful embodied actions (walking, breathing) and artefacts like art journals, meeting minutes, and photographs as sites for meanings that are not silent but rather "they speak up, get rowdy, act up" (Denzin, 2013, p. 354). From a posthuman perspective, they had agency that was entangled in meaning making with me (Barad, 2007). I was the creator of them then; I am the reflector upon them now.

Furthermore, these materials are performative (Spry, 2001) within the live action of writing as a method of inquiry (Richardson & St. Pierre, 2005). The words I pen in this story are forces constructing my view of reality and of my self. They are creative analytical processes that are to be viewed as "valid and desirable representations of the social writing process and the writing product deeply intertwined" (Richardson & St. Pierre, 2005, p. 962). I hold strong to this concept of *creative analysis* as a natural way to understand the juncture between experience and reflection, because once an experience is past, all we have is our reflection of that experience to create meaning.

I appreciate Caulley's (2008) boldness in saying that quite often "qualitative research reports [are] boring to read" (p. 424). Yet, such works are reporting on people who exist in a milieu of passions, intensities, emotions, and intellectualities that perch upon mountain tops, sink into the deepest of valleys, and traverse on pathways in between. We have had the techniques for expressing such aspects of our social research for many years through literary tropes and devices. Leavy (2020) asserted, "fiction has unique capabilities for creating and disseminating research because it is engaging, evocative, and accessible to broad audiences" (p. 60). At the core of these literary experiences is humans' unique ability to use *social imagination*, or "the ability to understand what others think, feel, and believe" (Lysaker et al., 2011, p. 522). This imaginative space is where empathy can emerge and be nurtured (Leavy, 2020).

In this chapter, I intentionally draw upon such devices with creative non-fiction memoir. I recognized my experiences as a literary story that has equipped me for living (Burke, 1973) – a full, flourishing, and nourishing life. Not far into this autoethnographic inquiry I noticed the connection to Joseph Campbell's (2008) monomyth, *the hero's journey*. With each dive into the monomyth, I came up with rich new understandings of my journey. I was also intrigued by Michael Wolff's concept of creativity as three muscles to be exercised – curiosity, appreciation, and imagination (Popova, n.d.). I exercised these muscles through creative reflection activities that are a part of my toolkit of contemplative practices. Thus, my heroism was born.

About a Hero's Journey Narrative

Much has been written about Joseph Campbell's (2008) *hero's journey*. In its basic form, the protagonist's journey comes in three stages – "a separation from the world, a penetration to some source of power, and a life-enhancing return"

Fighting Dragons with Contemplative Practices 79

(Campbell, 2008, p. 28). The journey begins with a call to adventure that the traveller resists until a mentor encourages them to take the leap of faith into an unknown world. After crossing the threshold into the strange land, the traveller encounters tests and battles. In their darkest hour, the traveller experiences a revelation of truth – a reward. The traveller must then journey home again, still facing difficulties but now armed with weapons and the knowledge to emerge victorious. As they travel across the threshold back into the known world, they have been transformed "into the master of the two worlds" (p. 29), ready to share their gifts with others.

Allison and Goethals (2017) described these three states as the transformation of the setting, of the self, and of society. These stages appeared in my own story. I had to first transform my setting, making physical space for the weapons that would allow me victories like paints, brushes, coloured pencils, Japanese papers, magazines, watercolour paper, journals, camera, walking shoes, and readings on self-care. I also transformed my time, making intentional time for self-care through contemplative practice. Finally, I arrived at the place where I sought to transform my social worlds, not in grandiose ways, but in small, personal ways.

Visual Narrative

Figure 8.1 My hero's journey (adapted from Herosjourney.svg)

80 *Melanie Reaves*

Connection to Visual Narrative

Three years ago, I was living with a fragile state of mental health. Anxiety became all-too-commonplace in response to work stressors. I found myself in the precarious situation of being in a caring profession without the capacity to teach those entering my profession how to care for themselves. This visual narrative tells of my journey to discover self-care in the realm of higher education and, in the process, to become the hero of my own story (Figure 8.1). As I entered the unknown world of anxiety in the workplace, I faced many dragons, such as adversarial leadership, lack of resources, and annoyances. My helpers became contemplative practices (Barbezat & Bush, 2013) that centralized creativity – mindful art journaling, reframing through story, use of curiosity through metaphors, and walkographies. Deep in the abyss, I learned that time itself was a key character in my story; I began to fight the Time Thief by setting an intentional schedule for each day. Through regular practice, I transformed. When I returned to my known world, I began sharing the gifts of creative reflection with my students, friends, and colleagues.

My Hero's Journey

I present my story in vignettes drawn from real-life experiences. Each vignette moves the story forward with *time* playing a key role. Following my story, I provide readers with two strategies they can use to embark on their own heroic journeys.

Time to Go: Call to Adventure

I sat down to my computer to virtual conference with my administrator about his approval of an in-house grant I had submitted a month before. After we exchanged pleasantries, he said, "We are willing to support this application since we have recently seen a change in you being less resistant to the work of the College and the Department." Immediately, I felt hurt, anger, and disbelief the size of a kumquat form in my throat. Panic set in. *What was he talking about?* Time stood still; silence on the screen; my mouth agape. He prompted, "Do you have something to say?"

Do I have something to say? I thought. I considered the fact that on any given work day, my car was usually the first in the parking lot and the last one to leave. I thought about all the weekends when my car was the only one there. I mulled over the three work-laden College and Department committees I had volunteered to Chair over the past year. Finally, I spoke. "What evidence do you have of resisting the work of the Department and College?"

His voice cracked, "Well, I've been told that you have been telling people you don't want to work weekends anymore." Finally, swallowing the kumquat, I forced my voice to sound calm, "It's true. I am working toward a better work/life balance by reclaiming weekends for personal time, but I'm not sure how this applies." He quickly responded, "We just don't understand why you are taking on this grant when you want to work less." I took my answer directly from the rationale I had

Fighting Dragons with Contemplative Practices   81

written, reiterating that the work was not additional; it would bolster students' cultural competence within a particular course. I had seen the grant as an opportunity to take the university up on its promise to support these efforts in a meaningful way.

As he kept talking, I realized his words were just that – and these words had nothing to do with me. I quickly thanked him for supporting my grant and clicked "end meeting." I sat there frozen, hand to chest feeling my rapid heartbeat and the hot swell of tears in my eyes. These anxious responses had become nearly a weekly occurrence; I realized that while I had no control over others' actions, I had to get control of mine. Adventure was calling, though I didn't yet view what was ahead of me as an adventure; it was a dark, scary unknown world.

Better Late than Never: Help through Creativity

My phone perched to my left with the timer set for 20 minutes. My charge: (1) Set an intention. (2) Play with art materials for 20 minutes. (3) Write reflectively for 20 minutes. (4) Reread what I wrote, underlining key words and phrases. (5) Give it a title (Rose, 2023). I thought, *Okay, Rachel Rose, I'm trusting you with this "Mindful Art Journaling."* My intention on this day? *Discovery.* My materials of choice? Art paper and oil pastels. Instinctively, I grabbed *Brown* with a fist grip and it zig-zagged diagonally from the top left to bottom right of the page. I recognized it instantly – a lightning bolt. I boldened the colour. *Green, Blue, Yellow* followed suit, each outlining the brown strike. Then, the strike stopped; my fist loosened. *Orange* and *Peach* made gentle alternating waves out towards the edge of the page. As the last stroke laid down, I was jostled back to reality with the beeping of the cell phone timer.

Timer reset, I began to write using my computer. The metaphor of lightning took centre stage and a new discovery rose from the ashes – peace and calm after a strike. The timer beeped again and I abruptly stopped. I reread highlighting words and phrases and then ended my session with a title. Finally, I compiled the title and highlighted words into a poem:

Lightning
Strike from nowhere!
Soul-sucked
Deep into the soil.
Spring of new growth
Water and sunshine nourish
Waves of peace carry it away.

My journey had begun; I had crossed the threshold into this unknown world armed with something that had brought me solace in the past, creativity. This felt different than the traditional mindful practices I had tried. I emerged hopeful, refreshed, renewed. My quest for other creative reflection activities propelled my journey forward.

82   *Melanie Reaves*

Moments in Time: Transformation Begins – Battles Ensue

Spurred on by mentors of creative reflection, I seized moments in time – each time battling a new dragon:

Battling the Dragon of Physicality

The somatic nature of my responses to stress were new. I began to recognize their earliest presences – a twinge in my chest, a thump in my eardrum, the clench of my hands into a fist. I often quickly identified the stressor bringing these markers on, but sometimes, they came with no identifier. This was one of those times – anxiety for no apparent reason. I was nestled snug in a cabin in the woods for a three-day get-away. The cast-iron stove brought warmth into the log cabin; I wore fluffy socks on my feet that reminded me of my mom, hot cocoa rested upon the table to my right, and a novel rested atop a plush blue blanket draped across my legs. The setting was idyllic, serene, even picturesque with the snow softly piling on pines outside of the picture window.

Not 10 minutes into my luxurious moment I felt them – those nasty twinges and thumps. I knew my future if I didn't intervene – a racing heart, the inability to catch my breath, and a pounding headache for hours after the anxiety subsided. But I had learned to recognize this dragon and was ready for combat. In this moment, my weapon of choice was *walkography* (Cutcher, 2018). Off flew the blanket, fluffy socks traded with wool socks and snow boots, on went my snow gear, and out the door I went with my phone-camera in hand. With each breath, the cold, crisp air loosened my tight chest. My clenched fists relaxed within the thick home-made mittens. My fingers caressed the silky bits of mohair I had woven within the strands of wool – *snap! Mitten image captured.* With each crunch of the snow beneath by feet, the twinges subsided. I noticed how my footsteps left dragging traces in the snow between the sunken vestiges of my presence – *snap! Traces of presence captured.* Then, the greatest gift of this moment – a doe and her fawn bounded out from the trees. I stopped. They stopped. *Snap! Wildlife gift captured.* The somatic grips on my body, mind, and emotions seemed years away as I stood motionless in the moment, breathing calm life into my body. *Snap! Selfie captured.*

Battling the Dragon of Fatigue

I'm tired, beaten down, exhausted. *Saturday's on the horizon* I reminded myself this Friday afternoon as I waded through grading and advising appointments. Saturdays had become my creative respite days. This Saturday I sat with a pile of *National Geographic* magazines, stick glue, scissors, paint, and stencils. Playing with the paint and stencils, I ended up with a background that seemed poised for a collage – green and yellow splashes with bright orange stencilled flowers. Having just taught my students about *found poetry*, I wondered, "Is there a poem for me here today?" Flipping through the magazines I happened upon several pages filled with butterflies. I began fussy-cutting around the delicate wings and bodies. When

Fighting Dragons with Contemplative Practices   83

I had freed enough butterflies from the pages, I searched for my poem within the text and it found me:

Butterflies can Help
BUTTERFLY PATTERNS are tough to quantify.
something's changed
Consistency is key: for what's going on
distinguish between lasting changes and year after year.
conditions cool nights
big news
butterflies came back
just a year's aberration.

The poem became the centrepiece of my collage in *ransom note* style text. I glued the bodies of the butterflies around the poem and bent their wings upward to create a 3-dimensional collage in which they were all poised for flight. I was poised as well.

Battling the Dragon of Annoyance

On this particular day, I had a three-hour flight and a book to dive into, *The Creative Act: A Way of Being* by Rick Rubin (2023). Even before take-off, Rubin's stream-of-consciousness style flowed through me. I found gems of truth, shards of challenge, and clouds of comfort that I scribbled occasionally in my journal. Although I was in a middle seat, I was in the flow (Csikszentmihalyi, 1990), lost in time, Rubin's words, and my journal.

I was jolted out of the flow with a sound, *schz, schz, schz...schz, schz, schz...* I turned to find the woman to my right filing her nails. I thought, *Oh! I get that. I've been in that spot when a nail breaks or chips.* I settled back into my book, thinking she'd take care of the problem. But the sound continued, *schz, schz, schz...*

I tried to ignore it. After 45 minutes, I closed my book and journal in full annoyance. *Doesn't she realize how annoying this is?* The longer it went on, the more I stewed. *Please, for the love of all that's holy, STOP!* I shouted in my mind. I plugged my ears for a bit of a respite from the scraping sound. I dug out my headphones, desperate to drown out the noise. Alas, I had forgotten to charge them.

I closed my eyes – *Why is she doing this? Is she nervous? Does she do this every time she flies? How does she even have nails left to file?* Curiosity rushed in to take the space that annoyance had occupied. I opened my journal and began writing "her story" and soon found myself enraptured! I imagined her sitting in her therapist's office, cringing with the thought of getting on this plane. The therapist would recommend she do something to busy her hands to distract herself from the fear. "Hm, I do like to file my nails," she might admit. The therapist then encouraged her, "Try that!" Now, here she is! *schz, schz, schz...* I start to tap along to the rhythm of her filing.

84 *Melanie Reaves*

Time is of the Essence: Battling the Outlook Time Thief

I was in the abyss, as Campbell (2008) described it. It was dark and doom loomed large. It had been a month since I had engaged in creative reflection, and I felt it deeply. I sat staring at my computer, considering the many anxiety dragons that had won recently. *Ding!* A calendar invitation popped into my email. *Click.* I accepted. I nearly jumped right out of my seat! Microsoft Outlook © was stealing my time! It was common practice for my colleagues (and me) to use Outlook to schedule meetings – and when these popped into my email, I clicked "accept" and BOOM! another moment from my week was gone!

My experiment began. On Monday mornings, I perused my calendar for the week and scheduled a meeting with myself for half an hour or an hour. When the calendar notification for my meeting with myself popped up, I stopped what I was doing, closed my office door, and put my "In a Meeting" sign up. When someone wanted to schedule a meeting during that time, I simply responded, "I'm not available. I have a meeting at that time." I was consistently working 10–11 hours a day. These meetings became a welcomed respite. After the first month of this practice, I just scheduled them in for the following month. I lived for these moments of solitude and creativity. Transformation was tangible!

Story Time: Finding Stories in Meetings

The dragons of anxiety had been kept at bay and my intentional use of contemplative practices seemed to be working. One of the last battle fields was contentious work meetings. As soon as the tone of the meeting turned accusatory towards anyone in the room, the twinges and thumps began. A few times, I had to dismiss myself to deal with the somatic responses in private.

I thought of Kenneth Burke's (1973) suggestion that literature is *equipment for living* and of my many colleagues who explored the roles of affect and imagination within literature-based experiences (e.g., Lysaker et al, 2011; McGinley et al., 2017). It dawned on me: *Story* is the answer! If I changed my frame of mind during a meeting to viewing the events that unfolded as a "story," could that make a difference?

I decided to try this method out at my next meeting. A half hour before the meeting, I packed my literal bags with a notebook and my favourite pen and packed my metaphorical bag with *story elements*. Eleven of us sat around the rectangular table. I promptly opened my notebook and recorded the characters and details of the opening scene. I assigned characters symbols so I could record the story quickly as it unfolded writing in a play-style structure. I had never been so eager for a meeting in my life; and this meeting did not disappoint! As I recorded the events, I pondered the motivation of the characters as they spoke. On several occasions, I noted "PLOT TWIST!" on my page – out-of-the-blue comments that moved the story in new directions. Most surprising to me was how I was in-the-moment and outside-the-moment at the same time during the meeting. I was fully present and engaged, a character with my own dialogue, *and* I was the reader of the characters

Fighting Dragons with Contemplative Practices 85

and the room. It was like zooming in and out of the story, giving me new perspectives of others to ponder.

The meeting ended. I slipped my notebook and pen back into my bag and filed out with the others. On the walk back to our building, I blurted out to a colleague, "That was fascinating!" She quipped back, "That was awful!" She shared her frustrations from the meeting, and I realized I had experienced those frustrations as interesting parts of this unfolding story. Since that meeting, I've pulled out this practice on several occasions; each time, I've kept the somatic markers of anxiety at bay and my notebooks are filled with fascinating characters and stories!

It's about Time: I'm Home

I am now home, transformed to whom I want to be. Stressors are still there, but I'm functioning in a better place. My friends and colleagues have noticed, too, with comments like, *you seem happier.* What I have is the emotional space to understand others' perspectives. I have power and agency to say *no* to the barrage of the potential anxiety-ridden "extras" of my work. Most importantly, I'm teaching my students this ethic of care as well so they, too, can be the heroes of their own stories as they enter the same caring profession. I've come full circle in my story. In Campbell's (2008) terms, I've returned home transformed, ready to share the gifts I received along the journey.

I recently had the opportunity to work with a group of teachers for two and a half days with a focus on creative reflection as self-care. None of us knew each other when our time together began. I worried, *Will these work for them? Will they find their time well-spent?* I was not disappointed in the process. Each morning, we learned the research behind these methods and then we spent the rest of our days engaged in creative reflection contemplative practices. Our product was called a Multimodal Reflective Memoir. Every few hours, we paused to share our work and, to my surprise, these interludes often brought tears, laughter, and even hugs. We ended our time together feeling refreshed, renewed, and ready to face our students, all through the practice of self-care.

My Gift to Readers: Time to Care for Yourself

The contemplative practices I undertook are not magical. Some I learned from mentors, like mindful art journaling from Rachel Rose (2023) and walkography from Alexandra Lasczik (Cutcher, 2018); others were developed with my friend and thought partner in this work, Dr. Karen Ventura-Kalen. In this section, I provide basic instructions for two of the generative activities that emerged from my journey – *collage reflection* and *found poetry.*

Collage Reflection Activity

1 Set a focus for the collage (see examples by Prasad, 2021).

   Questions:

86   *Melanie Reaves*

- A Hope Collage: What vision of learning do you want to reflect and project for your future learners?
- A Fear Collage: What fears, doubts, and/or questions are you wrestling with regarding teaching and learning with learners in your future classroom?
- An Integrated Collage: How do you negotiate your hope-filled vision of teaching and learning with your inner thoughts and dialogue with your fears, doubts, and questions about yourself and your future students? (pp. 331–332)

2   Gather collage materials of choice and search through them for items of interest.
3   Audition materials on the collage foundation – place materials on the foundation and play with different arrangements until you find one that makes sense to you.
4   Carefully glue materials onto the foundation, trying to maintain the arrangement.
5   Write a reflection. The following questions may be helpful, but anything you write works:

a   What title would you give your collage and why?
b   Why did you choose the materials you chose? What might they represent in relation to your focus?
c   What did you notice about your thinking and feeling during the creative process?
d   How were you surprised?
e   What new ideas do you have in relation to your focus?

Found Poetry Reflection Activity

1   Set an intention or just be open to the meaning of a new found poem.
2   Decide on a type of found poetry you want to compose (examples are easily found online):

a   Cut-up
b   Erasure
c   Blackout
d   Free-form excerpting/rewriting

3   Gather book pages, magazines, printed online articles, etc.
4   Skim the texts to identify words that stand out to you regarding your intention.
5   Compose your found poem by cutting, erasing, blacking out, etc.
6   Give your poem a title.

My hope for you, is that you become the hero of your own story through creative reflection as contemplative practice. Treat time as the unavoidable character it is in your life. Be intentional with it. Make meetings with yourself (even if they are only 15 minutes) and do not let yourself out of those meetings. Hold them with tenacity. Trust in this process. It will make a difference.

References

Albers, P., & Sanders, J. (Eds.). (2010). *Literacies, the arts, and multimodality*. National Council of Teachers of English.

Allison, S. T., & Goethals, G. R. (2017). The hero's transformation. In S. T. Allison, G. R. Goethals, & R. M. Kramer (Eds.), *Handbook of heroism and heroic leadership* (pp. 379–400). Routledge.

Barad, K. (2007). *Meeting the universe halfway: Quantum physics and the entanglement of matter and meaning*. Duke University Press.

Barbezat, D. P., & Bush, M. (2013). *Contemplative practices in higher education: Powerful methods to transform teaching and learning*. John Wiley & Sons.

Burke, K. (1973). *The philosophy of literary form* (3rd ed.). University of California Press.

Campbell, J. (2008). *The hero with a thousand faces* (3rd ed.). New World Library.

Caulley, D. N. (2008). Making qualitative research reports less boring: The techniques of writing creative nonfiction. *Qualitative Inquiry, 14*(3), 424–449. https//doi.org/10.1177/1077800407311961

Csikszentmihalyi, M. (1990). *Flow*. Harper and Row.

Cutcher, A. J. L. (2018). *Moving-with & moving-through homelands, languages & memory*. Brill Sense.

Denzin, N. K. (2013). The death of data? *Cultural Studies? Critical Methodologies, 13*(4), 353–356. https//doi.org/10.1177/1532708613487882

Docka-Filipek, D., & Stone, L. B. (2021). Twice a "housewife": On academic precarity, "hysterical" women, faculty mental health, and service as gendered care work for the "university family" in pandemic times. *Gender, Work & Organization, 28*(6), 2158–2179. https//doi.org/ 10.1111/gwao.12723

Dutro, E. (2019). *The vulnerable heart of literacy: Centering trauma as powerful pedagogy*. Teachers College Press.

Ellis, C., Adams, T. E., & Bochner, A. P. (2011). Autoethnography: an overview. *Historical Social Research, 36*(4), 273–290. https://www.jstor.org/stable/23032294

Herosjourney.svg (n.d.) Creative Commons Licensed Image. https://commons.wikimedia.org/wiki/File:Heroesjourney.svg?uselang=en#Licensing

Indiana General Assembly (2022). House bill 1134. http://iga.in.gov/legislative/2022/bills/house/1134#digest-heading

Leavy, P. (2020). *Method meets art: Arts-based research practice*, third edition. Guilford.

Lemon, N. S., & McDonough, S. (2021). If not now, then when? Wellbeing and wholeheartedness in education. *The Educational Forum, 85*(3), 317–335. https://doi.org/10.1080/00131725.2021.1912231

Lesh, J. J. (2020). Don't forget about yourself: Words of wisdom on special education teacher self-care. *Teaching Exceptional Children, 52*(6), 367–369. https://doi.org/10.1177/0040059920936158

Lysaker, J. T., Tonge, C., Gauson, D., & Miller, A. (2011). Reading and social imagination: What relationally oriented reading instruction can do for children. *Reading Psychology, 32*(6), 520–566. https://doi.org/10.1080/02702711.2010.507589

McGinley, W., Kamberelis, G., Welker, A., Kelly, M., & Swafford, J. (2017). Roles of affect and imagination in reading and responding to literature: Perspectives and possibilities for English classrooms. *Journal of Curriculum Theorizing, 32*(1), 67–85.

Popova, M. (n.d.). Michael Wolff on the three muscles of creativity [blog post]. *The Marginalian*. https://www.themarginalian.org/2011/03/28/michael-wolff-creativity-visual-life/

88 *Melanie Reaves*

Prasad, G. (2021). Collage as a pedagogical practice to support teacher candidate reflection. *LEARNing Landscapes, 14*(1), 329–345.

Richardson, L., & St. Pierre, E. A. (2005). Writing: A method of inquiry. In N. K. Denzin, & Y. S. Lincoln (Eds.), *The Sage handbook of qualitative research,* third edition (pp. 959–978). Sage.

Rose, R. (2023). *Creating stillness: Mindful art practices and stories for navigating anxiety, stress, and fear.* North Atlantic Books.

Rubin, R. (2023). *The creative act: A way of being.* Penguin.

Spry, T. (2001). Performing autoethnography: An embodied methodological praxis. *Qualitative Inquiry, 7*(6), 706–732.

9 Time Allocation and Job Satisfaction for Women Academics

Lessons Learned from the Pandemic

Aslı Ermiş Mert and Elif Yılmaz

During the pandemic, women academics' job satisfaction and their overall wellness was compromised due to the exacerbated paid and unpaid workload they were challenged with. This visual directly represents our experience during these turbulent times as women in academia in relation to self-care (or lack thereof), and as the photo clearly reveals (Figure 9.1), particularly the blurring boundaries between work and private life due to working from home at the time affected not only our mental but consequently overall health, compromising time spent for self-care to keep up with professional alongside home- and family-related

Figure 9.1 Reflections on wellbeing, self-care, work-life balance, and job satisfaction during the pandemic

DOI: 10.4324/9781032688633-11

90   *Aslı Ermiş Mert and Elif Yılmaz*

responsibilities. All of these also diminished our job satisfaction, both authors consequently leaving academia after the pandemic, which is a real-life example of the importance of overall wellbeing connected to practicing self-care in academia to maintain satisfaction at work as well, and that it is not sustainable when it is overlooked. When we highlight self-care in academia for women in this chapter, we refer to the time we spend for ourselves only, which could be spent to improve our health (such as adequate sleep, nutrition, movement etc.), for our hobbies/leisure activities, time spent with loved ones excluding the times allocated to care, or just to unwind after a long day of work and other responsibilities. (Photo credit: Elif Yılmaz)

Introduction

Crises that disrupt the normal flow of life impact various aspects of individuals' daily routines. During the Covid-19 pandemic, the way we spend our days was reshaped globally. Women, and women academics in particular, have faced unique challenges during this time as well, while trying to balance their professional and personal responsibilities amidst the uncertainties brought about by the pandemic. Many women in academia experienced increased housework and unpaid care responsibilities (King & Frederickson, 2021; Pereira, 2021). This process resulted in unprecedented changes in the time spent on different activities, including work, household chores, caregiving, and self-care for women academics in Türkiye and beyond.

There were many difficulties faced by women academics due to the pandemic. The expectation to undertake even more unpaid care work while they navigate the challenges of remote work (Docka-Filipek & Stone, 2021; Parlak et al., 2021) is expected to be related to profound implications concerning their job satisfaction. The pandemic has also disrupted the research productivity of women academics, especially in terms of publishing (Gabster et al., 2020). With the expanding neoliberal agenda in academia, the pressure for publication and research on academics is increasing (Tarabochia et al., 2022), and these expectations did not seem to stall during this period to a great extent. As the pandemic negatively affected the job satisfaction and subjective wellbeing of women academics (Szromek & Wolniak, 2020), we presume that changing working conditions and related time allocation dynamics also contributed to this pattern.

This chapter examines primarily the influence of the changes in time allocation patterns that emerged during the pandemic on women academics' satisfaction with their job in Türkiye. Understanding the dynamics between changes in time spent in different spheres and job satisfaction in academia is important as the former could potentially restrict self-care, which may subsequently diminish the latter. Therefore, based on data obtained from a sample of 328 women academics in this context, we examine how changed paid workload, controlling for other relevant indicators namely age, hopefulness for one's career, and financial satisfaction, predict job satisfaction levels for all respondents and for those with extended unpaid domestic work.

Literature Review

While the definition of self-care varies in the literature, it is found to be highly associated with job satisfaction (Acker, 2018; Cassie & DuBose, 2023). As we argue that increased time spent in other areas of life decreases the time we spare for self-care, it is significant to investigate job satisfaction patterns of women academics in relation to changes in time allocation, to be able to understand the ways in which their wellness can be improved overall[1] and through promoting self-care. Scholars emphasize that job satisfaction affects individuals' general wellbeing and happiness (Calaguas, 2017; Chiva & Guinot, 2021). It is directly related to subjective wellbeing (Cannas et al., 2019) and inversely related to burnout (Anbar & Eker, 2008). There are different findings on women's and men's job satisfaction in academia. Some studies reveal that men in academia have higher job satisfaction (Bender & Heywood, 2006; Bilimoria et al., 2006), while others find no significant discrepancy between the job satisfaction of women academics and that of their male colleagues (Okpara et al., 2005; Sabharwal & Corley, 2009). Overall, studies confirm that the pandemic resulted in significant disruptions in the academic environment, and also changed academics' job satisfaction levels (Ahmadi et al., 2022; Walters et al., 2022), in the form of a continuous decrease (Feng & Savani, 2020).

In academia, women have more difficulties balancing familial responsibilities and academic duties than their male colleagues (Minello et al., 2021; Schiebinger et al., 2008), while balancing different responsibilities is significant for academics' job satisfaction and wellbeing (Shadab & Arif, 2015). Women academics also most tend to be in the academic profile characterized by lowest work-family life balance and job satisfaction and highest intentions of turnover (French et al., 2020), as these components are somewhat interrelated: the disturbed balance between familial and academic responsibilities may result in lower job satisfaction (Machado-Taylor et al., 2014) and higher turnover rates (Deutsch & Yao, 2014), as well as more stress and feelings of burnout for women academics (Bender & Heywood, 2006; Liu & Lo, 2017). During Covid-19, with school closures and increasing care responsibilities, women in academia had further issues concerning this double burden (King & Frederickson, 2021; Utoft, 2020), and the conditions during the pandemic diminished the boundaries between professional and personal aspects of their lives, negatively affecting their job satisfaction (NASEM, 2021).

How academics allocate their time is critical for understanding the job satisfaction patterns in academia (French et al., 2020). For example, time devoted to research and teaching is found to be positively affecting their job satisfaction levels (Feld et al., 2015; Szromek & Wolniak, 2020), as research activities and productivity are critical to their satisfaction at work (Albert et al., 2018), possibly since engaging in research allows academics to follow their intellectual interests, contribute to knowledge, and gain career development. During the pandemic, there was a disproportionate decrease in the time dedicated to research for women compared to men in academia (Deryugina et al., 2021), which could have impacted their feelings of satisfaction and fulfillment adversely during this period. Also, increased time allocated to administrative roles negatively affects job satisfaction

92 *Aslı Ermiş Mert and Elif Yılmaz*

of academics overall (Szromek & Wolniak, 2020) unlike time spent for research, potentially due to increased workload, time constraints it creates for research and teaching, and decreased autonomy. For women academics in particular, the rise in the time allocated to administrative tasks affected job satisfaction levels in a negative way during the pandemic (Ronnie et al., 2022).

Data and Methodology

This part of the chapter presents the data and methods used for the analyses. The aim to collect this data was to understand how the pandemic has influenced the wellbeing of women academics primarily in relation to their changing workload and productivity (mainly concerning research) and time spent in unpaid work. The following subsections will provide information on the content and structure of the data and the methods employed in the study.

Data

Based on a 95% confidence interval and 4% margin of error, taking the total number of women in academia by 2020 ($N = 79.914$) (Council of Higher Education, 2020) into account, the ideal size of the sample was found as 596, decided as the nearest whole number of 600, which ended up being 601 as a result of proportioning at the city level during the sampling process. To prevent the risk of not reaching the targeted response rate, an addition of 30% was made, making the final sample size 784 (3 of whose contact information we could not reach). The data for this study was collected between November 2021 and January 2022 in Türkiye, through the implementation of an online questionnaire by distributing its link via email, following a pilot study in which 16 participants completed the questionnaire. Multistage cluster sampling was employed as the method based on academic rank (instructors and research assistants, assistant professors, associate professors, professors) since the expectation was that there would be varying experiences in terms of wellbeing for women in different stages of their lives and careers.[2] Women academics were randomly selected in also randomly chosen universities from one chosen city among 12 NUTS 1 (Nomenclature of Territorial Units for Statistics – level 1[3]) regions (12 cities in total) in the country, for which the process was undertaken in a random pattern as well. To elaborate, the sample size was proportioned between the 12 cities by considering the total number of women academics in each of these contexts, and the number of universities to be selected in each city was determined based on the principle of selecting 25 respondents at most in each university since the sample size was small for some of the cities and universities. The total number of participants in each city was distributed equally between universities. Finally, women academics were randomly chosen in these universities, by proportioning the total (university level) sample size to the number of women academics in each rank in every university. At the end of the data collection process, 328 respondents out of 400 who participated in the study completed the questionnaire by answering all of the questions.

Methods[4]

This study mainly implements two multiple regression models to predict the reported job satisfaction levels of women in academia in Türkiye after the pandemic had begun, in relation to primarily the changes in the academic workload. In both regression models, residuals are found to be approximately normally distributed. In the first model, age, hopefulness for career, financial satisfaction, and extended academic workload are used as predictors, and the model includes all respondents. To evaluate how a high level of increase in time allocated to domestic responsibilities relates to job satisfaction, the second model predicts the effect of the changes in same independent variables, yet the model includes those who claim their time spent in housework and/or unpaid care work had increased after the pandemic. This group of participants are those who either agreed or completely agreed to an increase in at least one of the domestic responsibility components (housework and care responsibilities).

Results and Discussions

This section will primarily discuss the two multiple regression models predicting women academics' reported job satisfaction levels mainly based on changed time allocation patterns/workload. Descriptive statistics and Spearman's (1904) correlation coefficients will be presented within the discussions where necessary. While 15.8% of women academics in our sample agreed that their job is the biggest source of happiness in their lives (corresponding to a score of 80 and over out of 100), 37.5% of the respondents stated that their current job satisfaction is at a high level (a score of 80 and over out of 100), and only 23.5% claimed that their job satisfaction was not affected by the pandemic (a score of 80 out of 100 for agreeing with the statement 'The pandemic did not negatively affect my job satisfaction'). As seen, only a little more than 1 in 3 women academics claim to have a high level of job satisfaction, while experiencing no negative effect in relation to the pandemic concerning satisfaction at work is also reported at a relatively low level.

Table 9.1 presents the multiple regression model predicting the reported job satisfaction of women academics, by using age, hopefulness for career, financial satisfaction, and increased workload in research, administrative roles, and teaching as the independent variables. The predictors in the model explain 42.2% of the variance in women academics' reported job satisfaction.

As presented in the first model, one unit increase in age enhances women academics' satisfaction with their job by .39 points, as a higher level of hopefulness about career prospectively has the strongest statistically significant and positive effect on job satisfaction of women in academia. One unit increase in the reported hopefulness for career, job satisfaction increases by .51 points, as there is a relatively strong positive correlation between job satisfaction and career hopefulness (rho: 0.5548). Regarding financial satisfaction, there is also a statistically significant improving impact of increasing satisfaction with pay, with one unit increase

94 Aslı Ermiş Mert and Elif Yılmaz

Table 9.1 Multiple regression model predicting women's job satisfaction levels based on components related to workload and other relevant components (for all women academics in the dataset)

Age	.39 (.12)***
Hopefulness for career	.51 (.05)***
Financial satisfaction	.24 (.04)***
Increased workload in research	.07 (.04)
Increased workload in administrative work	−.07 (.03)*
Increased workload in teaching	.04 (.04)
Cons.	12.02 (4.08)**
N	327
F (6, 320)	40.64
Prob > F	0.0000
Adj. R-Squared	0.4218

*p value ≤ 0.05, **p value ≤ 0.01, ***p value ≤ 0.001.

displaying an improvement by .24 points. This finding is important to emphasize the need to improve women's income overall (only 14.6% of the respondents reported a score of 80 and over for being financially satisfied with their job) and to challenge the gender pay gap in academia and beyond.

The results for expanded workload predictors are somewhat more mixed. Firstly, spending more time undertaking research since the beginning of the pandemic yields no statistically significant result. This could be due to academics (both women and men) viewing research activities in a positive light, meaning that it is a default part of their job, which they also mostly consider a time investment in self as an academic, essential for development as well as fulfilling. Indeed, research productivity is found to be enhancing job satisfaction (Albert et al., 2018), and with regard to specifically publishing, it is related to professional satisfaction for tenured and nontenured men academics and tenured women academics (Hesli and Lee, 2013). When it comes to extended administrative responsibilities, a statistically significant diminishing impact is observed. With one unit rise in claiming to have increased workload in administrative roles since the beginning of the pandemic, there is a decrease in the reported job satisfaction levels of women in the Turkish academia by .07 points. Administrative roles are generally viewed as auxiliary in academia, and related duties could be considered as disruptive to academics' main roles, taking time away especially from research overall and for women academics. There is also evidence that the lack of time to undertake research and time dedicated to administrative duties relate to job dissatisfaction among academics (Schulze, 2006). While these responsibilities are extensively expected of women in most academic settings, having increased time spent could even be more diminishing to their occupational satisfaction, also because performance indicators are to a considerable extent based on teaching and/or research in academia. The result for increased workload in teaching is also not statistically significant, which could be explained similarly to the impact of expanded research workload since the beginning of the pandemic.

Time Allocation and Job Satisfaction for Women Academics 95

Table 9.2 Multiple regression model predicting women's job satisfaction levels based on components related to workload and other relevant components (for those who reported increased time spent on housework and/or care responsibilities in relation to the pandemic)

Age	.48 (.15)***
Hopefulness for career	.47 (.06)***
Financial satisfaction	.24 (.05)***
Increased workload in research	.11 (.04)**
Increased workload in administrative work	−.10 (.04)**
Increased workload in teaching	.06 (.05)
Cons.	10.00 (4.83)*
N	255
F (6, 320)	29.73
Prob > F	0.0000
Adj. R-Squared	0.4043

*p value ≤ 0.05, **p value ≤ 0.01, ***p value ≤ 0.001.

In this study, there is a high rate (74.5%) for reporting (agreeing or completely agreeing) increased time spent on housework since the pandemic has begun, which is 48.6% for unpaid care responsibilities. It is significant to note that alongside work-related responsibilities, this increase is also expected to contribute to the diminishing levels of self-care. As women academics' difficulties to balance work and family life by also extensively compromising self-care as a consequence are expected to influence their job satisfaction, it is crucial to investigate how increases in academic workload impact those with a relatively heavier domestic burden. Therefore, an additional model was created to predict the reported job satisfaction levels of women academics, who reported to have increased time spent for housework and/or unpaid care responsibilities based on the same indicators. In this model, predictor variables explain the variance in reported job satisfaction levels by 40.4%.

As seen in Table 9.2, for women academics with extended housework and/or care responsibilities, the effects of increasing age and being more hopeful for career on job satisfaction are similar to the model presented in Table 9.1, the impact of improved financial satisfaction being identical. However, findings for changes in the academic workload show differences. Results are not statistically significant in both models for teaching despite that the highest rate for increased workload was reported for this role. Undertaking more administrative work since the beginning of the pandemic decreases the reported job satisfaction levels, slightly stronger than the first model. The main difference between the two models could be seen in the result for increased research workload. One unit increase in the reported expansion of research-related work, job satisfaction improves by .11 points. The finding being statistically significant in this model could mean that with an even extra hectic schedule, women academics could be more evidently satisfied when they have the opportunity to engage in further research activities, as it is more challenging for them with enhanced unpaid domestic responsibilities. In other words, this could be related to being able to find time to contribute to one's career and undertaking a task that is fulfilling (especially for parents whose time allocation patterns are more complex).

Conclusion

This chapter primarily focused on women academics' job satisfaction as a core element of their wellness based on the changed workload/time spent in different areas of life during the pandemic in the Turkish context. The importance of this study was understanding the dynamics between the shifts in time allocation patterns and academics' level of satisfaction with their job as also how we spend our time as academics potentially determines whether or to what extent self-care is practiced, which in turn relates to job satisfaction as discussed above. The findings suggest that how women in the Turkish academia spend their time in terms of work-related duties predicts their job satisfaction successfully to a certain extent. Intensified roles that do not directly relate to their main academic responsibilities were found to be associated with a decrease in their job satisfaction overall, while being able to save more time for research was enhancing reported satisfaction with one's job for those with relatively higher time limitations and possibly more cramped schedules due to expanded unpaid work, who are also expected to have no to little room for self-care. These results, aligned with our own experiences as academics (until recently), bring about the following recommendations:

- Administrative and bureaucratic duties should be equally distributed between women and men in academia, and a gendered division of academic labour should be avoided to allow women in academia time for research as well as self-care with the goal of preventing burnout.
- During performance evaluations, time spent on administrative and related duties needs to be recognized considering the interruption they cause for especially research responsibilities.
- Flexible work arrangements and remote work opportunities need to be available when and where possible.
- Providing accessible support for care responsibilities is a key issue such as offering day care in the campus or financial support for receiving paid help so that those with such responsibilities have an equal opportunity to allocate time for research and practicing adequate self-care.
- Increasing the job satisfaction of academics should be among the institutional performance indicators as it is also connected to the extent of self-care they are able to practice. These indicators need to be regularly measured, as well as actions need to be taken for the related short-term and long-term goals by adopting a gender-sensitive approach.

Ethical Approval

The ethical approval for this study was provided by the Koç University Committee on Human Research (Decision no. 2020.479.IRB3.197).

Funding

This chapter is based on the research that was funded by The Scientific and Technological Research Council of Türkiye (TÜBİTAK) (project no. 220K276).

Notes

1 A Spearman correlation test showed that there is a statistically significant positive and moderate relationship between job satisfaction levels of women academics and their reported happiness levels after the pandemic has begun (scale of 1–100, mean: 58.19, std. dev: 17.33) in our study (rho: 0.3389).
2 A one-way analysis of variance (ANOVA) test was used to determine whether job satisfaction levels of women academics from different ranks vary, and while a statistically significant difference was found, the Tukey test demonstrated that there were only two pairwise comparisons that presented a significant variation: assistant professors versus research assistants (contrast: 11.56 standard error: 3.71) and professors versus research assistants (contrast: 17.41, standard error: 5.54). Since no extended differences were discovered, analyses in the chapter are conducted without regarding ranks.
3 For further information on NUTS 1 regions in Türkiye, please visit: https://ec.europa.eu/eurostat/documents/345175/7773495/TR.pdf
4 Please see the Appendix for the details of the variables.

References

Acker, G. M. (2018). Self–care practices among social workers: Do they predict job satisfaction and turnover intention? *Social Work in Mental Health, 16*(6), 713–727. https://doi.org/10.1080/15332985.2018.1494082

Ahmadi, F., Zandi, S., Cetrez, Ö. A., & Akhavan, S. (2022). Job satisfaction and challenges of working from home during the Covid-19 pandemic: A study in a Swedish academic setting. *Work (Reading, Mass.), 71*(2), 357–370. https://doi.org/10.3233/WOR-210442

Albert, C., Davia, M. A., & Legazpe, N. (2018). Job satisfaction amongst academics: The role of research productivity. *Studies in Higher Education, 43*(8), 1362–1377. https://doi.org/10.1080/03075079.2016.1255937

Anbar, A., & Eker, M. (2008). An examination of relationship between burnout and job satisfaction among Turkish accounting and finance academicians. *European Journal of Economic and Political Studies (EJEPS), 1*(1), 46–67.

Bender, K. A., & Heywood, J. S. (2006). Job satisfaction of the highly educated: The role of gender, academic tenure, and earnings. *Scottish Journal of Political Economy, 53*(2), 253–279. https://doi.org/10.1111/j.1467-9485.2006.00379.x

Bilimoria, D., Perry, S. R., Liang, X., Stoller, E. P., Higgins, P., & Taylor, C. (2006). How do female and male faculty members construct job satisfaction? The roles of perceived institutional leadership and mentoring and their mediating processes. *The Journal of Technology Transfer, 31*(3), 355–365. https://doi.org/10.1007/s10961-006-7207-zCalaguas, G. M. (2017). Satisfied and happy: Establishing link between job satisfaction and subjective well-being. *Asia Pacific Journal of Multidisciplinary Research, 5*(1), 104–111.

Cannas, M., Sergi, B., Sironi, E., & Mentel, U. (2019). Job satisfaction and subjective well-being in Europe. *Economics and Sociology, 12*, 183–196. https://doi.org/10.14254/2071-789X.2019/12-4/11

Cassie, K. M., & DuBose, E. M. (2023). An exploratory examination of the effect of self-care practices on job satisfaction and organizational commitment. *Journal of Evidence-Based Social Work, 20*(2), 258–271. https://doi.org/10.1080/26408066.2022.2156832

Chiva, R., & Guinot, J. (2021). *Well-being, happiness, satisfaction, burnout and the future of work* (pp. 163–182). https://doi.org/10.1108/978-1-80071-298-020211019

Council of Higher Education. (2020). Council of Higher Education statistics. https://istatistik.yok.gov.tr/

Deryugina, T., Shurchkov, O., & Stearns, J. (2021). Covid-19 disruptions disproportionately affect female academics. *AEA Papers and Proceedings, 111,* 164–168. https://doi.org/10.1257/pandp.20211017

Deutsch, F., & Yao, B. (2014). Gender differences in faculty attrition in the USA. *Community, Work & Family, 17,* 392–408. https://doi.org/10.1080/13668803.2014.885880

Docka-Filipek, D., & Stone, L. B. (2021). Twice a "housewife": On academic precarity, "hysterical" women, faculty mental health, and service as gendered care work for the "university family" in pandemic times. *Gender, Work & Organization, 28*(6), 2158–2179. https://doi.org/10.1111/gwao.12723

Feld, L. P., Necker, S., & Frey, B. S. (2015). Happiness of economists. *Applied Economics, 47*(10), 990–1007. https://doi.org/10.1080/00036846.2014.985374

Feng, Z., & Savani, K. (2020). Covid-19 created a gender gap in perceived work productivity and job satisfaction: Implications for dual-career parents working from home. *Gender in Management: An International Journal, 35*(7/8), 719–736. https://doi.org/10.1108/GM-07-2020-0202

French, K. A., Allen, T. D., Miller, M. H., Kim, E. S., & Centeno, G. (2020). Faculty time allocation in relation to work-family balance, job satisfaction, commitment, and turnover intentions. *Journal of Vocational Behavior, 120,* 103443. https://doi.org/10.1016/j.jvb.2020.103443

Gabster, B., van Daalen, K., Dhatt, R., & Barry, M. (2020). Challenges for the female academic during the Covid-19 pandemic. *The Lancet, 395.* https://doi.org/10.1016/S0140-6736(20)31412-4

Hesli, V., & Lee, J. (2013). Job satisfaction in academia: Why are some faculty members happier than others?. *PS: Political Science & Politics, 46*(2), 339–354. doi:10.1017/S1049096513000048

King, M. M., & Frederickson, M. E. (2021). The pandemic penalty: The gendered effects of Covid-19 on scientific productivity. *Socius, 7,* 1–24. https://doi.org/10.1177/23780231211006977

Liu, H., & Lo, V. (2017). An integrated model of workload, autonomy, burnout, job satisfaction, and turnover intention among Taiwanese reporters. *Asian Journal of Communication, 28,* 1–17. https://doi.org/10.1080/01292986.2017.1382544

Machado-Taylor, M. de L., White, K., & Gouveia, O. (2014). Job satisfaction of academics: Does gender matter?. *Higher Education Policy, 27*(3), 363–384. https://doi.org/10.1057/hep.2013.34

Minello, A., Martucci, S., & Manzo, L. K. C. (2021). The pandemic and the academic mothers: Present hardships and future perspectives. *European Societies, 23*(sup1), S82–S94. https://doi.org/10.1080/14616696.2020.1809690

National Academies of Sciences, Engineering, and Medicine (NASEM). (2021). *The impact of Covid-19 on the careers of women in academic sciences, engineering, and medicine.* The National Academies Press. https://doi.org/10.17226/26061

Okpara, J. O., Squillace, M., & Erondu, E. A. (2005). Gender differences and job satisfaction: A study of university teachers in the United States. *Women in Management Review, 20*(3), 177–190. https://doi.org/10.1108/09649420510591852

Parlak, S., Çelebi Çakıroğlu, O., & Öksüz Gül, F. (2021). Gender roles during Covid-19 pandemic: The experiences of Turkish female academics. *Gender, Work, and Organization, 28*(Suppl 2), 461–483. https://doi.org/10.1111/gwao.12655

Pereira, M. do M. (2021). Researching gender inequalities in academic labor during the Covid-19 pandemic: Avoiding common problems and asking different questions. *Gender, Work & Organization, 28*(S2), 498–509. https://doi.org/10.1111/gwao.12618

Ronnie, L., du Plessis, M., & Walters, C. (2022). Women academics and the changing psychological contract during Covid-19 lockdown. *Frontiers in Psychology, 13*. https://www.frontiersin.org/articles/10.3389/fpsyg.2022.940953

Sabharwal, M., & Corley, E. (2009). Faculty job satisfaction across gender and discipline. *The Social Science Journal, 46*, 539–556. https://doi.org/10.1016/j.soscij.2009.04.015

Schiebinger, L., Henderson, A. D., & Gilmartin, S. K. (2008). *Dual-career academic couples: What universities need to know*. Stanford University.

Schulze, S. (2006). Factors influencing the job satisfaction of academics in higher education. *South African Journal of Higher Education, 20*(2), 318–335.

Shadab, M., & Arif, K. (2015). Impact of work-life balance on job satisfaction: A case of health care services in Pakistan. *Developing Country Studies, 5*(9), 132–138.

Spearman, C. (1904). The proof and measurement of association between two things. *The American Journal of Psychology, 15*(1), 72–101. https://doi.org/10.2307/1412159

Szromek, A. R., & Wolniak, R. (2020). Job satisfaction and problems among academic staff in higher education. *Sustainability, 12*(12), Article 12. https://doi.org/10.3390/su12124865

Tarabochia, S. L., Brugar, K. A., & Ward, J. A. (2022). Running, writing, resilience: A self-study of collaborative self-care among women faculty. In N. Lemon (Ed.), *Creative expression and wellbeing in higher education: Making and movement as mindful moments of self-care* (pp. 87–104). Routledge.

Utoft, E. H. (2020). 'All the single ladies' as the ideal academic during times of Covid-19? *Gender, Work & Organization, 27*(5), 778–787. https://doi.org/10.1111/gwao.12478

Walters, C., Mehl, G. G., Piraino, P., Jansen, J. D., & Kriger, S. (2022). The impact of the pandemic-enforced lockdown on the scholarly productivity of women academics in South Africa. *Research Policy, 51*(1), 104403. https://doi.org/10.1016/j.respol.2021.104403

Appendix

Outcome Variable

Job satisfaction: Scale of 1–100 (from agreeing the least to agreeing the most), mean: 63.64, std. dev: 25.50, level of agreement with the statement 'I am satisfied with my job'

Predictor Variables

Age: Min. 24, max. 86

Hopefulness for career: Scale of 1–100, mean: 61.99, std. dev: 24.29, level of agreement with the statement 'I feel hopeful about the future regarding my career'

Financial satisfaction: Scale of 1–100, mean: 47.47, std. dev: 26.79, level of agreement with the statement 'I am financially satisfied with my job at the moment'

Increased research workload: Scale of 0–100, mean: 52.62, std. dev: 32.14, level of agreement with the statement 'Since the beginning of the pandemic, my research workload (writing papers, participating in seminars/conferences, funding applications, etc.) has overall increased.' (0 corresponding to having no research workload) (30.6% of the respondents reported a score of 80 or above out of 100)

Increased teaching workload: Scale of 0–100, mean: 61.01, std. dev: 31.13, level of agreement with the statement 'Since the beginning of the pandemic, my educational workload (teaching and related responsibilities, master's/doctoral student supervision, etc.) has overall increased' (0 corresponding to having no educational workload) (39.6% of the respondents reported a score of 80 or above out of 100)

Increased administrative workload: Scale of 0–100, mean: 46.46, std. dev: 35.14, level of agreement with the statement 'Since the beginning of the pandemic, my administrative (departmental chair, director of research center, board member, committee work, non-academic assistant responsibilities, etc.) workload has increased in general' (0 corresponding to having no administrative workload) (26.7% of the respondents reported a score of 80 or above out of 100)

Increased time spent on housework: 'During the pandemic, the time I spent on housework has increased.' (0 – I have no housework responsibilities, 1 – Strongly disagree, 2 – Disagree, 3 – Neither agree nor disagree, 4 – Agree, 5 – Strongly agree.)

Time Allocation and Job Satisfaction for Women Academics   101

Increased time spent on unpaid care responsibilities: 'During the pandemic, the time I spent on unpaid care work has increased.' (0 – I have no care responsibilities, 1 – Strongly disagree, 2 – Disagree, 3 – Neither agree nor disagree, 4 – Agree, 5 – Strongly agree.)

Note: The responses corresponding to having no responsibility (0 out of 100) in the above-mentioned work-related and unpaid domestic responsibilities are kept in both models (and for other statistical calculations), as involving those with no such responsibilities was considered to be important for predicting particularly job satisfaction in this study. In the second model, we are only taking those with highly increased unpaid work into account, thus, keeping those with no such responsibilities in the variables did not generate any difference.

10 Interstate Dialogues

Chronicles of Rhythms of Time and the Art of Self-care of a Mobile Academic

Narelle Lemon and Sharon McDonough

Introduction

Significant research has concentrated on examining how geographic mobility influences the wellbeing of family members, encompassing aspects such as their physical health, professional performance and contentment, as well as the quality of their marital and familial bonds (Frame & Shehan, 1994; Sagi et al., 2021; Townes Mayers, 2022). Illuminated are those groups with strong place attachment and for whom relocation may increase, not reduce, vulnerability (Farbotko et al., 2020). Scholarly interest in the transnational movement of individuals within higher education dates back to the 1950s, with initial emphasis primarily on international students (Nash, 1976; Pace, 1959). Research on the mobility of academic staff began to emerge in the 1990s (Teichler, 1996; Welch, 1997), gaining increasing attention over the past two decades (e.g., Franzoni et al., 2015; Huang & Welch, 2021; Richardson & McKenna, 2002; Richardson & Zikic, 2007; Shen et al., 2022). However, the empirical knowledge regarding the migration and mobility of 'teachers in higher education', 'scholars', 'academics', or 'researchers' has remained limited (Teichler, 2015) but we are now entering into a new phase of more interest in cross-border (state and country) mobility (Franzoni et al., 2015; Shen et al., 2022). Within these realms, some studies are delving into the social and psychological dimensions of mobility, with particular emphasis on its economic, cultural, political, and social ramifications (Amaro et al., 2024; Andresen et al., 2020; Herschberg et al., 2018; Joshi, 2023; Shen et al., 2022; Sulaimanova et al., 2023). Academic mobility is a significant feature of modern higher education; however, we rarely hear about the intricacies from a self-care and wellbeing perspective. In particular, we are interested in how the movement of academics might intersect with time, and how use of time and making time for self-care and wellbeing might be impacted by such movement.

We are writing this chapter as a duo-ethnography. We are two scholars who have had a long-standing collaboration, and we are close friends. We advocate for placing wellbeing at the centre of the educational endeavour and both our individual and collaborative works have a focus on building skills, knowledge, and awareness of wellbeing and resilience processes at the individual and systemic level

DOI: 10.4324/9781032688633-12

(Lemon & McDonough, 2020, 2021, 2023; McDonough & Lemon, 2021, 2022b, 2022a). We are also advocates of voice that embrace vulnerability, noting:

> One of the best ways to embrace this is to learn with and from one another as we individually and collectively build our capacity to truly care for ourselves. What does being an advocate for yourself and a self-care activist for the academy look like for you? What small act can you embrace, that over time when repeated daily or often interrupts those badges of exhaustion being placed on our chest and rather replaces them with a badge of play and rest?
>
> (McDonough & Lemon, 2021, p. 95)

We both have lived in the same state of Victoria for ever, but recently, one of us accepted a new job interstate to the west of the country in what some call the most remote city in the world, Perth in the state of Western Australia. So began a new time in our friendship and work collaboration. Additionally for Narelle, a shift in how time is utilized in the work space, with a move from a senior leadership role in service to a School with four departments and two research centres on one campus to a research intensive position in one school across three campuses building a research community from the ground up. To capture this moment in time, we are writing this chapter as a dialogical conversation live (captured in the first 3 months or 11 working weeks during October to December 2023) and it is presented in the format of a diary, reflecting on the impact of time, in this moment of time.

This chapter captures a pivotal juncture in the trajectory of an academic career, often regarded with anticipation and enthusiasm – a relocation interstate for a professional opportunity. While the allure of novel prospects in terms of work and influence is evident, scant attention is typically paid to the multifaceted challenges encountered by mobile academics. This encompasses the complete upheaval and resettlement of not only oneself but also one's family: securing new accommodation, navigating unfamiliar neighbourhoods, establishing essential services such as healthcare providers and amenities, and adapting to a different social milieu. Amidst the excitement, there exists a profound cognitive burden, manifesting in prolonged days and an overwhelming sense of disorientation. Furthermore, the transition entails not only acclimatizing to a new professional environment with its attendant cultural nuances but also negotiating the unfamiliarity of personal domains. While romanticized by some, the toll exacted on wellbeing and self-care cannot be overstated.

Exploring Methodology: Navigating the Unfolding Research and Writing Journey

In the realm of research and writing, we draw from the work of Helin (2016) who offers a profound perspective on dialogical writing, asserting that it marks a shift in emphasis from finalized narratives to emergent ones. It is this emergent nature that we find valuable as it functions as a means of inquiry, a conduit for emotions, a channel for attentive listening, and a bridge to connect with others (Helin, 2016). The use of dialogical writing also challenges philosophical paradigms that seek to create "stable, solid, and enduring texts" (Helin, 2016, p. 3). Dialogue, in this context, emerges as the fertile ground where tentative, developmental, and emergent conversations and writings unfold, enabling individuals to collaboratively test ideas, explore concepts, and develop new meanings (McDonough & Brandenburg, 2019; Smith, 2015).

In this chapter, we are not reporting empirical findings but instead, we aim to draw readers into our dialogical journey in order to understand our experiences and our interpretation of those. In order to do this, we use an approach we have previously employed (McDonough & Lemon, 2021), where we depart from a traditional academic structure and we seamlessly interweave literature into our dialogue, using it to frame and enrich the ongoing evolution of our exploration.

As we delve into the exploration of creating spaces for self-care and wellbeing within higher education contexts, we perceive dialogic writing as the initial step towards opening up a space (Lemon, 2021). It also represents an invitation to others to join in the conversation that is "shared, collective and systemic responsibility that invites us to stand in a shared vulnerability" (McDonough & Lemon, 2021, p. 185).

Through this duo-ethnography using dialogical writing, we wanted to explore the ways that this move for one of us from one state to another might connect to concepts of time, how we spend it, how it intersects with beginning a new job in a new place, and how it is connected with self-care and wellbeing. To structure our dialogic writing and conversation, we initiated our journey with a series of question prompts related to our focus of time, self-care, and wellbeing:

- What are you noticing about the rhythm of your days in this new job and place?
- How are you maintaining old and forming new habits and routines?
- What are you noticing about how you form new collaborations and invest time in new collegial relationships while continuing to foster ongoing collaborations?

Throughout this chapter, these prompts are highlighted in bold text. We share some of our diary entries, presented under our prompts to guide the reading and journey. Italics Aerial font represents Sharon's diary entries, and Narelle is represented in Times New Roman. We also identify the authors of each section by using our respective names. Ultimately, we conclude the chapter by presenting key insights derived from our collective conversation.

Habits in Flux: Balancing Old and New in the Daily Routine

2 October 2023

Sharon: I wanted to send Narelle a text message wishing her well for the first day of the new job. The first thing I did was check the time difference on my phone – was it too early to text? She's an early riser I figured or would have her phone on silent if she was still sleeping.

Narelle: To wake up to a message on my phone was so comforting. First day of new job vibes. I have butterflies in my tummy – anticipation, excitement, newness, familiar, and unfamiliar. My daily routines are a little different as well. I'm walking to walk. Something I have never ever done in my entire life; I've always lived away from the work zone, a conscious decision to split personal and professional. But in a new city, there is little choice in where you can rent, and well we found a house to rent that happens to be a ten-minute walk away. So, new daily routines have me walking in my Birkenstocks (at the moment Perth is around 36 degrees Celsius), carrying a bag with my heels, and carrying out a wish I have always wanted to live out, not carrying a laptop rather leaving my writing to live in the cloud and syncing work and personal computers to enable this. Living the dream of morning routines – a walk and coffee with my lovely, shower then walk to work. A new daily norm.

4 October 2023

Sharon: I sent Narelle an Instagram post about how friends keep in touch long distance by sharing the seemingly mundane, everyday things – I DM'd it with a short message 'it's us'. But the ideas of it have been resonating for me throughout the day – is this how we maintain connections in the face of distance by continuing to message the small, seemingly inconsequential aspects of the day? I like this idea so much as it reminds us about the importance of the small moments – all the small moments build up to the bigger connections.

Narelle: Living life through digital spaces at the moment. A selfie shared here, an observation noted there. Photos of clouds, blue skies, names of street signs that remind me of friends. Maintaining connections. Feeling like we are there even though we can't touch each other. Treasured moment in the balancing of new rhythms and habits. I am missing touching friends in real life; that knowing comfort.

Noticing the Rhythm of Days in a New Job and Place

22 October 2023

Narelle: Time is such an interesting concept at the moment. I'm writing this on day 21 of what I am calling "project relocation to Perth". That's not long, 21 days, but it feels like a lifetime. So much has happened. Each day is new, unfamiliar but familiar.

Time to get to know oneself in a new role. I'm research intensive. This is a dream, but I keep finding myself checking the diary to make sure I haven't missed a meeting. The last three years I've held an Associate Dean role with back-to-back meetings. I'd sneak in writing or reading for my research, in small pockets of time, between virtual appointments, early in the morning.

The liminal space between time zones. I'm still living in two. My mind, body, relationship with self (I'm hungry at 4 pm in Perth and all I can think is that it is 7 pm in Melbourne or I rise at 6 am in Perth and it's already 9 am in Melbourne, I'm running late). I get to 6 pm in Perth for dinner with friends and my body is telling me I should be in bed (I'm a 9 pm go-to-bed person). My body pays the price, as does my mind.

9 October 2023

Narelle: Day 24 in new city, Day 7 new job. Time for self-care required. Routines have totally changed.

Time and the concept of speed of work. Slower pace. That's not bad, I'm attracted to it, and to be honest feel close to it. I have days when I embrace it. I'm grounded. Other days when I have a mind fog, a haze over my eyes, and I feel overwhelmed with what I need to do, my to-do list grows at a rapid pace, things seem slow, one problem solved uncovers five other things. I find myself frustrated by the lack of processes. I move into the negative bias, fast-paced, hectic vibes that I'm so not wanting to be or experience. I wonder if it's release, getting out, a cleansing with this time of transition. Almost a right of passage. A cleaning out. A resetting.

Sharon: Oooh so interesting to read this. I'd wondered how the working between timezones with colleagues was going. I'm trying to be mindful of when is your working time on the other side of our wide brown land – of when the best times are for us to connect across the country. Perhaps some of the fast and slow are your body and brain shedding one role and way of being to another – the packed calendar, the heavy administrative demands that required you to be 'on' versus a slower pace of writing and thinking that has to come with research (despite all the associated institutional pressures to produce... but more of that below).

*I think there's something even in the language we use to describe the roles that we have that implies the time we are meant to be giving to things – you're now research **intensive** – the nomenclature itself implies the intensity of time that you will be giving in this role, but as we know, in academia the intensity is not just about time but about **productive use of time**, so from an institutional perspective the name implies that there will be an intensity of production too – and I wonder if or how that manifests in these early days or what tension there is between taking things slow, finding your feet, building connections versus the need to have things up and running quickly?*

Maintaining Old and Forming New Habits and Routines

14 October 2023

Narelle: It is the end of week four (day 29) in Perth and I've hit homesickness. I'm feeling a bit down. The tears are sitting there. Change overload. Newness overload. Nothing specific has occurred but it is a bit much. I'm tuning into my body and mind and what it is telling me right now, I don't want to move into glazed over, not present mode. Such a funny time. Funny, not hilarious funny, so maybe not the right word, more **bewildering**, **exciting**, **fascinating**, and **unusual** all in the one moment of time (can I claim this as a BEFU moment??!?). My book of wisdom is being called upon. What is it I know I need to do at this time? I know what my go to strategies are for when I feel sad, for when I feel frustrated, or exhausted, or tender, but overwhelmed homesickness, I'm not sure. I guess this is a good opportunity to be curious. I'm noticing I am breathing from my shoulders, not my belly. I'm holding tension in my jaw. Release I tell myself, but it is not.

16 October 2023

Narelle: I actually found myself turning to poetry and baking on the weekend. Poetry is an expressive, almost journaling-like tool in my toolbox. My emotions flow through the words as they emerge on the page, almost like a transfer of flow from my emotional energy through the pencil onto the page. Baking is familiar, associated with fond childhood memories of learning to bake with my nana, and something I do to share with others (Figure 10.1).

Figure 10.1 Instagram post juxtaposed with a poetic response from Narelle

Time to bake
Follow recipe
Measure ingredients
  Slow down
    Gentle with each ingredient
      Made with love
        An act of self-care
Time to make
      An act of self-care
Making for others
Altruism
  Sharing
    Smiles
    A treat
    Joy
    Savour
Time together, bonding, chatting
      An act of self-care
Time
Small choices
 Repeated daily
  Change slowly over time
A routine, ritual, proactive action
Making time to bake
Making time to make
      An act of self-care

Narelle: The irony is in my BEFU moment, I baked and totally didn't even follow the recipe that I was actually reading as I was making at the time. I was not present in the act of my self-care. That was a reality check. Productive use of time, pressure to perform (self, institutional, and others), pressure to change a culture. It's a lot. And my baking mishap (actually both cookies are delicious, just different consistencies) is a great metaphor of things looking the same at this time but they are not. The ingredients, or what is pulling everything together or what is a part of the environment is the same but different. The job is familiar, but the context is not. The act of researching is familiar, but the context of being research intensive is not. The institutional hurt and healing is familiar, but this hurt and healing is not my hurt and healing. How do I cultivate and create the person I want to be in my new environment personally and professionally?

108 *Narelle Lemon and Sharon McDonough*

Sharon: I see a post about the baking and I wonder if the change is feeling all a bit much at the moment. I send a screenshot of a book I'm reading where the author, Stacie Bloomfield (2020) describes as their personal motto this idea of giving yourself margin. They take it from the language of sewing, where you need to include seam allowance, and they explore how this might function in our lives, how if we give ourselves margin, we build in time for space, for reflection, for creativity and for growth. From an outsider watching you navigate new space, new place, new roles, new people it feels like giving yourself margin is something that might enable the space and time to be held and set aside. Maybe the baking is a way to give yourself margin, but I wonder how might the new rhythm and structure of your days hold the opportunity for giving yourself margin. Can we capture margin in our calendars? In our mindsets? In our collaborations?

Rhythm

3 November 2023

Narelle: Putting rhythm into your life in the day. Rhythm is a pattern of being, being with the moment, sending a message to the brain of familiarity in a grounding way: being present in this moment. For me, my rhythms are my green tea drinking routine in the morning. Now, in Perth, this has changed. I consume a teapot quietly, with my husband, at a cafe, sitting outside early in the morning after a walk. No laptop. No notebook. No thinking about writing. No phone for email or social media scrolling. Just being with each other, in the fresh air, in the crispness of the new day. Saying hello to locals walking by, chatting to the barista, or patting a dog. My rhythm for writing and green tea routines happens later, on campus usually in my new office or at the campus cafe. Writing new words, the click on the computer, the flow. My rhythm in the day connects to my breath. Slow inhale and exhale. Feeling my feet on the ground, wiggling my toes in my shoes. This rhythm I can do anywhere anytime. Helping me come back to the present moment. Daily rhythms bring a calmness, a familiarity amongst the unfamiliar.

Rhythms in how I walk
Rhythms in where I walk
Slowing down, feeling the ground under my shoe
    barefoot, the sand between my toes, the grass blades brushing the outer foot

Rhythms in my green tea daily ceremonies
Rhythms in my green tea locations
    Tea bag dipping, tea leaf extraction
    The pour, multiple pours
        The feel of the ceramics in my palm, soothing

Rhythms in my breath
Rhythms in my head and heart connection
    the rising of my abdomen, deep, slow

Rhythms in day, night, cool, heat
Rhythms sun expectations, assumptions on self by others
Rhythms in making new connections, maintaining old
Rhythms in listening to the body, ups down, cycles, energy
Rhythms in familiar, unfamiliar, expats, locals, new state, familiar country

Rhythms that sooth
Rhythms that slow time down
Rhythms that ground
Rhythms that bring a deeply rooted listening to own needs

Sharon: Oh I love this. So often our rhythms are mindless – the habits we've formed that we fall into without question. We don't think about how our time is framed by them and how our time is stolen or grown by the rhythms we follow. There's so much in here about an awareness of the rhythm, of the time, of the embodied way you inhabit each of these moments – 'the grass blades brushing the outer foot'... the idea of being familiar and unfamiliar reminds me of a book I read where people wrote about being between worlds, not quite at home in a new home, no longer quite belonging to the old. Here, in this liminality, you're able to look at everything anew. So often we might think of it as a loss, but there's much to gain from that too – insight, understanding, meaning, new beginnings. I'm thinking about that for you at the moment when I know you're back for a while in Victoria. That moving between worlds, identities, ways of being, rhythms. Which ones continue to serve you? Which ones can you lay down and return to at a later date?

Collaborative Shifts: Forming New Bonds, Nurturing Existing Ones

5 December 2023

Narelle: The rhythms of collaboration are changing. There is a soothing feel with the familiar – those collaborators who have been sustained writing and researching partners. Soothing. This is nudged by the side of new rhythms, habits, connections, and everything that comes with the unknown. I'm adapting my rhythm (the speed, ways of working, expectations, and assumptions) of collaboration to the existing culture and ways of being and working that are unfamiliar to me. I feel like a Chameleon, changing skin colour based on their surroundings, or in this case, changing my ways of working in order to fit in while also ever so gently modelling new ways of working to support cultural shifts while also making new collegial relationships that will lead to collaborations. But like a Chameleon I have a limited colour palette or starting again with everything when it comes to collaborations. I have this little moment of panic every now and then. 'Oh no, collaborations in the new environment aren't happening', then I remind myself I've only been here for three months. So, I'm living a collaboration mixed life – my torso and tail are hanging out in the green of sustained and familiar collaborative familiarity and rhythms of working that are just continuing with a strength that is comforting and forward

110 *Narelle Lemon and Sharon McDonough*

moving at usual speeds of how I work, while my head and shoulder are hanging out in another environment, with a tonal colour not matching the rest of me as I transition to form new bonds, connections, and shared interests.

Concluding Remarks: Adaptation, Connection, and Time in Academic Life

Engaging in a duo-ethnographic exploration, we, two scholars and close friends, embarked on a reflective journey as one of us transitioned to a new job interstate. This transition signified a profound shift in our collaborative endeavours and daily experiences of time, self-care, and wellbeing. We are forever learning about ourselves, and this dialogical exchange illuminates the way that time, self-care, and wellbeing are associated with an intricate balance between familiar routines and the adjustments necessitated by new circumstances.

Through the dialogical exchange we identify the role of time and geography in academic identity and in self-care and wellbeing practices. While Bennett and Burke (2018) describe higher education as a timescape "in which participants manage their own and others' time according to normative frameworks" (p. 914), in the entries, we can see that in different contexts, and within different job descriptions, that timescape manifests differently. For Narelle, there is a tension between previous experience and professional identities relevant to working in higher education, and how these fit with her new roles and identities as an educator and researcher (Williams et al., 2012). The process and time that it takes to transition to, and adapt to a novel job and locale, highlight the inherent challenges and opportunities in acclimating to unfamiliar environments and roles (Sharon & Narelle, 2 October 2023; Narelle, 22 October 2023). It also highlights that the way we spend our time is mediated by the geography and culture of a place and that new rhythms and routines in both personal and professional life are influenced by place, culture, and time.

The role of digital platforms in preserving social connections and nurturing relationships across geographical and temporal distances, emphasizes the significance of what could be considered mundane everyday interactions, but instead function as glimmers, hope, and expressions of love in maintaining relational continuity despite geographical and temporal separation (Sharon & Narelle, 4 October 2023; Narelle, 22 October 2023). Furthermore, our dialogical conversation highlights the way that the establishment of new daily rituals and rhythms operates as a means of anchoring oneself amidst a time of transition and uncertainty. Including practices such as morning routines and mindful exercises (Narelle & Sharon, 3 November 2023), intentional time can be made for self-care and wellbeing. In particular, the role of taking time for a pause through strategic acts of self-care, such as poetry and baking, is highlighted as a means of addressing the emotional terrain associated with transitions (Narelle, 14 October 2023). Through our vulnerability and sharing of our journaling, the discourse sheds light on the evolving dynamics of collaboration within academic spheres, highlighting the challenges of adapting to new cultural norms and professional expectations while navigating institutional structures and identities in a new context (Narelle, 5 December 2023).

As we draw together our concluding remarks, we share key strategies that supported self-care and wellbeing during a time of change, and we share these in the hope that others may incorporate them into their own daily wellbeing and self-care practices.

1 Using digital platforms to foster continued social connections and relationships despite geographical and temporal distance.
2 Making intentional time each day for self-care and wellbeing practices through daily morning routines and mindful exercises.
3 Taking a pause when overwhelmed by engaging in self-care practices that foster and support creativity.
4 Journaling as a means of reflection.

This dialogical exchange underscores the intricate dance between continuity and change in academic life that comes with being a mobile academic, emphasizing the crucial intersection of self-care and wellbeing with the passage of time and rhythms of academic life.

References

Amaro, D., Caldeira, A. M., & Seabra, C. (2024). Exploring higher education mobility through the lens of academic tourism: Portugal as a study case. *Sustainability, 16*(4), Article 4. https://doi.org/10.3390/su16041359

Andresen, M., Pattie, M. W., & Hippler, T. (2020). What does it mean to be a 'self-initiated' expatriate in different contexts? A conceptual analysis and suggestions for future research. *The International Journal of Human Resource Management, 31*(1), 174–201. https://doi.org/10.1080/09585192.2019.1674359

Bennett, A., & Burke, P. J. (2018). Re/conceptualising time and temporality: an exploration of time in higher education. *Discourse: Studies in the Cultural Politics of Education, 39*(6), 913–925. https://doi.org/10.1080/01596306.2017.1312285

Bloomfield, S. (2020). *Give yourself margin: A guide to rediscovering and reconnecting with your creative self.* Andrews McMeel Publishing.

Farbotko, C., Dun, O., Thornton, F., McNamara, K. E., & McMichael, C. (2020). Relocation planning must address voluntary immobility. *Nature Climate Change, 10*(8), Article 8. https://doi.org/10.1038/s41558-020-0829-6

Frame, M. W., & Shehan, C. L. (1994). Work and well-being in the two-person career: Relocation stress and coping among clergy husbands and wives. *Family Relations, 43*(2), 196–205. https://doi.org/10.2307/585323

Franzoni, C., Scellato, G., & Stephan, P. (2015). *Global mobility of research scientists.* Academic Press.

Helin, J. (2016). Dialogical writing: Co-inquiring between the written and the spoken word. *Culture and Organization, 25*(1), 1–15.

Herschberg, C., Benschop, Y., & Van den Brink, M. (2018). Precarious postdocs: A comparative study on recruitment and selection of early-career researchers. *Scandinavian Journal of Management, 34*(4), 303–310.

Huang, F., & Welch, A. R. (2021). (eds). *International faculty in Asia: In comparative global perspective.* Springer.

112   *Narelle Lemon and Sharon McDonough*

Joshi, P. (2023). *Faculty transfer and its association with mental well-being in academia* (SSRN Scholarly Paper 4625461). https://doi.org/10.2139/ssrn.4625461

Lemon, N., & McDonough, S. (2020). *Building and sustaining teaching career strategies professional experience wellbeing and mindful practice.* Cambridge University Press.

Lemon, N., & McDonough, S. (2021). If Not Now, Then When? Wellbeing and Wholeheartedness in Education. *The Educational Forum, 85*(3), 317–335. https://doi.org/10.1080/00131725.2021.1912231

Lemon, N., & McDonough, S. (2023). "I Feel Like Nothing Else Will Ever Be This Hard": The dimensions of teacher resilience during the COVID-19 pandemic. *The Educational Forum,* 1–15. https://doi.org/10.1080/00131725.2023.2178564

McDonough, S., & Brandenburg, R. (2019). Who owns this data? Using dialogic reflection to examine an ethically important moment. *Reflective Practice, 20*(3), 355–366. https://doi.org/10.1080/14623943.2019.1611553

McDonough, S., & Lemon, N. (2021). Stepping into a shared vulnerability: Creating and promoting a space for self-care and wellbeing in higher education. In N. Lemon (Ed.), *Creating a place for self-care and wellbeing in higher education: Finding meaning across academia* (pp. 187–196). Routledge. https://doi.org/10.4324/9781003144397-17

McDonough, S., & Lemon, N. (2022a). Creating care-full communities after COVID: supporting care as a strategy for wellbeing in teacher education. In M. Shoffner & A. W. Webb (Eds.), *Reconstructing care in teacher education after COVID-19* (pp. 179–188). Routledge. https://doi.org/10.4324/9781003244875-20

McDonough, S., & Lemon, N. (2022b). 'Stretched very thin': The impact of COVID-19 on teachers' work lives and well-being. *Teachers and Teaching, ahead-of-print* (ahead-of-print), 1–13. https://doi.org/10.1080/13540602.2022.2103530

Nash, D. (1976). The personal consequences of a year of study abroad. *The Journal of Higher Education, 47*(2), 191–203.

Pace, C. R. (1959). *The junior year in France: An evaluation of the University of Delaware-Sweet Briar College program.* Published for Sweet Briar College by Syracuse University Press.

Richardson, J., & McKenna, S. (2002). Leaving and experiencing: Why academics expatriate and how they experience expatriation. *Career Development International, 7*(2), 67–78.

Richardson, J., & Zikic, J. (2007). The darker side of an international academic career. *Career Development International, 12*(2), 164–186.

Sagi, L., Bareket-Bojmel, L., Tziner, A., Icekson, T., & Mordoch, T. (2021). Social support and well-being among relocating women: The mediating roles of resilience and optimism. *Revista de Psicología Del Trabajo y de Las Organizaciones, 37*(2), 107–117. https://doi.org/10.5093/jwop2021a11

Shen, W., Xu, X., & Wang, X. (2022). Reconceptualising international academic mobility in the global knowledge system: Towards a new research agenda. *Higher Education, 84*(6), 1317–1342. https://doi.org/10.1007/s10734-022-00931-8

Smith, D. (2015). Exploring interprofessional collaboration and ethical practice: A story of emancipatory professional learning. *Reflective Practice, 16*(5), 652–676. https://doi.org/10.1080/14623943.2015.1071246

Sulaimanova, N., Csereklye, E., Győri, J. G., & Horváth, L. (2023). 'To go or not to go': Organizational determinants of academic staff participation in teaching mobility – a structural equation modelling approach. *European Journal of Higher Education.* https://www.tandfonline.com/doi/full/10.1080/21568235.2023.2294742

Teichler, U. (1996). Research on academic mobility and international cooperation in higher education: An agenda for the future. In P. Blumenthal, C. D. Goodwin, A. Smith, &

U. Teichler (Eds.), *Academic mobility in a changing world* (pp. 338–358). Jessica Kingsley Publishers.

Teichler, U. (2015). Academic mobility and migration: What we know and what we do not know. *European Review, 23*(S1), S6–S37. https://doi.org/10.1017/S1062798714000787

Townes Mayers, B. (2022). *Qualitative Case Study of Relocation Experiences of Active-Duty Military Families* [Doctor of Education, Northcentral University]. https://www.proquest.com/openview/808492e66e04f016324e19e65f9e6a67/1?pq-origsite=gscholar&cbl=18750&diss=y

Welch, A. R. (1997). The peripatetic professor: The internationalisation of the academic profession. *Higher Education, 34*(3), 323–345.

Williams, J., Ritter, J., & Bullock, S. M. (2012). Understanding the complexity of becoming a teacher educator: Experience, belonging, and practice within a professional learning community. *Studying Teacher Education, 8*(3), 245–260. https://doi.org/10.1080/17425964.2012.719130

Part 3

Time Investing in Self

116 *Time Investing in Self*

Embracing Balance: Nurturing Academia's Soul

Narelle Lemon

In academia's grip, where time's relentless churn,
Heavy workloads and stress so often burn,
Physiological strains, psychological plight,
As scholars toil through day and night.

Sharing our wisdom, a beacon bright,
In self-care's embrace, finding respite.
For time invested in nurturing the soul,
Is not a luxury, but a vital integration, worthy, ever so worthy.

Our insight, piercing and clear,
Reveals a truth we hold so dear,
Overwork, not passion, in academia's fold,
A system that neglects self-care, we're told.

In this intricate dance, where academia thrives,
We seek to understand, to thrive, to survive.
With nuanced eyes and hearts alight,
We forge new paths in scholarly flight.

For in this nexus of work and care,
Lies the key to a future fair,
Where academics flourish, hearts aglow,
In a culture of wellness, they'll proudly show.

DOI: 10.4324/9781032688633-13

11 In and out of Time

Practising Self-care When Leaving and Re-entering Higher Education

Charlotte Bilby

Introduction

It is not often that I am floored by a question, but this was such a shock that I felt my jaw gape, as though I was in a cartoon. I floundered for an answer. I was at an interview for a part-time research job in the voluntary sector: the first outside a university for 20 years. The organisation wanted someone to collect data from projects run to support people who encountered criminal justice agencies or needed additional help with managing sometimes chaotic lives. There was an understanding that employees' wellbeing was essential, primarily because of the challenging problems that might be disclosed.

I was asked how I practised self-care, and I did not know the answer.

Since the mid-1990s, my research has considered different elements of the criminal justice system in England and Wales. As part of a generation of criminological researchers who benefited from the 1997 to 2010 Labour governments' priority to evaluate the effectiveness of crime reduction and prevention policies, we were rarely short of research funding. At one point the money spilled over to teaching, with fully funded postgraduate opportunities for prison, probation and police officers who worked with sexual offenders. I managed a course, supervised research students, and taught the ever-increasing numbers of undergraduates, all looking to explore who commits crime, why they do it, and how they are punished, rehabilitated and failed by states and communities.

At the turn of the century, when going on a lot of 'mini breaks' with friends, it felt as though I could navigate my way to any self-catering cottage by the location of probation offices, community service workshops and prisons I had visited for work. My housemate stopped me watching *CrimeWatch*, a television programme dedicated to supporting the police solve often violent crimes with public tip offs, as he was unable to bear the running commentary on the 'sensationalised' cases explored. As you can begin to see, I was not good at developing healthy boundaries between work and time away from it.

This chapter explores my decision to leave a constantly pressurised university environment with high, and increasing student numbers and the need to research and publish, through a series of part-time roles, where the dysfunctional working practices of higher education were laid bare, to the consideration of my future

DOI: 10.4324/9781032688633-14

118 *Charlotte Bilby*

career and return to study. It explains how my understanding of time and self-reflection, a crucial part of my research focus, did not, while I was enmeshed in university life, provoke me to consider my own behaviour and wellbeing. It draws together criminological and design literatures, my 'old' and 'new' disciplines, to demonstrate how criminal justice researchers have begun to reflect on the emotional impact of their research and suggests tactics for a healthier return to work in higher education.

The chapter shows how I now understand the interview question posed, and what I would offer in response.

Visual Narrative

These three pieces are part of my doctoral work, *Keeping in touch*, that considers the aesthetics of care and harm in craft pieces made by women in and outside the criminal justice system (Figure 11.1). Here are two envelopes and one badge, made from fabrics, found objects, sewing and embroidery threads. While these were made as suggestions of the work I hoped to make with workshop participants, they have meaning beyond simply being samples. They have allowed me to reflect on

Figure 11.1 Three mixed-media, hand-crafted items: two envelopes and a badge. Made with hand and machine embroidery

In and out of Time 119

my own relationship with different concepts and theoretical positions about craft, care and harm, while introducing me to research through making practices (Durrant et al., 2017). Something that has reignited my joy in research.

Envelopes have multiple meanings. The enveloping care of a family, or the malign reach of a total institution (Goffman, 1961) depriving you of personal autonomy (Sykes, 1958). They can hold things of excitement and engagement, such as celebratory cards, or things of fear and worry – court summons, final demands for money or medical test results. These two envelopes show my frustration and burgeoning reconciliation with my ageing and recovering body.

The most influential reason for me leaving academia in 2019 was that two years previously I had been treated for breast cancer, including surgery, chemotherapy and radiotherapy. I collected the many appointment envelopes, all with the same institutional postmark: even now they provoke a surprising level of anxiety when the drop through my door. During the consultation when I was told the surgery has been successful in removing all the cancerous cells, my surgeon noticed I had become quiet and asked why. I was wondering when I could return to work. She, the two nurses and my mother all spluttered in disbelief, and gently suggested I may need a little more time to recuperate. I went back to work only a month after the end of active treatment and found my short-term memory was shot. I could not hold more than one idea in my mind at a time, and the abilities to multi-task and task-switch had disappeared too.

Now, years later, and following a medically induced menopause, changes to my memory continue to frustrate. After one bout of forgetfulness brought me to tears, I rage made the larger envelope from linen and cotton, with a machine embroidered faux address that includes an expletive. If you have never tried it, dropping the feed dogs on your sewing machine and going heavy on the pedal is recommended for exorcising frustration. The choice of a stitched paper aeroplane on an envelope suggests both the dynamic and friable nature of the objects, the memories and their meanings contained within.

The smaller envelope is made from mixed-media including found objects. It is an example of a craft approach to making; making use of the things to hand (Marshall, 2021). The motif in the middle is from a bright pink delivery envelope, which assured me of its environmental credentials. In the United Kingdom, the phrase 'old bag' is an insult for a woman in the later part of life, and this truncated message was a tense expression of my self-identity. While parts of me do not function as they originally did, I am deep in middle age and, post-pandemic, more attached to elasticated waistbands than expected, I do feel able to state my boundaries and reaffirm them without worry. I am near to a new 100%.

Yet, I still need courage that the badge brings. In the early part of my academic career, when carrying out evaluations for central government, I spent and wasted time writing long reports that clearly were not read or used. This exercise in futility has had a long-lasting effect on my ability to complete writing tasks. I often believe that writing is a chore, and waste time, putting it off, only then to find that my new disciplinary voice makes the process much easier and enjoyable. In Design, the critical friend and process are keys to crafting writing and provoking engagement with

120   *Charlotte Bilby*

others who are interested in your transdisciplinary thoughts and ideas. The badge is homage to these timely reflections. During the pandemic, artist Alinah Azadeh's healing activities for the Craft in Common project[1] included making 'medals for everyday courage'. She demonstrated how small medals could be made to send to loved ones, acknowledging their everyday acts at an extraordinary time. When I embarked on my doctoral research, I understood that my challenge might come from writing and 'showing up every day'. This small, hand embroidered pencil, on a piece of white and blue striped fabric, reminiscent of men's prison shirts, backed with felt and held in place with a safety pin, is my call to courage.

Doing Time Inside

Safely pinned with my medal of courage, this chapter includes criminological and design literatures exploring time, creativity and wellbeing. It will consider the different ways in which time is experienced in and outside prison, and how creativity and making enables us to spend and 'waste' time differently. Lastly, learning from academics from my first home discipline, who challenge the ways in which they do research, and ideas drawn from participatory design, I draw together elements important for me when preparing for change. I question whether the influences of neoliberalism, productivity and economic activity in higher education and prison robs us of opportunities to pause and reflect, both of which are critical to self-care and nuanced research.

Time is a peculiar concept in prisons. It ordinarily runs slowly; dragging until the time you are close to release. Earle (2014, p. 434) a former imprisoned man, now a prison researcher and founder of the ConCrim group,[2] explains that "prison is a place so removed from the rhythms of the social world that temporality … is heavily distorted". The women taking part in Chamberlen's (2017) research noted that while prison life is slow, the ageing impact on your own body feels accelerated. The stress and institutional carelessness of prisons (Crawley, 2005) has a significant impact on physical and mental health, and the "pervading sense of boredom and torpor" (Earle, 2014, p. 434) has the effect of temporal and corporal stasis.

Government prison ministers, the prison inspectorate and reform and campaigning groups acknowledge that time inside is not used well. A government paper referred to the "enforced idleness" of prisons (Ministry of Justice, 2011, p. 3), and while this language might be archaic, the effect is not. There are complex relationships between serving time and poor mental health, problematic substance use, regime rule breaking and violence, aggression. The 'purposeful activity' that prisons should provide or enable, whether through work, learning and training activities or hobbies, to challenge incarcerated torpor are not always available (HMCI of Prisons for England and Wales, 2022; Howard League, 2021), with their provision cut because of resourcing and staffing shortages.

Because prison deprives people of autonomy as well as liberty (Sykes, 1958), people who are imprisoned are not able to make positive choices about where and how to spend time, this is managed by the institution. Experiencing prison is living in a meantime, an interstitial time where everything is in a state of flux, and waiting is the norm (Bailey & Suddaby, 2023). It is a time when "we must live with confusion and make do with partial answers" (Akomolafe & Leberecht, n.d.). This expression of time, that is neither one thing nor another, is prevalent in prisons. Time and waiting are weaponised. The stretch of time allows imagination to wander, rumination to occur, and for people to build a picture of life outside where they are excluded. The institution also plays with time, with prisoners perpetually waiting for something to occur, yet hoping that it does not. James (2005), a journalist and former prisoner, notes that disruptions to prison routines causes disproportionate distress in an already stress-filled space.

Bailey and Suddaby (2023, p. 1033) associate reflection, wandering and meandering while looking for inspiration with meantime, and this is much more akin to my experience. My meantime was the space between leaving my full-time, secure job in a university and returning to a university as a postgraduate researcher. It included acknowledgement of the inspiration from the 'before times'. I regularly met former students at my new workplaces, and they would tell stories of how their jobs were fulfilling and the benefits of their degrees. If I had not taken time out of higher education, I would not have known the impact that my colleagues and I had.

The meantime is about waiting, experiencing neither one thing nor another, that is acknowledged as stressful, yet I found it a time to change and to make grand decisions about future plans. It was a positive experience that provoked excitement rather than anxiety. The change came after a meeting with a former student and friend, where we talked about her research methods and findings. I revelled in the discussion and exploration of theoretical positioning. It was at this point I understood that what I had been experiencing in my new jobs was transitory. The meantime allowed me to reconsider what I had enjoyed, what could nourish me in the future, and how a balance might be restored. My reflection required me to (re)consider my identity and my relationships with others.

Exploring temporality inside and outside does not equate my life experiences with those of people who have been criminalised and traumatised through harm they have experienced and enacted. Rather it is a conversation between familiar concepts and practices, and novel ones. This conversation takes me further to unpick how desistance from crime, a theoretical concept that explains how people change their own behaviour, helped me to enable changes in my own behaviour before I returned to a university setting.

Desistance involves changes to the way that people act, identify and relate to others (Nugent & Schinkel, 2016). Changing the way in which you act, which means stopping offending is considered the first step and often is the result of a trigger or hook for a desire to change. Identity desistance is about the way in which you understand and express your sense of self. Lastly, relational desistance explores how you fit within communities and how others react to you to form new relationships. This can also be related to the Good Lives Model, that explores people's primary needs in order to have a fulfilled (and crime free) life (Mallion et al., 2020). Desistance is not a linear process, and the research is littered with references to zig-zagging and diversions, which could also be considered as meantimes or waiting periods, of stopping and starting.

122   *Charlotte Bilby*

Returning to Toofast?

After the meantime, I applied to be a research student. During this process, I considered how to restart working in an environment that was both toofast and tooslow (Goodman & Manning, 2022). I use toofast to mean neoliberalism's drive for production and consumption, where things need to be completed with urgency, whether they are emergencies or not. This contrasts with Goodman and Manning's alternative toofast of "connecting to the bursts of liveliness" (p. 578), that seems vibrant and energising, and that I wanted to experience again as a research student. How then, to avoid the perceived, and actual, unproductive, 'unacceptable' behaviours of tooslow, that happen in the summer period after teaching and examining are finished? Exhaustion is the consequence of toofast. Here, tooslow is not an act of resistance or even one of self-care, rather a malignant wellbeing, where the body demands rest. The toofast renders us unable to find the capacity to write, research or do anything other than to recover in preparation for the next toofast.

Time inside prison is also toofast and tooslow. People are moved from prison to prison with little notice. Government policies are to be implemented immediately, and short- and long-term changes are made before and after the prison inspectors visit. Yet prisons also exist at a pace where new bedding to keep you warm from the bighting North East English cold finally arrives on the hottest summer day for many years. In prison, tooslow is not active, agentic resistance as might be practised in the face of institutional toofast. Tooslow is the manifestation of structural carelessness and is not supportive or beneficial. This tooslow does not help people travel through the prison gate; people are "thrust into a world that seems to be moving fast, and [experience] feeling out of kilter with it" (Doxat-Pratt et al., 2022, p. 4), posing danger and difficulties for settling into a different pace of living (McNeill et al., 2022) with new or altered communities.

Making Time Inside and out

Slowness, or as Goodman & Manning put it, trying to find the intersection between toofast and tooslow, is an increasingly considered element in craft and the slow stitch movement (see, for example, Wellesley-Smith, 2015). Slowness in making *is* resistance. Slowness can demonstrate a protest against consumption, but it can also be used to make things with which to protest, as can be found in the craftivist movement (Corbett, 2017). But if the slow stitch movement is about resisting the state of the modern world – that is speed with the attendant consumption – what role does slowness have in prison, where inertia is often the typical state, and how might this link to wellbeing and self-care?

Before I left higher education in 2019, my research focussed on the impact of creativity on reducing reoffending. Do painting, creative writing or embroidery stop people from committing crime again? How could they support self-management and the creation of a new identity, which are both important in cessation of offending?

In and out of Time 123

Arts and crafts practice have a long history within and prisons: from arts therapy, being used as regime compliance incentives (Bilby, 2014). If a prisoner takes part in an arts activity, they may then be allowed to rent a television from the prison (Bilby et al., 2013). Goffman (1961, pp. 67–68) described enjoyable events as, "little islands of vivid, encapturing activity" in the tedium of the prison day. My making interests are sewing and textiles, which have more complicated relationships with criminal justice systems. For example, in the 19th and early 20th centuries, imprisoned women in England were taught how to sew in order improve employment prospects post-release. In the contemporary Global South, women are 'rescued' from sex work by offering a sewing machine and suggesting that this work is a more acceptable way of making money. Prisoners who embroider soft furnishings for boutique hotels, hangings for heritage sites and work for internationally renowned artists,[3] speak of starting stitching for the wage it offers and continue because they find it a helpful and enjoyable way to pass the time inside. These examples tangle the links between making for pleasure and making for profit, via making for redemption or making for a new identity.

As noted above, doing something creative is associated with prison allowances, and making is also couched in terms of gaining qualifications and reducing reoffending (Ministry of Justice, 2014), rather than simply spending leisure time, as people in the community do. During an interview with a prison art teacher, I was told that the man who just wanted to sit in the art class, watch what others were doing, and read art history books was no longer allowed to attend because he was not engaged in a qualification course. His time was not his own to manage and leisure was not an option. It was a waste of time.

In the same group, men spoke of the impact that taking part in painting sessions had. One explained that sharing craft supplies was possible in prison where lending things usually came at a cost. Another said that time in art class could be used to work through his issues piqued by the mandatory offending behaviour programmes. A third, who had previously lent me a slashed, monochrome picture of a screaming zombie-like head to put in an exhibition, explained that he knew that if he could not decide what to include in his collage, it was an indication that he should not make any more important decisions that day. While wellbeing and self-care were not explicitly stated, it is clear that time spent in art classes offered allowed contemplation while doing something enjoyable.

Within wellbeing movements, there is a suggestion of the transformative powers of craft and making. I understand this and try to ensure that I make time each day to stitch or knit, as it calms and delights me. Sometimes, it helps to make sense of research processes and data. These are examples of Bryan-Wilson (2017) and Hemmings' (2018) assertions. Craft should not always be viewed as a reified form of activity. Sometimes the impact is small and is certainly unable to battle against the elements that cause myriad harms to people and non-humans. Making sometimes does not have the power, intention, or time to disrupt.

124   *Charlotte Bilby*

Going Back Inside

Craft had not disrupted my life, but it played a part, along with time to work through the chaos that illness had brought to my career. Once I had made the decision to return to higher education and secured a place that enabled me to research intersections between participatory design and making and criminology, I understood that this would come with continued challenges to my self-identity. I had anticipated that I would meet old colleagues and would have to negotiate our new relationships. I had not understood that many of them would set my student status aside and try to map our previous ways of working on to my new boundaries.

I believed that working in a different place and department would be beneficial, but what I had not expected was to be introduced to ways of working that so clearly fitted my (re)instated boundaries and consideration of how my time and energy should be spent. The feedback received on my research ethics application, questioned why nothing about my personal psychological care had been considered. Of course, my physical safety had been explored but I had not expressed how to deal with working in a prison for a prolonged period. Working in prisons was something that I had been doing for 20 years, and there had never been any discussion about this before. I knew that the journey home from a high-security prison would be past a shopping centre, where I would buy the pinkest thing I could find – often just a bag of jelly sweets shaped like pigs – but I had not explored *why* this was part of my routine. Now, guided by feminist and social justice design praxis, I express these elements of work that were not spoken of; how I silenced myself and the people who gave their time to take part in my research to fit in with a research orthodoxy (Ahmed, 2009) that demonstrates good results without the chaos or confusion of fieldwork.

Before I left academia, there was little work exploring how criminological research effected researchers' wellbeing. A handful of articles (see for example, Crewe, 2014; Farrant, 2014; Jewkes, 2012) highlighted the prison researcher's emotional labour, but the 2020 special edition of *Methodological Innovations* was devoted to this. While previous articles considered the ethics and morals of carrying out research with exceptionally vulnerable populations, this special edition considers how researchers might manage experienced emotions in the field. There is clearly a need to critically consider research carried out in unusual, powerful settings, with people who have harmed and have been harmed by others, while managing the demands of the neoliberal academy and world that exhausts the emotional labour of researchers. If you are swept up in the bustle and rush of researching and publishing favoured in some disciplines in some parts of the world, then finding the time to consider the impact of the work on your wellbeing is difficult.

Akama and Light's (2018) work draws these ideas together. They explore punctuation and poise, times and spaces where breaths need to be taken and directions changed. Their cross-cultural examination of the "boundless potentiality and imagination" (p. 7) of the in-between things, spaces and times is essential to their participatory design work. You privilege your readiness to become attuned to the needs of research participants, but also consider the importance of the elements that

In and out of Time 125

do not yet exist that might enable meandering towards new meaning. This finds the convergence between toofast and tooslow and points us to embrace the importance of waiting in the meantime, which should ensure that we recalibrate our relationships with work boundaries.

Concluding Thoughts

I am privileged to have had an interesting and purposeful career. I enjoyed teaching, but the support offered to students was diminished by stress, physical and emotional ill-health. Now, as a research student, I supplement my income by hourly-paid teaching, working from semester to semester, and am part of the higher education's precariat. Yet, I am free from administrative duties, the pressure to write a certain number of impactful articles per year, or to hit research income targets. I am careful to provide the support asked of me by students and colleagues, and because of my levels of experience, I can do that efficiently and effectively.

However, I need to remind myself regularly that I should not take on tasks not required of me, simply because I have the ability or time to do them. This is part of the self-imposed care package that I keep with me. But what would I offer in response to the interview question that sparked the self-searching? Rather than static answers, I continue to ask questions.

1   What will returning to a university offer you? It may not be possible to get past the question of keeping yourself fed and housed, but other jobs can offer that. Try to explore what needs a university post will fulfil. For me, it was about finding the intellectual joy in research and its theoretical underpinnings that I did not find elsewhere.
2   Can your ego manage a change in status? This took a great deal of introspection and repositioning, but releasing some responsibilities for things that you enjoy might counter this.
3   How will you protect yourself and your boundaries from encroachment of old pressures? Universities expect you to progress and apply for promotions, but do you have a plan for maintaining your position if you do not want to have more responsibility?
4   Is it possible to have an academic support group? In the past, the groups I have belonged to have not always nurtured the things important to me. They were often about staving off stress or discussing anxieties. The new groups I have found are supportive, invigorating, and challenging in equal measure.
5   With this in mind, can you go to other research groups or departments to find people who might have a different perspective on your work? The inter and transdisciplinary nature of research is encouraging. It asks questions of your entrenched positions that might set you off in new directions.

These questions require you to take some action to improve your self-care, much of which may be difficult to explore while in the business of a university career. But try to reflect and take a breath in the meantime.

126 *Charlotte Bilby*

Notes

1 https://vimeo.com/426232882?embedded=true&source=video_title&owner=1912844.
2 Within the British and American criminological societies, there are groups that support the work of formerly imprisoned academics. See for example https://concrim.org/about/british-convict-criminology/.
3 Fine Cell Work is a charity that teaches imprisoned people how to stitch. Work is then sold and proceeds divided between the maker, the charity, and victim-survivor charities. https://finecellwork.co.uk/.

References

Ahmed, B. (2009). Not telling it how it is: Secrets and silences of a critical feminist researcher. In R. Ryan-Flood, & R. Gill (eds.), *Secrecy and silence in the research process: feminist reflections*. Routledge: 96–104.

Akama, Y., & Light, A. (2018). *Practices of readiness: Punctuation, poise and the contingencies of participatory design*. Proceedings of the 15th Participatory Design Conference: Full Papers – Volume 1, Hasselt and Genk, Belgium. https://doi.org/10.1145/3210586.3210594

Akomolafe, B., & Leberecht, T. (n.d.). The power in losing hope. House of beautiful business. https://houseofbeautifulbusiness.com/read/the-power-in-losing-hope

Bailey, C., & Suddaby, R. (2023). When time falls apart: Re-centring human time in organisations through the lived experience of waiting. *Organization Studies, 44*(7), 1033–1053. https://doi.org/10.1177/01708406231166807

Bilby, C. (2014). Creativity and rehabilitation: What else might work in changing sex offenders' behaviour? In K. McCartan (ed.), *Sexual offending: Perceptions, risks & responses*, Palgrave McMillan: 189–205.

Bilby, C., Caulfield, L., & Ridley, L. (2013). *Re-imagining futures: Exploring arts interventions and the process of desistance*. Report for the National Criminal Justice Arts Alliance. http://www.artsevidence.org.uk/evaluations/re/

Bryan-Wilson, J. (2017). *Fray: Art and textile politics*. University of Chicago Press.

Chamberlen, A. (2017). Changing bodies, ambivalent subjectivities, and women's punishment. *Feminist Criminology, 12*(2), 125–144. https://doi.org/10.1177/1557085116689134

Corbett, S. (2017). *How to be a craftivist: The art of gentle protest*. Unbound.

Crawley, E. (2005). Institutional thoughtlessness in prisons and its impacts on the day-to-day prison lives of elderly men. *Journal of Contemporary Criminal Justice, 21*(4), 350–363. https://doi.org/10.1177/1043986205282018

Crewe, B. (2014). Not looking hard enough: Masculinity, emotion, and prison research. *Qualitative Inquiry, 20*(4), 392–403. https://doi.org/10.1177/1077800413515829

Doxat-Pratt, S., Schliehe, A., & Laursen, J. (2022). 'Thank you for having me': The experiences and meanings of release from prison in Norway and England & Wales. *Incarceration, 3*(2), 26326663221104996. https://doi.org/10.1177/26326663221104996

Durrant, A. C., Vines, J., Wallace, J., & Yee, J. S. R. (2017). Research through design: Twenty-first century makers and materialities. *Design Issues, 33*(3), 3–10. https://doi.org/10.1162/DESI_a_00447

Earle, R. (2014). Insider and out: Making sense of a prison experience and a research experience. *Qualitative Inquiry, 20*(4), 429–438. https://doi.org/10.1177/1077800413515832

Farrant, F. (2014). Unconcealment: What happens when we tell stories. *Qualitative Inquiry, 20*(4), 461–470.

Goffman, E. (1961). *Asylums: Essays on the social situation of mental patients and other inmates*. Penguin.

Goodman, A., & Manning, E. (2022). Social dreaming: Fabulating ecologies. *Qualitative Inquiry*, *28*(5), 578–585. https://doi.org/10.1177/10778004211065799

Hemmings, J. (2018). Rereading and revising: Acknowledging the smallness (sometimes) of craft. *Craft Research*, *9*(2), 273–286.

HM Chief Inspector of Prisons for England and Wales (2022). *Annual Report 2021–2022* (*HC 411*). https://www.justiceinspectorates.gov.uk/hmiprisons/wp-content/uploads/sites/4/2022/07/HMIP-Annual-Report-web-2021-22.pdf

Howard League (2021). *'Time well spent' in prisons*. https://howardleague.org/blog/time-well-spent-in-prisons/

James, E. (2005). *A life inside: A prisoner's notebook*. Guardian Books.

Jewkes, Y. (2012). Autoethnography and emotion as intellectual resources: Doing prison research differently. *Qualitative Inquiry*, *18*(1), 63–75.

Mallion, J. S., Wood, J. L., & Mallion, A. (2020). Systematic review of 'Good Lives' assumptions and interventions. *Aggression and Violent Behavior*, *55*, 101510. https://doi.org/https://doi.org/10.1016/j.avb.2020.101510

Marshall, J. (2021). *Crafting the commons and/or designing the commons?* https://commoners.craftspace.co.uk/research-network/crafting-the-commons-and-or-designing-the-commons/

McNeill, F., Thomas, P. C., Frödén, L. C., Scott, J. C., Escobar, O., & Urie, A. (2022). Time after time: Imprisonment, re-entry and enduring temporariness. In N. Carr & G. Robinson (eds.), *Time and punishment: New contexts and perspectives*. Springer International Publishing: 171–201. https://doi.org/10.1007/978-3-031-12108-1_7

Ministry of Justice (2011). *Breaking the cycle: Government Response* (CM8070). https://assets.publishing.service.gov.uk/media/5a7ac90be5274a34770e71cb/breaking-the-cycle-government-response.pdf

Ministry of Justice (2014). *Justice Data Lab Re-offending Analysis: Prisoners Education Trust Art and Hobby Materials*. https://assets.publishing.service.gov.uk/media/5a7ca242ed915d6969f46425/prisoners-education-trust-report.pdf

Nugent, B., & Schinkel, M. (2016). The pains of desistance. *Criminology & Criminal Justice*, *16*(5), 568–584. https://doi.org/10.1177/1748895816634812

Sykes, G. M. (1958). *The society of captives: A study of a maximum security prison*. Princeton University Press.

Wellesley-Smith, C. (2015). *Slow stitch: Mindful and contemplative textile art*. Batsford.

12 Overwork Is Not Evidence of Passion

Nicole Melzack

Introduction

While working in higher education we are told that it is a vocation, that we are driven by passion. While true, this is often used as an excuse to underpay, especially PhD students and those on casual contracts. It is used to justify the expectations to go 'above and beyond' contracted duties. This chapter explores what it means to weaponise our passion and how it has created a culture of overwork. As the topics discussed throughout this book are nuanced, words can have subtly different meanings and loadings. Therefore, this chapter begins with some definitions. The hope is that this chapter is understood as it was intended, that it is clear, concise, free from ambiguity – and a tool that enables reflection, action, and change. This chapter is specifically about the UK higher education and focuses on academic research and teaching staff as well as students.

The Collins dictionary states "If you have a passion for something, you have a very strong interest in it and like it very much" (Colins Dictionary, 2023). In this chapter, I would also expand this definition to encompass enthusiasm, excitement, and motivation. This can be applied to work in many ways: the topic we study (enthusiastic to learn and talk about our topic); the environment within which we work (motivated to exist in the academic culture, in our office; excited to talk to other people, to socialise, to be part of something collective); and the way in which we work (driven to change or foster strong relationships, support networks, inclusive understanding). The passion itself is often a strong internal driver for the things we do and brings us joy, as well as satisfaction within our lives.

When thinking of overwork, it can be split into both the practical and personal. Practically, overworking means working for more hours than you are either contracted to or have agreed (internally or externally) to. Personally, overwork can be seen as working at the detriment to other factors within your life (neglecting to eat properly, nurture relationships, look after our health), regardless of how many hours that is for. Personal overwork can be applied to both the time worked, as well as the emotional and mental component to overwork. If we work to the extent that we are too fatigued, distressed, or otherwise mentally overwhelmed that we cannot do the things in our lives that we both need and want to do – then we are overworking. We may only spend three hours on a piece of work, but if the topic is difficult,

DOI: 10.4324/9781032688633-15

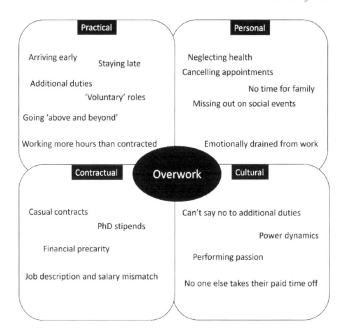

Figure 12.1 Non-exhaustive examples of practical, personal, contractual, and cultural overwork

draining, or distressing, this may be too much time, we may be overworking and be unable to cope for the rest of that day. In Figure 12.1, I provide my illustration of how overwork can present itself. We see overwork in academia encouraged through the culture and the contracts within which we work. It is interesting to note that the practical examples are often the addition of actions and extra responsibility, and the personal examples are a decrease in actions, and avoidance of certain responsibilities (such as having to cancel medical appointments). Throughout this chapter, both practical and personal overwork will be discussed and will be identified as such.

In more recent years, self-care has been seen as nice-to-haves, a warm bubble bath or a pamper session. However, the core meaning of self-care and its inception is based in the Black community, as it relates to meeting your basic health and well-being needs by yourself and within your community (Houseworth, 2021). Self-care refers to the maintenance elements of our day-to-day, looking after yourself that only you can do. This includes brushing your teeth, staying hydrated, following up on medical needs, and sorting out your financials. Treating yourself to nice things is great for wellbeing, but in this chapter, that is not what self-care refers to.

Exploring Academic Overwork

The Culture, Power Dynamics, and Overwork

Within any life situation, there are power structures. An employer and employee, a supervisor and supervisee, a manager, and their direct reports. It is also prudent

130   *Nicole Melzack*

to note that privilege outside of the workplace structure can bring power dynamics into the workplace, and academia too – popular and unpopular people, gender, race, sexuality, disabilities, social status, and even accents can all play into power structures and create dynamics which work to weaponise 'passion' and encourage overwork in an academic environment. The well-known adage of 'publish or perish' within academia further illustrates the pervasiveness of continual overworking. If an academic is not writing and publishing academic articles (which is often in addition to the research and teaching they do – practical overwork), then their career will stagnate (Nicholls et al., 2022).

Further, academia for researchers is full of competition. Competing for funding, grants, and awards. Being continually made to compete for these to maintain your job causes anxiety, fear, and overwork, impacting mental health and wellbeing. If your job depends on you securing a grant – you will work and work to ensure you get that grant (Danielle et al., 2014). Unfortunately, though, there is always something new to bid or apply for. So, this competitive undercurrent drives those in academia to push themselves more and more to be eligible for these awards. Within the constraints of grant applications and awards, future contractual overwork is often planned right into the request. Grant applications are costed based on the work required, then, through reviews, these valid costs are often deemed too expensive – the cost needs to reduce to get the funding. So, two posts become one, or roles are merged, principal researcher time is reduced, etc. If this grant is thus awarded, the contracts created and the expectation from everyone will already be 'above and beyond' what has been asked for – which is exactly what the academic culture makes acceptable. An ouroboros of overworked academic researchers.

The culture within the academic environment has been fostered with a historical, stereotypical worker in mind: The male academic, who is able to work long hours on their passions and intrigues with a wife at home looking after the children and the housework, who organises everything else so the male academic can focus on work. Although the demographics of the academy have changed (only slightly with 70% of professors in the UK identify as being male (HESA, 2022)), and academics often have many other responsibilities in their life on top of their research – those at the top, and those setting the standards, are often from the generation of 'kept men', and while these men do not recognise their privilege, they are in a position to demand the same working ethic as was expected of them. This expectation has a hidden support network embedded, support which many minoritised groups do not have. Therefore, many academics feel pressure to overwork, pressure to neglect their family, friends, caring responsibilities, and self-care, resulting in personal overwork, due to the culture. This pressure, whether it translates to neglect, can lead to increased anxiety. The pressure leads to guilt – both for neglecting their life outside research, and for not working enough on their research. When the power dynamics at play create an environment that takes 'passion' and morphs it into anxiety, we create an academic on the verge of burnout, unable to reach their potential and unable to truly enjoy their passion for research (Barkhuizen et al., 2014).

There is an expectation that if you are a cis white man in academia, you belong there. There is also an expectation that if you are anything else, that you don't belong unless you prove yourself (Savigny, 2014). This puts increased pressure on those who have been historically marginalised and minoritised, to perform passion and show you are 'just as good, if not better' than others in the academy. While in the UK about 15% people are black and 20%–25% have disabilities, only 3% of staff in UK universities are black, 6% have disabilities (HESA, 2022). As a minoritised person, you may also be asked to take part in a range of initiatives that aim to celebrate or encourage others like you in academia. You may be asked to give a talk on what it's like being you, doing your job (not actually about the work you do though). Women in STEM are often asked what it's like to be a woman in STEM; Black academics are often asked to talk about their experiences navigating a system that is, inherently, racist. You will be asked to do this, as an additional piece of work, for which you are unlikely to be paid extra or given any help with other commitments (overwork, by design). You will do this, you are told, because surely you are passionate at getting more people like you represented in academia. You will do this because this is important, not important enough to be paid for though. These initiatives that many minoritised people get pressured into doing perpetuate the inequity they aim to correct (Manzo et al., 2022). They take a marginalised person and further exploit them, specifically because they are marginalised. They put the work of making change on the people who are being oppressed. Most minoritised folk in academia want more representation, want to be considered on merit, and want to be treated equally. Of course they do. But weaponising this desire to further inequity is never okay, and yet it happens everywhere in academia and beyond. The overall structure and culture within academia remains set up for the cis straight white man, and until there are structural changes, there will always be pressure to overwork for anyone not holding those identities (Arday, 2021; Arday, 2022; Wang & Widener, 2019).

From X (formally Twitter) – which is itself a small, biased, sample – many examples of overwork culture have been shared. One tweeter discussed that while on maternity leave, they still worked on and submitted a paper, both they and their supervisor thought nothing of it. Later, when interviewed by the ATHENA Swan group (an organisation dedicated to ensuring inclusion and diversity), the committee were shocked that they were expected to work while on leave, although it is not uncommon (Maxwell et al., 2019). Another tweeter shared how they were often told that if you were passionate enough about the work, you won't experience burnout – yes, an academic deciding not to consult studies on how burnout manifests. Many shared how they found themselves working late, checking emails on weekends, and shared a general sense of unease when they were not working. Another tweeter told the story of a supervisor 'showing off' about their sleeping habits (only sleeping once every 48 hours) and how they were surprised when this was met with concern, not congratulations.

Many academics can revel in these identities, love to struggle through and see it as a rite of passage, or a badge of honour. They see it as their hard work being rewarded and that others should be doing the same. There is a toxicity in this view, as it only serves the few who survive, and those who do not make it, cannot take it, leave academia and so their voices are no longer heard. Those who see overwork

132   *Nicole Melzack*

as passion are the ones who stay in academia; subconsciously or otherwise, they want to re-create the conditions they succeeded in. If you make the game 'easier', create a less hostile culture, their win may feel less meaningful. This only serves to perpetuate the culture that you must overwork to succeed. Instead of asking 'who isn't in the room anymore, who left quietly and overwhelmed?', we continue to listen to those who survive through academia, while they claim they are thriving.

Contractual Overwork for Staff

In calling out the culture as a means of weaponising passion and encouraging overwork, universities and other institutions can easily dismiss this as specific to certain research groups or individuals and argue it is not a problem that exists at the higher levels. However, when we look at specific use of contracts (specifically in the UK), we can see that the written voice of these institutions also creates a culture of overworking. Over the last decade, there has been an increase in casual contracts for academics. This reduces the amount of full-time, salaried positions and replaces them with a culmination of smaller part-time fixed term positions to deliver very specific pieces of work. Over 66% of academic research staff and 45% of teaching staff are on these casual contracts in UK universities in 21/22 (HESA, 2022).

The University and Colleges Union (UCU) in the UK reports four key costs of casualisation – findings 3 and 4, lack of agency, and an inability to project into the future are major factors in causing overwork (Megoran & Mason, 2020). The financial precarity these contracts put people in, in addition to the stress involved in delivering work in a short period of time, strips people of their passion for the job and renders people tired, burnt-out, continually anxious for their future, and no longer able to find job satisfaction through their passions.

An example job listing posted on March 2023 at a top British university is for a 9-hour-a-week role lecturing in Hindi studies. This role requires four hours of teaching per week, with five hours remaining for preparing lectures, preparing coursework, marking work, organising tutorials, writing reports on student progress, preparing and delivering examinations including oral exams, conducting research in order to meet scholarship and professional development targets, as well as admin, office hours, serving on faculty committees and taking part in open days. Reading through the job description, you'd be forgiven for thinking that it sounds like an impossible amount of work given the contracted time, and you would be right. Imagine an academic requiring four such roles, potentially at different institutions, to make a full-time salary. This is contractual practical overwork; the role itself is asking for more time than it will pay for.

Even within full-time, open-ended contracts – the overwork is pervasive. The means of calculating workload often do not consider many duties. Mentoring, outreach, activism, time spent doing peer review, and often paper writing itself are not considered but are expected of academic staff. Thanks to the overwork culture baked into the system, this overwork is seen as normal. During 2019, the UCU participated in 'Action short of Strike (ASOS)'; this was defined as doing only what their contracted role was, for the time it was contracted for. To many people outside of academia, this does not sound like ASOS at all, it sounds like how many people behave at work. As a response to the ASOS, many universities threatened pay deductions, specifically for refusing to reschedule anything that was missed during ASOS (Chitty et al., 2019). The huge disruption caused by ASOS at universities is proof that overwork is baked into the contracts and is expected by many academics. Here, we see that the underlying culture and expectation of academia being a passion-driven vocation creates contracts that do not fully list the duties, because why wouldn't someone want to go above and beyond for something they are passionate about?

Often, the small benefits within our contracts that aim to give balance, such as paid time off, are not used. This is where culture takes precedent over the contracts, where the culture of practical and personal overwork lead to helpful contractual terms being unused. The implied view that if one is motivated and satisfied by their research, they shouldn't need time off. This can be seen as competitive suffering, the need to perform overworking, to show dedication to the job. Where most of a contract encourages overwork, having time off stipulated is counter intuitive, and often seen as a test, not a right.

Postgraduate Students, Research, and Overwork

In the UK, the annual stipend given to a PhD researcher in 2023 from UKRI (UK research and innovation) is £17,688. UKRI is the largest funder of PhD stipends in the UK, funding around 8000 studentships every year. This amount equates to about £340 a week, and, assuming a PhD researcher works 37 hours on their PhD each week, they are being paid £9.18 per hour – below minimum wage for the UK. Assuming a PhD researcher in the UK is worth about £15 per hour, they should be working about 22 hours a week and spend the rest of their time on other paid work. But how many of us know a full-time PhD researcher who spends 22 hours a week on their work. A 2005[1] in-depth study of postgraduate researchers in Oxford found that "28% spend 30 or less hours a week on their research, 43% spend between 31 and 45 hours, and 29% spend more than 45 hours a week on their research" (Trigwell & Dunbar-Goddet, 2005, p. 28). Further, this study found that those who spent less time on their research also felt less supported by their department and in their work. We would not expect that PhD students are valuing themselves below minimum wage – and they are not. The same study found that those who spent more than 30 hours a week on research saw their research as better than those who worked less. Therefore, working for more hours equates to a perceived increase in research value but an actual decrease in their hourly wage. This all shows quite clearly that however you look at it, PhD researchers in the UK are undervalued and overworked.

The PhD is meant to be an introduction into academic life, into research, academic writing, teaching, and, I suppose, the overwork culture. During a PhD, the student must keep a good relationship with their supervisor, as this is the person who approves your work and can help shape your future within the field. Because

134   *Nicole Melzack*

of this power dynamic at play, PhD students will find it hard to say no to their supervisor when new aspects of work are suggested, or when additional work is proposed. Often, a PhD student may find themselves supporting their supervisor in work unrelated to their project, be that in helping masters students or providing research and experimentation. This is done in addition to the work required for the PhD project and creates extra pressure on the student. Saying no to a supervisor may damage the relationship but will free up time to work on the PhD. Saying yes to a supervisor will improve the personal relationship, will show that you are passionate about the field of work, not just your PhD work. However, your own research, your personal life, and general wellbeing may suffer. The UK produced 26,980 PhDs in 21/22 (HESA, 2022), while many of them won't pursue further academic jobs, for those that do, the competition is fierce, and PhDs often find there are at least 250 applicants per job. Therefore, all the extra work, 'above and beyond' experience and other proof of passion feels necessary to have a chance at an academic career. But a career based on the unhealthy overworking ethic cannot be sustainable.

Those undertaking postgraduate roles also have practical overwork baked into their stipend agreements, setting students up to expect to be paid for a fraction of the work they do. This makes postdoctoral jobs acceptable within a framework of overwork. We see further that student advisors, who themselves were brought up in the same culture, see no issue demanding yet more work and unrelated work from their students – further squeezing the capacity of the student and leading them to neglect their self-care and wellbeing. PhD students have a high rate of depression and suicide in the UK with 40% of PhD students at risk of suicide (Hazell et al., 2021), and many cite the pressure to continually be working and performing passion as a major driver. Increased levels of anxiety and depression for PhD students was also found for those spending more time on their research per week (over 41 hours) (Berry et al., 2021). This culture is harming passionate academics. We need to change.

The Author's Perspective

We don't all have the same 24 hours in a day. As a disabled PhD candidate, I experience that first hand. I need to manage my energy, my symptoms, and of course, my work. I live with dissociative identity disorder (DID), I have chronic migraines, nerve damage, and I am autistic. These are all called invisible disabilities since they are not apparent at first glance. However, I can assure you they are not invisible to me.

One key impact of being disabled is that my time becomes limited. I lose time through medical appointments, through having migraines, through dissociating. I lose time through having to chase down medical tests or prescriptions. I lose time through needing to rest and recover from dissociative episodes. I also lose time talking to the university disability offices, requesting accommodations, chasing those accommodations, and complaining about my accommodations and access needs not being met – something felt by many disabled academics (Price, 2021).

Overwork Is Not Evidence of Passion 135

I also lose time talking about being disabled in academia and being disabled in STEM, because I feel guilty if I do not take these opportunities, as discussed earlier. Therefore, the amount of work I can do is time-limited for me. This does not stop me feeling pressure to work more, and even when I do push myself and overwork – I still work far less than many other PhD students. I struggle with this. In December 2020, my medication was unavailable, so I took two weeks off sick with debilitating anxiety and withdrawal symptoms. I felt guilty, I started thinking that a PhD wasn't for someone like me, that I would never make it in academia. I was lucky in that my supervisor was (and continues to be) supportive. We set long-term goals so that I do not feel pressured to get everything done at once. This doesn't always help – because I see other students, other researchers. I see them coming in on weekends to do experiments or staying late at the office reading paper after paper. Something I cannot do, something I know isn't sustainable for them, and yet something I feel jealous of, and guilty about.

On average, I spend about 30 hours a week on my PhD. It feels strange admitting that, like admitting a huge crime, making a terrible confession. I know if I push myself to work for longer hours, I risk my health but that doesn't stop the continual thoughts that I should be doing more. Heck, I'm writing this book chapter when my main research area is in batteries and energy storage. I am working on this because it is important, and because I am passionate about this topic – I am falling into the exact same way of thinking that this chapter presents. I exist within the overwork culture of the academy, I have internalised it, and in that, you get to read this chapter. Is that irony? I'm not sure. Is it okay? Probably not. Will it continue? Yes. Because my drive and motivation to make a difference in this space has led me to work for free, on a topic not related to my PhD.

Conclusions, Reflections, and Calls to Action

As we move forward, can we rethink our place of passion? Consider the reflection questions posed in Table 12.1.

Final Thoughts

The exploitation of passion transforms it into anxiety – the motivation and drive to perform is still there but it no longer comes from a place of excitement but a place of fear. The fear that others will not view them as passionate enough, that they are not performing their passion as well as others in their field (Hall & Bowles, 2016). But for passion to truly be explored and realised, for our wellbeing to be supported through our work, all other aspects of our lives need to be supported too. Creating an environment of overwork causes people to resent what they previously loved, leading to guilt and shame and a feeling of "I should be enjoying this, I'm spending all my time on a topic I am passionate about". This leads to burnout, mental health issues, and the loss of brilliant, brilliant people from academia.

136　*Nicole Melzack*

Table 12.1 Reflection questions

For everyone	Look at the figure for this chapter, do you recognise any of this in yourself? Can you talk to your peers (students, colleagues) about how you're feeling? Have you noticed your mood is tied to your work? Do you feel guilt when you are not working? Do you feel safe to talk to your supervisor/manager about this? If not, do you have someone you can talk to about this? Can you do less? Can you cut part of your project and still produce good work? Are you passionate about your topic? What do you need to help find that passion? How much time do you spend doing voluntary or additional roles? Are you neglecting yourself? Your wellbeing and your self-care?
For staff	Does your current contract reflect the work you do and the time you spend doing it? Do you know who to talk to if not? Are you taking your paid time off? If not, why not? Can you book something off now, even a half day? Are your colleagues on casual contracts? If so, how can you support them? Are you expecting your students to overwork? Are you assuming passion based on the time they spend working? Do you or your colleagues have marginalised identities? How can you be supported or support others to limit overwork?
For senior staff	Why are you reading this book, this chapter? What did you want to get out of it? Do you know how many members of staff are on casual contracts? How do you calculate workload for staff? How can you take account of 'extra duties'? Do you encourage others to take their paid time off? Do you judge staff based on their working hours, perceived passion, and eagerness to go 'above and beyond'? Are you asking for even more from your minoritised staff? How can you change the culture in your organisation?

Note

1 While this study is now nearly 20 years old, it is the most recent in-depth study found.

References

Arday, J. (2021). Fighting the tide: Understanding the difficulties facing Black, Asian and Minority Ethnic (BAME) Doctoral Students' pursuing a career in Academia. *Educational Philosophy and Theory, 53*(10), 972–979. https://doi.org/10.1080/00131857.2020.1777640

Arday, J. (2022). 'More to prove and more to lose': Race, racism and precarious employment in higher education. *British Journal of Sociology of Education, 43*(4), 513–533. https://doi.org/10.1080/01425692.2022.2074375

Barkhuizen, N., Rothmann, S., & van de Vijver, F. J. R. (2014). Burnout and work engagement of academics in higher education institutions: Effects of dispositional optimism. *Stress and Health, 30*(4), 322–332. https://doi.org/10.1002/smi.2520

Berry, C., Niven, J. E., & Hazell, C. M. (2021). Personal, social and relational predictors of UK postgraduate researcher mental health problems. *BJPsych Open, 7*(6), e205. https://doi.org/10.1192/bjo.2021.1041

Chitty, A., Callard, F., & Rocha, L. (2019). University management tactics on strike and ASOS pay deductions – and ways to push back. *USSbriefs, 87*. https://medium.com/ussbriefs/university-management-tactics-on-strike-and-asos-pay-deductions-and-ways-to-push-back-c23e9c296003

Danielle, L. H., John, C., Philip, C., Nicholas, G., & Adrian, G. B. (2014). The impact of funding deadlines on personal workloads, stress and family relationships: a qualitative study of Australian researchers. *BMJ Open, 4*(3), e004462. https://doi.org/10.1136/bmjopen-2013-004462

Hall, R., & Bowles, K. (2016). Re-engineering higher education: The subsumption of academic labour and the exploitation of anxiety. *Workplace*, 30–47. https://doi.org/10.14288/workplace.v0i28.186211

Harper Collins (2023). Passion, In *Collins COBUILD Advanced Learner's Dictionary* (10th Ed.)

Hazell, C. M., Niven, J. E., Chapman, L., Roberts, P. E., Cartwright-Hatton, S., Valeix, S., & Berry, C. (2021). Nationwide assessment of the mental health of UK Doctoral Researchers. *Humanities and Social Sciences Communications, 8*(1), 305. https://doi.org/10.1057/s41599-021-00983-8

HESA. (2022). 2021/2022 Statistics. *Higher Education Statistics Agency, HESA* www.hesa.ac.uk.

Houseworth, L. E. (2021). The radical history of self-care. *Teen Vogue*. Retrieved from https://www.teenvogue.com/story/the-radical-history-of-self-care.

Manzo, G., Piña-Watson, B., & Kim, S. Y. (2022). Minority stress and academic outcomes among ethnic minority college students: Anxiety as a mediating mechanism. *Journal of American College Health*, 1–8. https://doi.org/10.1080/07448481.2022.2128683

Maxwell, N., Connolly, L., & Ní Laoire, C. (2019). Informality, emotion and gendered career paths: The hidden toll of maternity leave on female academics and researchers. *Gender, Work & Organization, 26*(2), 140–157. https://doi.org/10.1111/gwao.12306

Megoran, N., & Mason, O. (2020). *Second class academic citizens: The dehumanising effects of casualisation in higher education.* Retrieved from https://www.ucu.org.uk/media/10681/second_class_academic_citizens/pdf/secondclassacademiccitizens

Nicholls, H., Nicholls, M., Tekin, S., Lamb, D., & Billings, J. (2022). The impact of working in academia on researchers' mental health and well-being: A systematic review and qualitative meta-synthesis. *PLoS One, 17*(5), e0268890. https://doi.org/10.1371/journal.pone.0268890

Price, M. (2021). Time harms: Disabled faculty navigating the accomodations loop. *South Atlantic Quarterly, 120*, 257–277. https://doi.org/10.1215/00382876-8915966

Savigny, H. (2014). Women, know your limits: Cultural sexism in academia. *Gender and Education, 26*(7), 794–809. https://doi.org/10.1080/09540253.2014.970977

Trigwell, K., & Dunbar-Goddet, H. (2005). The research experience of postgraduate research students at the University of Oxford. *Institute for the Advancement of University Learning*. 1–76, Oxford University.

Wang, L., & Widener, A. (2019). The struggle to keep women in academia. *Chemical and Engineering News, 97*, 19. Retrieved from https://cen.acs.org/careers/diversity/struggle-keep-women-academia/97/i19

13 Deep Dive on Boundary Setting

Time for Maintaining and Thriving

Mandy Dhahan

Imagine if you will, the sun is shining down on you (Figure 13.1). The faint sounds of cars start to fade. You are finally able to leave the hustle and bustle of the city behind and embark on a new adventure. It is as if time stops, even if it is only for a moment. You take in all the beautiful surroundings on your hike through the Tucson Mountains. There are magnificent Saguaros, which are native to the Sonoran Desert and belong to the cactus family (Arizona-Sonora Desert Museum, 2008), welcoming you and gazing down at you, all around you. There are uneven rocks beneath your feet, but it does not bother you too much, as you just keep walking. A bird is flying above you, and you notice a small clear cloud just on the horizon. You feel gratitude for the positive choice you made, something just for

Figure 13.1 Flourishing Tucson Saguaros, as photographed by M. Dhahan

yourself. A choice that was not graded or posted online, just something for you to feel peace.

The overwhelm of all that you must do, all that needs to be done is no longer in the forefront of your mind. I come to this trail as part of my self-care. I choose to slow things down here, and just breathe. Now I share this with you. I hope throughout this chapter you will learn not only how to set time aside for yourself, but a little bit about some of the lived experiences of the folks attempting to survive and thrive in the academy.

Introduction

When thinking about boundaries and self-care, it is tempting to envision calling off work or class and staying home. Brewing a nice warm cup of coffee/tea, while lying in a nice warm bubble bath, with your favorite music streaming in the background, as you drift away to your happy place. However, self-care is not a one-time act but a daily necessity. True self-care is internal and will not be soothed externally if not but for a temporary moment of bliss, like the first bite of your favorite dessert. While self-care is in all aspects of our lives, and we should be cognizant of the many ways we want to use it, this chapter is focused on making time for self-care as doctoral students of color in higher education, and how to maintain boundaries while doing so.

The educational journey can vary for those who are in it, as the foundation of higher education is filled with an elitist-exclusionary origin (Thelin, 2011), that has primed the path toward a new age of academic capitalism. The struggles doctoral students of color endure are often overshadowed by the meritocracy of higher education, attributing personal ambition above anything else, not considering the structural inequities and lived experiences of students of color. However, when we factor in intersectionality and consciously include the myriad of identities doctoral students embody, we must consider how it all fits into the academy. How are various doctoral students of color, who may be women, first-generation students, immigrants, English language learners, international scholars, anchored in diverse feminist ideologies received and represented? Subsequently, what can self-care and boundaries look like for this group? Using these questions as a guide, the literature was reviewed along with recommendations for interventions to support compassion, authenticity, and wellness for doctoral students and faculty alike.

Literature Review

Intersectionality is defined as, "The interconnected nature of social categorizations such as race, class, and gender, regarded as creating overlapping and interdependent systems of discrimination or disadvantage..." (in *Oxford Dictionary*, 2023b). Kimberle Crenshaw pioneered intersectionality because of the omission of oppression Black women faced in employment practices due to the segregation of their identities as either Black or Women, but not both – discounting double discrimination. Crenshaw (1991) builds off her notion of intersectionality

140 *Mandy Dhahan*

to include the "Need to account for multiple grounds of identity when considering how the social world is constructed" (p. 1245) as we are not one dimensional but are intertwined among individual and collective structures which can make some groups more vulnerable. For example, I am a part of the Asian race, when compared to others in the same racial category of Asian – which includes around 22 origin groups according to the 2021 Pew Center (Budiman & Ruiz), my experiences will be unlike those from a different origin group or gender, even though we may be in the same racial category. While there are similarities within a group, there will also be differences, and we must honor these considerations as when we do not, then people are not seen nor treated for who they are and risk generalizations and inequity.

The lived experiences of doctoral students are nuanced, and for doctoral students of color, there are multiple identities and subsequent choices that require time to assess. For instance, Zeligman et al.'s (2015) study exposed the additional barriers women of color contest with when considering higher education such as lack of representation, gendered pressure, and funding, and bell hooks (2014) also noted racial tension and less support for academic pursuits, which Ju et al. (2020) also concluded with the added pressure of "tokenism". Tokenism refers to "Rare persons of their demographic groups within the context, especially in contrast with majority, numerical dominants" (Flores-Niemann, 2016, p. 452). Being tokens can amplify differences and stereotypes of the group they represent, as well as positioning them as the go-to-for racial matters causing unfair power dynamics (Flores-Niemann, 2016).

Given the numbers, doctoral students of color are often in the minority and can fall into the token category and subsequently will have contrasting experiences from their white peers who belong to the majority in higher education. Zeligman et al. (2015) revealed "Racial minorities make up over 41 percent of the United States population. Despite this representation, however, they represent only 6.5 percent of those who earn doctoral degrees" (p. 67). With these stark numbers, the history and access of higher education need to be examined to better understand the intricacy of the system, especially within the framework of intersectionality. Utilizing Relational-Cultural Theory as a theoretical orientation can yield support for doctoral students of color and faculty to build safe spaces, mitigate feelings of isolation, and "othering".

History of Higher Education

John Thelin (2011) wrote about the transformation of higher education which links institutions of higher education as a symbol of success and as a timeless lure of a rite of passage. Furthermore, Thelin's research illustrates the university's prevalence in preserving colonialism. As a result, when non-White people such as Native Americans entered higher education, they had to choose between keeping or forsaking their cultural values and many other intersectional groups were not even allowed in Thelin (2011). The ethos of the academy remains intact, but the distribution of funding and principles changed drastically (Thelin, 2011).

Rise of Academic Capitalism

Garry Rhoades and Lesile Slaughter have written about academic capitalism and the impact it has had on faculty and students. For example, Rhoades and Slaughter (1997) argued less investment in retaining and supporting faculty manifested because of academic capitalism. Munch (2014) confirmed this notion as, "Researchers and teachers are no longer independent actors in this competition, but rather human capital..." (p. 49).

This shift has caused universities to disincentivize taking the necessary time to cultivate mentoring, teaching, and community among faculty as they are prompted to "publish or perish" (Ju et al. 2020). With the promotion of U.S. college score rankings, there is a culture that is to be maintained. There can be additional labor placed on faculty to become indispensable (Santa-Ramirez, 2022). Whereas before the demand of academic capitalism Munch (2014) asserted, there was a reciprocal process among the academic community, where faculty shared without quid pro quo. However, there is a *performance profile* to maintain which has fueled the scaling of research in such a way that it is being *quality controlled* through administrative means, which further exacerbates how time is spent in the academy, often rooted in survival (Munch, 2014; Rhoades & Slaughter, 1997).

Given the pressure faculty face, such as job security (Rhoades & Slaughter, 1997), their relationships with doctoral students can be unpredictable and unstable (Santa-Ramirez, 2022). Considering doctoral students of color experiences and subsequent compromising of roles and responsibilities, especially as tokens in some spaces, they would benefit from purposeful mentorship that is grounded in their intersectional identities and epistemologies (Ju et al., 2020; Santa-Ramirez, 2022).

Doctoral Students of Color Experiences

The intent of examining the transformation of the academy is to support doctoral students of colors' need for self-care, as higher education was not developed for them. Additionally, reflecting on how faculty may negotiate time, as their roles may be delegated, which may impact their presence. For example, Lee and Lenior (2016) share the experiences of immigrant Asian women who navigated higher education in the United States as they were outcasted due to their "othered" intersectionality accumulating from their citizenship to language acquisition while trying to teach and survive. The experiences of immigrants can vary, and many face the constant need to prove themselves (Lee and Lenior 2016).

Furthermore, lingering uncertainty can loom over the thoughts of many immigrant Asians, who endure stressors from xenophobia, acculturation stress, and gender stereotypes (Lee and Lenior 2016). Mlambo (2016) also confirmed this in their research and added that many international students rely on graduate funding and have pressure to perform as the tokens of their race. One Asian immigrant

142   *Mandy Dhahan*

woman graduate student shared their experience working with a faculty member who threatened their funding and made threats such as,

> I will stop your funding tomorrow…You can go home and visit your family. But my research cannot stop. If you go home, I will hire someone else to take your place. When you come back, there will be no more funding for you.
>
> (Lee & Lenior, 2016, p. 199)

The perpetual state of fear many students of color suffer is unfathomable, in addition to being constantly berated, they must come to terms with knowing their abuse can come from someone who is supposed to be a part of their support system. Moreover, being told you are not going to graduate, nor should you even be here, is something bell hooks (2014) endured during her graduate experience and when addressing it was met with colorblind responses – negating any attempts to foster justice. The power imbalances are rampant within the academy and adheres to a hierarchical structure that due to the nature of academic capitalism, can position some students to be viewed as *commodities* over learners (Rhodes and Slaughter, 1997), and when we factor in race and gender, it exacerbates stress for students of color – something their white peers do not often contend with (hooks, 2014; Mlambo, 2016). While not all students of color experiences are the same, they almost unanimously shared feelings of *isolation* (Ju et al., 2020; Lee & Lenior, 2016; Zeligman et al., 2015), *marginalization* (hooks, 2014; Ju et al., 2020; Lee & Lenior, 2016; Santa-Ramirez, 2022; Zeligman et al., 2015), and the need to validate their existence in higher education (hooks, 2014; Lee & Lenoir, 2016; Mlambo, 2016).

Hence, the framework of intersectionality, which can include gender, race, social class, citizenship, and sociopolitical values, ought to be holistically assessed and validated as people are not a one-size-fits-all clothing garment but highly complex individuals. For instance, Mlambo (2016) shares that in African feminism, women are honored as "superwomen" who can devote enough attention to what they need to do, while in American standards, Women are seen as "fragile" needing to forgo certain aspects of themselves to find true balance. While both perspectives can and do exist at the same time, Mlambo (2016) recommends faculty honor their students' personal boundaries and trust the discretion of their students' timelines and aspirations – instead of forcing students into one category. Nevertheless, this understanding takes time to fully develop and will demand faculty to take the time to consider how the intersectionality of their students will impact their graduate experience as well as how they can support students and not further perpetuate harm (hooks, 2014; Santa-Ramirez, 2022).

Doctoral students of color need access to diverse affirming mentoring as well as compassion as they face sociopolitical challenges and need intentional support that takes into consideration the power imbalances, racism, sexism, and token status they may encounter. For example, when I attended an awards ceremony at my previous graduate school, as excited as I was to be honored – that excitement dissolved when I was quickly and subtly power checked. While at the ceremony,

Deep Dive on Boundary Setting: Time for Maintaining and Thriving 143

I went to get food and was taking note of what foods were available before putting them on my plate, when a White woman immediately stopped me and roared, "The vegetarian food is on the other side" and it was said in such a condescending tone, that the impact "othered" me and invalidated my presence. The aim was to draw attention to the fact that I should not be allowed to freely roam around and pick what I want. The way microaggressions work are that they are so subtle, as they are "Brief and commonplace daily verbal, behavioral, and environmental indignities, whether intentional or unintentional, that communicate hostile, derogatory, or negative racial slights, and insults to the target or group" (Sue et al., 2007, p. 273). I was immediately dismissed, and not given the courtesy to exist as an awardee in a ceremony where I was invited to be honored. Furthermore, this White woman was a member of the faculty (while not anyone from my department), I did not witness her tell the other guests where the vegetarian dishes were – just me. Her behavior serves as a reminder that faculty are not immune to implicit bias and their impact can outweigh their intent.

Boundaries in Relation to Care

Tawwab (2021) shares how boundaries can bring feelings of "love, safety, respect" and peace. Yet, if we are told and made to feel that we *don't* **belong**, it may be more difficult to be vulnerable and stand firm in our boundaries, and as Tawwab (2021) proclaims, "Boundaries…are a safeguard to overextending yourself" (p. 8).

To maintain boundaries, the parameters must be specified. Thus, the definition of a boundary is "That which serves to indicate the bounds or limits of anything whether material or immaterial; also the limit itself" (in *Oxford Dictionary*, 2023a). Boundaries provide freedom, but when we are isolated, or set up to feel fear of losing our place in the academy, constantly pushed to prove our worth, and fight for our right to exist in academic spaces, that freedom quickly dissipates.

Boundaries are essential for self-care and shape roles in multiple relationships (Tawwab, 2021); in terms of academia, roles may be imposed or already established. Therefore, time is needed for graduate students of color to think about how their identity will be encouraged (hooks, 2014; Santa-Ramirez, 2022), as well as what parameters will be considered for culturally relevant mentorship (Purgason et al., 2018), especially as mentorship is an essential component of retention (Bril et al., 2014), and with the low numbers of doctoral students of color, there must be intentional support. Moreover, there are numerous factors to consider while working with doctoral students of color, especially as they may experience "Both overt and covert racism" (Ju et al., 2020, p. 585). For this reason, nurturing safe, authentic spaces is called upon as a foundation of self-care.

While the focus of this chapter is boundary setting, time for maintaining and thriving for doctoral students of color, the omission of faculty support is to do a disservice to the collective experience that is higher education, especially as faculty relations can deeply impact their students. Boundaries address acceptable and unacceptable behaviors, but they cannot exist in a vacuum and must be given time to be discussed without retribution, as perpetual states of fear and people

144 *Mandy Dhahan*

pleasing give rise to greater polarization of extreme boundaries (Tawwab 2021), which won't induce thriving. This chapter helps serve as a guide to consider how time can be used daily to develop and nourish boundaries while in higher education through the lens of intersectionality. For instance, Tawwab (2021) declares boundaries change as people move through different life stages. As such, when doctoral students of color move through their journey throughout higher education, it is vital to nurture true fellowship that extends beyond their first year. Hence, the theoretical orientation I am suggesting is Relational Cultural Theory to nurture and maintain cohesion among faculty and doctoral students of color.

Relational Cultural Theory

Relational Cultural Theory (RCT) is a counseling framework that is applicable to the relationships among faculty and doctoral students. For example, counselor-client dynamics are similar to faculty and doctoral student dynamics as faculty can be viewed as seasoned guides who can offer counsel in how to move through doctoral programs. RCT values individual lived experiences which are seen as assets rather than deficits which can springboard genuine healing (Frey 2013). Furthermore, RCT, "Posit that disconnections may occur as a result of relational interactions, racism, cultural oppression, sexism, and other social injustices" (Cholewa et al., 2014, p. 578). Restoration is possible through positive connections that acknowledge and honor one's identity, roots, and history, which flourishes when in community rather than isolation (Cholewa et al., 2014; Frey, 2013). Thus, providing space and time for faculty and doctoral students to discuss their lived experiences in the classroom through community circles in the notion of RCT framework supports holistic connections. As bell hooks (2000) profoundly stated, "Rarely, if ever, are any of us healed in isolation. Healing is an act of communion" (p. 215). As research has concluded, doctoral programs have increased feelings of isolation, and building intentional community can help unpack those experiences.

Community Circles as Groundwork for Connection

Feelings of isolation are notoriously felt in doctoral programs and can be higher for marginalized doctoral students of color (Zeligman et al. 2015). Often, one of the most crucial connections for doctoral students are faculty relationships and have been associated with academic completion (Brill et al., 2014; Purgason et al., 2018). However, as Gretzky and Lerner (2021) found in their study, faculty are promoted as "mentors" automatically and called upon to uplift student resilience but are not necessarily given the tools for it. There is a lot of pressure placed on professors to be mentors, but how often are professors trained or given the time on how to provide mentorship? In fact, as Parker-Jenkins (2016) found, faculty are usually assigned graduate students as advisees without student consultation.

Mentorship is the common factor among all doctoral programs that promote student success (Brill et al., 2014; Ju et al., 2020; Purgason et al., 2018; Zeligman et al., 2015). Moreover, mentorship for doctoral students of color has demonstrated

Deep Dive on Boundary Setting: Time for Maintaining and Thriving 145

an elevated level of belonging and self-worth (Purgason et al., 2018; Zeligman et al., 2015). Sharing experiences is vital, especially as doctoral students of color may endure several forms of microaggressions. Therefore, imagining classrooms as foundations for freedom, embracing vulnerability, and the soul (hooks, 1994) can manifest in higher education if we make the time for it, as demonstrated in Silverman and Mee's (2018) article, in their use of community circles. Community circles were a part of teaching pedagogy for aspiring teachers and were introduced to graduate students (Silverman & Mee, 2018). By utilizing meaningful community circle guides, which can consist of different prompts and activities that support getting to know one another as well as understanding values, and beliefs that embrace the essence of "wholeness" (hooks, 1994) through different modalities like storytelling, openness can be nurtured in such a way that students, "Felt safe voicing their thoughts with their peers…They liked realizing they were not alone in their emotions as they heard from one another during community circles" (Silverman & Mee, 2018, p. 4).

Edber (2022) also recommends using community circles as a part of building classroom culture, while their study was on implementation in primary and secondary schools, it can be intentionally adapted for higher education as was demonstrated by Silverman and Mee (2018). By implementing this practice, doctoral students will have more opportunities and time to purposely build fellowship as a form of self-care. Moreover, if students need to find mentors and/or change advisors, they may have a better sense of who they may align with after spending time forging deeper connections.

Choosing a mentor requires time to cultivate as some doctoral students of color have attested to feeling more comfortable with faculty from similar backgrounds; however, some have experienced harm if their intersectionality is invalidated (Santa-Ramirez, 2022). Furthermore, Parker-Jenkins (2016) and Purgason et al. (2018) recommend transparency regarding expectations from both mentors/mentees' roles, commitments, and modalities of accountability to sustain boundaries that support appropriate development.

Peer Networks

Peer to peer support has been shown to be effective for doctoral students (Brill et al., 2014) and faculty (Himelein & Anderson, 2020). Furthermore, Dollarhide et al. (2013) study on doctoral student development in counselor education recommended peer groups to honor students throughout the transitional stages of their program, as they gain more clarity on their roles. Additionally, connecting through peer networks may promote collegiality and address barriers to the "socialization" process through peer mentoring; confronting doctoral students challenges with racial/ethnic identity in academia (Ju et al. 2020). Peer networking provides opportunities for doctoral students to feel seen and serves as support for social-emotional and academic interventions (Brill et al., 2014). Moreover, Ju et al. (2020) advocates for peer groups that extend beyond doctoral programs and offers various suggestions such as "race-based campus organizations" to encourage inclusion and advocacy.

146 *Mandy Dhahan*

Himelein and Anderson (2020) found that faculty also face isolation in academia. Learning circles were instituted for faculty to support their teaching practices, in addition to reducing stress by providing time to talk through concerns with their peers, which subsequently led to increased feelings of belonging for faculty members who attended (Himelein & Anderson, 2020). Students and faculty should both receive multimodal levels of support through peer networks and community circles as self-care.

Daily Boundary Practice

Time management can be a common block for doctoral students. As Brill et al. (2014) reported, many doctoral students shared time management as being a contributing factor to their ability to persevere. Julia Cameron (2016) suggests implementing a daily practice of writing to encourage productivity and creativity which as a result can influence time management. For instance, she developed a program called *Artist's Way* and you do not need to be an artist to use any of her approaches. While her book has a recommended course, there are two interventions anyone can utilize.

The first recommendation she shares is called *Morning pages*, and this is where as soon as you wake up you write, and you write, and you keep writing until you have completed three pages. This writing does not need to be linear. The purpose as Cameron (2016) describes is to offer a "brain dump" so that you can eliminate unnecessary clutter in your mind and focus on what you need to. We must be purposeful, and dedicate daily time for writing, which is two-fold in that it offers time to let go and maintains a personal boundary for ourselves.

The second strategy Cameron (2016) recommends is a "Artist date" with yourself and only yourself. This can be anything that lights you up, with a dedicated time ranging up to two hours a week consistently – imagine it as your sacred time, serving to "refill your well" (Cameron, 2016). For example, the picture I shared for this chapter was of my artist date. By committing to these tools and strategies, you are making the time in your day to day, as well as weekly planning to maintain boundaries that support thriving and growth. Tawwab (2021) also recommends daily uninterrupted lunches to help protect your time to be present and renourish yourself. Additionally, her book, *Set Boundaries, Find Peace* provides many tools to consider in maintaining boundaries. Another great resource is the book written by Dr. Cloud and Dr. Townsend, *When to Say YES and When to Say NO, to Take Control of Your Life.*

Conclusion

While this chapter was a deep dive into boundary setting, the dive needed to first take place into the development of the academy to consider how limited time constraints may be imposed onto faculty due to profit quotas which may affect their relationships with doctoral students, moreover marginalized students of color. As such, time is needed to nurture fellowship, as well as to make space for self-care.

Deep Dive on Boundary Setting: Time for Maintaining and Thriving   147

Furthermore, time is required to mitigate feelings of isolation by first acknowledging structures through an intersectional framework, thus calling in and attending to systemic opportunities for allyship, including identity empowerment through an RCT theoretical orientation. Lastly, maintaining time for boundaries that uplifts the spirit from surviving to thriving.

References

Arizona-Sonora Desert Museum. (2008). *Saguaro Cactus Fact Sheet*. Desertmuseum.org. https://www.desertmuseum.org/kids/oz/long-fact-sheets/Saguaro%20Cactus.php

Brill, J., Balcanoff, K., Land, D., Gogarty, M., & Turner, F. (2014). Best practices in doctoral retention: Mentoring. *Higher Learning Research Communications*, 4(2). http://dx.doi.org/10.18870/hlrc.v4i2.186

Budiman, A., & Ruiz, G. N. (2021). *Key facts about Asian origin groups in the U.S.* Pew Center. Retrieved from: https://pewrsr.ch/2EoOpWe

Cameron, J. (2016). *Artist's way: 25th anniversary edition*. Penguin Books.

Cholewa, B., Goodman, R. D., West-Olatunji, C., & Amatea, E. (2014). A qualitative examination of the impact of culturally responsive educational practices on the psychological well-being of students of color. *The Urban Review*, 46(4), 574–596. https://doi.org/10.1007/s11256-014-0272-y

Cloud, H., & Townsend, J. S. (1992). *Boundaries: When to say YES when to say NO to take control of your life*. Zondervan.

Crenshaw, K. (1991). Mapping the margins: Intersectionality, identity politics, and violence against women of color. *Stanford Law Review*, 43(6), 1241–1299. https://doi.org/10.2307/1229039

Dollarhide, C. T., Gibson, D. M., & Moss, J. M. (2013). Professional identity development of counselor education doctoral students. *Counselor Education and Supervision, 52*(2), 137–150. https://doi.org/10.1002/j.1556-6978.2013.00034.x

Edber, H. (2022). Community circles in response to restorative justice research and critique. *Journal of Educational Research and Practice, 12*, 28–38. https://doi.org/10.5590/JERAP.2022.12.0.3

Flores-Niemann, Y. (2016). The social ecology of tokenism in higher education. *Peace Review*, 28(4), 451–458. https://doi.org/10.1080/10402659.2016.1237098

Frey, L. L. (2013). Relational-cultural therapy: Theory, research, and application to counseling competencies. *Professional Psychology: Research and Practice, 44*(3), 177–185. https://psycnet.apa.org/doi/10.1037/a0033121

Gretzky, M., & Lerner, J. (2021). Students of academic capitalism: Emotional dimensions in the commercialization of higher education. *Sociological Research Online, 26*(1), 205–221. https://doi.org/10.1177/1360780420968117

Himelein, M. J., & Anderson, H. L. (2020). Developing community among faculty: Can learning circles provide psychosocial benefits? *Journal of Faculty Development*, 34(1). https://link.gale.com/apps/doc/A622153394/AONE?u=uarizona_main&sid=bookmark-AONE&xid=5bf37799

hooks, b. (1994). *Teaching to transgress: Education as the practice of freedom*. Routledge.

hooks, b. (2000). *All about love: New visions*. William Morrow.

hooks, b. (2014). *Talking back: Thinking feminist, thinking black*. Taylor & Francis Group.

Ju, J., Merrell-James, R., Coker, J. K., Ghoston, M., Pérez, J. F. C., & Field, T. A. (2020). Recruiting, retaining, and supporting students from underrepresented racial minority backgrounds in doctoral counselor education. *Professional Counselor, 10*(4), 581–602. https://doi.org/10.15241/jj.10.4.581

Lee, P.-L., & Lenior, G. C. (2016). Asian foreign-born women scholars experience a triple threat to work-life balance. In K. C. Mansfield, A. D. Welton, & P.-L. Lee (Eds.), *Identity Intersectionalities, Mentoring, and Work-Life (Im)Balance: Educators (re)Negotiate the Personal, Professional, and Political (Work-Life Balance)*. (pp. 191–204). Information Age Publishing.

Mlambo, Y. A. (2016). Interrogating work-life balance discourses: An alternative explanation for Black African, female, international students in the United States. In K. C. Mansfield, A. D. Welton, & P.-L. Lee (Eds.), *Identity Intersectionalities, Mentoring, and Work-Life (Im)Balance: Educators (re)Negotiate the Personal, Professional, and Political (Work-Life Balance)*. (pp. 217–229). Information Age Publishing.

Münch, R. (2014). *Academic capitalism: Universities in the global struggle for excellence*. Routledge.

Oxford University Press. (2023a, August). Boundaries. In *Oxford English dictionary*. Retrieved August 23, 2023.

Oxford University Press. (2023b, August). Intersectionality. In *Oxford English dictionary*. Retrieved August 23, 2023.

Parker-Jenkins, M. (2016). Mind the gap: Developing the roles, expectations and boundaries in the doctoral supervisor–supervisee relationship. *Studies in Higher Education, 43*(1), 57–71. https://doi.org/10.1080/03075079.2016.1153622

Purgason, L. L., Lloyd-Hazlett, J., & Avent Harris, R. J. (2018). Mentoring counselor education students: A Delphi Study with leaders in the field. *Journal of Counselor Leadership and Advocacy, 5*(2), 122–136. http://doi.org/10.1080/2326716X.2018.1452080

Rhoades, G., & Slaughter, S. (1997). Academic capitalism, managed professionals, and supply-side higher education. *Social Text, 51*, 9–38. https://doi.org/10.2307/466645

Santa-Ramirez, S. (2022). Sink or swim: The mentoring experiences of Latinx PhD students with faculty of color. *Journal of Diversity in Higher Education, 15*(1), 124–134. https://psycnet.apa.org/doi/10.1037/dhe0000335

Silverman, J., & Mee, M. (2018). Using restorative practices to prepare teachers to meet the needs of young adolescents. *Education Sciences, 8*(3). https://doi.org/10.3390/edusci8030131

Sue, D. W., Capodilupo, C. M., Torino, G. C., Bucceri, J. M., Holder, A. M. B., Nadal, K. L., & Esquilin, M. (2007). Racial microaggressions in everyday life: Implications for clinical practice. *The American Psychologist, 62*(4), 271–286. https://doi.org/10.1037/0003-066X.62.4.271

Tawwab, N. G. (2021). *Set boundaries, find peace: a guide to reclaiming yourself*. TarcherPerigee.

Thelin, J. R. (2011). *A history of American higher education* (2nd ed). Johns Hopkins University Press.

Zeligman, M., Prescod, D. J., & Greene, J. H. (2015). Journey toward becoming a counselor education doctoral student: Perspectives of women of color. *The Journal of Negro Education, 84*(1), 66–79. https://doi.org/10.7709/jnegroeducation.84.1.0066

14 Self-care

A Guilty Pleasure or Required Academic Work?

Dangeni

Introduction

The impacts of academia on mental health are garnering increasing attention, both in scholarly research (Ayres, 2022; Buizza et al., 2022; Mackie & Bates, 2019) and everyday conversations (Mittelmeier, 2023; Shaw & Ward, 2014). Doctoral researchers have emerged as a focal point in this discussion. Pursuing a PhD can be a highly stressful endeavour, with both doctoral researchers and their supervisors expecting rigorous work, impeccable tasks, and effective time management (Appel & Dahlgren, 2003; Elliot et al., 2016a; Mackie & Bates, 2019). Academics, as a broader group, are also no strangers to mental health issues (Sakurai & Mason, 2022; Urbina-Garcia, 2020). Work demands, the increasing pressure to compete for research funding and publish in high-impact journals, a lack of work–life balance, isolation, career and financial insecurity, interpersonal conflicts, and a lack of support systems all contribute to a mental health crisis.

Habits, the keyword of this chapter, is defined as "something that you do often and regularly, sometimes without knowing that you are doing it" (Cambridge Dictionary, n.d.). When examining the habits of doctoral researchers and academics, the narrative often revolves around their successes and failures in completing academic tasks, such as research projects and publications. This is also reflected in the literature, where habit research has predominantly focused on formal academic contexts, such as study habits (i.e., activities undertaken by learners during the learning process to enhance learning). Examples of these study habits include planning, note-taking, concentration, and preparation (Bhat, 2016; Dey, 2014).

A cursory search of grey literature using keywords such as 'doctoral researchers', 'academics', 'PhD', and 'habit' in platforms like YouTube channels and blog posts reveals numerous resources and suggestions on the importance of habits for academic success. These resources often concentrate on the formal aspects of academic life, intensifying the perception that success in higher education (hereafter HE) necessitates the development of effective habits within a high-pressure environment, such as '3 habits that helped me finish my PhD'. However, it is imperative to acknowledge that informal, non-academic habits are equally indispensable for individuals within HE, including overlooked groups like doctoral researchers and early career academics. These informal habits serve as invaluable tools

DOI: 10.4324/9781032688633-17

150   *Dangeni*

for self-care and nurturing overall wellbeing (Ayres, 2022; Casey et al., 2022; Siddiquee et al., 2016).

By discussing and examining the intricacies of habits and their impact on our daily lives, particularly within the academic sphere, this chapter emphasises the significance of cultivating self-care habits and prioritising our wellbeing. It urges readers to reconsider how everyone could allocate time and energy, advocating for a healthier balance between personal care and academic pursuits. Reflecting on my experiences as a recently graduated international doctoral researcher and now as an early career researcher in various UK higher education institutions, this chapter delves into the realm of informal self-care practices and reflections. It explores strategies to alleviate the mental burdens, carve out time for self-care, foster supportive communities, engage with peers, prioritise physical health, and reflect on overall wellbeing. In particular, this chapter discusses the challenges that international scholars may face in developing self-care habits and the benefits of these habits for holistic wellbeing. The chapter concludes by offering self-reflection tools, including audio diaries and metaphorical drawings, encouraging individuals in HE to incorporate them into their self-care routines.

Navigating the Context for Cultivating Habits

Living and surviving in higher education can be taxing. Whether as a PhD researcher or an academic, the time and energy required for everyday work, such as managing the endless time and tasks and living with the common imposter feelings, can easily and naturally lead to a toxic working mode. We sometimes (and very often) fail to manage the time and tasks and struggle to take care of ourselves, both physically and psychologically (Ayres, 2022; Casey et al., 2022; Lau & Pretorius, 2019). PhD scholars, who are an important part of the academic community and contributors for society and economy (Hazell et al., 2020), have been extensively researched and identified as a cohort that experiences mental health challenges (Casey et al., 2022; Mackie & Bates, 2019). The stressors are multifaceted, for instance, transition to doctoral studies and being a doctoral researcher can bring concerns and uncertainties through unfamiliarity of the doctoral processes (Mackie & Bates, 2019) and the hidden curriculum, i.e., the various unintended, implicit, and hidden messages sent to students (Elliot et al., 2016b; Leask, 2009). For example, the supervisory relationship, networking, research skills, and even wellbeing can be stressful and demanding to grasp. Balancing personal life with academic/researcher life adds further complexity, including considerations of family and friends, financial circumstances, and relocation. Early career researchers (ECRs) and early career academics (ECAs) have been found to experience similar mental health issues related to wellbeing, burnout, and stress. They face added layers of stressors, including excessive workloads, job insecurity, teaching pressures, administrative burdens, leadership and management demands, all within the rapidly changing landscape of higher education settings (Sakurai & Mason, 2022; Urbina-Garcia, 2020).

Self-care: A Guilty Pleasure or Required Academic Work? 151

Furthermore, international PhD scholars and ECRs/ECAs experience 'otherness', awkwardness, and other difficulties (Elliot et al., 2016b) that have been explored and highlighted, including being thousands miles away from family and friends, and the demanding processes of becoming a researcher in a new academic environment using a foreign language, and working with culturally different expectations and requirements. The constant pressure to fit into their new roles can strain their wellbeing. Despite a growing body of literature emphasising the importance of coping strategies and self-care routines (Ayres, 2022; Moses et al., 2016), there remains limited understanding and reflection on how international scholars develop self-care practices, particularly in informal aspects.

Doctoral researchers often grapple with the feeling of never being free from their PhD work, espousing feelings such as, "research was always hanging over them and giving them a guilty conscience ... there is no clear dividing line between work and leisure time" (Appel & Dahlgren, 2003, p. 107). Though engaging in leisure activities has been observed to support mental health by promoting physical health, relieving stress, uplifting mood, and offering multiple identities (Begun & Carter, 2017; Hazell et al., 2020; Mackie & Bates, 2019), dedicating time to such non-PhD activities is often viewed as indulgent.

'Pick up a Habit': Cultivating Habits as an International Doctoral Researcher

Before embarking on a PhD journey in the UK, I pursued a master's degree in the UK with dedication. The brevity of the 12-month programme (a common duration of masters' programmes) left little room for self-care, and I was not even familiar with the concept of wellbeing. Given that it was my first time to study abroad, the short length and high demands of the master's programme left me fully immersed in the necessity to acquire essential skills and complete tasks in a foreign language and a completely new environment. I paid scant consideration to my wellbeing. Frankly speaking, I expected such an intense experience considering the financial and emotional investment my family and I had made towards this international journey. I thought, "I am here and I am supposed to experience these challenges". I vividly recall the tears shed during an exam period that demanded three written 4,000-word assignments in a single month. My self-doubt clashed with my identity as a high-achieving undergraduate. It was in a lonely transitioning stage when I was still in the process of finding a peer community where I could share my struggles and seek support. It was even harder to share these challenges with family, who were thousands of miles away from me and could only provide their unwavering belief in my ability to succeed.

It was not until I embarked on my PhD that I began to engage with discussions on mental health and wellbeing. I was introduced to helpful guides by my supervisor, such as *How to get a PhD* (Phillips & Johnson, 2022) and *The Unwritten Rules of PhD Research* (Petre, 2010), which helped me better understand this academic journey ahead. As I navigated relationships with supervisors, managed time and tasks independently, and sought opportunities for self-development, I grappled

152 *Dangeni*

with imposter syndrome and found myself spending excessive hours in the office and library. I felt guilty about taking weekends off, believing that my slower reading and writing pace, as an international student, placed me at a disadvantage. I believed I needed to spend as much time as possible to quickly familiarise myself with academic and research knowledge. This led me down a path where, paradoxically, the more I read, the more inadequate I felt as a doctoral researcher.

I proactively sought scholarly suggestions and searching for tips in grey literature (e.g., social media, webpages etc.) to see how others like me experienced and coped with similar struggles and challenges. One of the highlighted terms I found useful was "third space", which refers to a space for relaxation and recreation that engages learners and scaffolds learning, not oriented towards family, education, and work (Elliot et al., 2016b). The idea of having such a third space that engaged me in informal activities sparked my exploration into supporting my wellbeing and maintaining my mental health throughout my doctoral journey.

For example, while I was reading about potential research techniques to seek a nuanced understanding of participants' multifaceted and complex experiences for my PhD project, the methodological literature (e.g., Bell, 2010; Butler-Kisber, 2018) I read opened up a new world for me and encouraged me to try creative tools for self-reflections, not only as a researcher but also as some useful tools for my life. For example, I explored the use of audio diaries, i.e., using audio recording devices to record thoughts following reflection on personal aspects of life and stories (Dangeni et al., 2021), poetic enquiry (Butler-Kisber, 2018), visual methods, e.g., collage, photos, and images (Bell, 2010; Butler-Kisber, 2018). I started by using visually guided methods (which I will share in the end of the chapter), by drawing down and ordering the things I enjoyed most in non-academic life and life before the doctoral journey, keeping creative format of diaries to record my journey, and curating my reflections and thoughts.

Additionally, I made a deliberate decision to cultivate a habit. I explored informal and enjoyable activities that I could engage in regularly. I allocated a few time slots in my diary and ventured into trying different things. I started by blocking two to three 30-minute slots in my weekly schedule, allowing myself to pause and go for a walk. Seeking advice from peers who had embarked on their PhD journey before me, I inquired about activities they enjoyed, so I could get new ideas. I discovered a multitude of fitness classes at the university gym and, being in Scotland with its numerous natural wonders, I compiled a list of places as motivations for me to visit during the weekends and holidays (Visit Glasgow's Parks and Gardens – People Make Glasgow, n.d.).

Embracing the Habit: Reaping the Benefits of Self-Care Practices

At the beginning of 'in a self-care habit' stage, it was not easy to break away from my relentless pursuit of academic and research tasks to embrace self-care. I often found myself questioning whether I had done enough for the day or if I truly deserved a moment of relaxation, free from reading and writing obligations. Weekends, in particular, posed a dilemma. Was I entitled to take a day off when I could utilise that time to catch up on the work I had not completed during the week? It

Self-care: A Guilty Pleasure or Required Academic Work? 153

took courage and determination for me to combat these mental burdens to enjoy the habit, partly (and mainly) because I considered the PhD as the only and most important thing for the coming years.

The turning point arrived during the first dance class I joined at the university gym, an activity that initially carried a tinge of guilt. Although the class started at 4:30 pm, conflicting with my 9–5 routine, I made the bold decision to conclude my work at 4 pm that day, despite a mounting list of tasks awaiting my attention. From the outset, the dance class was a game-changer. The instructor's warm welcome and emphasis on enjoyment rather than perfection immediately eased my apprehensions. To my delight, I discovered that I was a quick learner, effortlessly following the steps, memorising choreography, and even outperforming my own expectations. This sense of immediate progress, witnessed in the mirror with a genuine smile, provided a refreshing contrast to the relentless pursuit of academic achievements. For the first time, my thoughts were free from PhD-related concerns. The engagement and motivation were invigorating, encouraging me to explore as many sessions as possible. Consequently, I attended all three weekly dance sessions provided in the gym, using them as motivation to maintain focus and productivity during office hours. I also introduced my doctoral colleagues to these sessions, and many continued to participate.

As my PhD journey progressed and my workload expanded, my appreciation for the time invested in the self-care habits deepened. The "guilt" that had plagued me gradually dissolved as I recognised the essential role of such "third spaces" in maintaining my mental and physical wellbeing. These activities not only kept me physically active but also cared for my psychological and emotional needs. With these newfound practices, I felt at ease exploring different activities, knowing that they were vital for my doctoral journey. I understood the necessity of incorporating self-care habits, whether through cooking a delightful meal, making a cup of tea, or taking comforting breaks. My perspective evolved, emphasising that the PhD is but a fraction of life, and to nurture it, we must care for ourselves and those around us.

Disrupted Habit During the Pandemic

The unexpected global pandemic struck during the final stages of my PhD. While some of my colleagues faced significant disruptions in their research projects, I considered myself fortunate as I focused on thesis writing in my studio rooms in the student accommodation. However, the anxieties triggered by the lockdown and the uncertainties in my home country and in the UK posed new challenges, particularly when my self-care routines were disrupted due to the closure of the university gym in line with government guidelines. I, like many international scholars, had to navigate ways to continue self-care routines within my confined living space alone. Fortunately, the gym quickly adapted to the new reality by offering online dance classes. This shift came with its own set of challenges. In an online setting, interactions with the instructor were limited to typed messages during water breaks. Despite these challenges, I found that the dance sessions continued to serve as a motivating habit, providing a semblance of normalcy during chaotic times. I also sought out other online resources, such as neighbour-friendly dance classes,

154   *Dangeni*

to maintain my routines. Upon the gym's reopening after the lifted lockdown regulations, renewing my membership was my first priority. It was so cherished to physically go back to the gym as a normal practice, meeting up with old dance mates and getting to know new people. I got the feeling that my PhD was also back in normal, and I could balance and manage it well.

With my PhD completed and a job offer accepted recently, I embarked on a new journey as an early career researcher in a different city. I have prepared my mind to explore a new context as a professional, inevitably experiencing rapid changes and identify shift (from a doctoral scholar to a professional). I value and deliberately plan my life in a new environment. My first action was to investigate the availability of fitness classes at the local gym and diligently slot those times into my diary to establish a new routine. Now, a year after, I never regret or feel guilty about the time I spend in the gym and other leisure activities. I can comfortably take weekends off. I also realised that self-care is even more essential in a 9–5 work pattern. The increased time spent in teaching, meetings, and administrative tasks meant longer hours at my desk. Consequently, I grew even more eager to return to the gym after a day of sitting. Three times a week, navigating local cafes and exploring a coastal town is always enjoyable and relaxing, and these enjoyable and personal moments became my cherished respite.

Conclusion

The journey I have shared in this chapter is a reflective account of my personal experience as an international doctoral researcher and an early career researcher in the UK. Through reflecting on the transformative power of self-care habits in mitigating the toll of academic stressors and enhancing overall wellbeing, I would love to highlight the importance of creating time and space for self-care. By sharing my experiences and the activities I found valuable and engaging, I hope to inspire international PhD scholars and ECRs to embark on a journey of self-care exploration. In the realm of self-care, there is no one-size-fits-all solution. What works for one may not work for another, and that is perfectly fine. The essence of self-care lies in discovering the habits and practices that resonate with us individually, both physically and psychologically. I encourage scholars, including doctoral researchers and early careers who share similar concerns and experiences of navigating new educational and cultural contexts, to embark on your unique self-care voyage, cultivate a habit, explore the practices, and prioritise your wellbeing in your academic and professional journey. Self-care is not a luxury but a fundamental requirement for anyone living in higher education. The slotted time for informal and non-academic habits could be the compass that guides us towards a balanced and fulfilling academic journey, ensuring that we flourish not only as scholars but also as individuals.

Potential Reflection Tools for Self-care Practices

For those who still grapple with the same nagging guilt as my former self, the initial step in nurturing self-care practices involves carving out time, space, and techniques for self-reflection. This process enables us to explore our feelings about our current

Description:

This activity is designed to help capture an in-depth reflection of your self-care practices, including the enjoyable moments and things in everyday life, and how you can create time and space to make these enjoyable moments happen continually, as part of your life routine.

What to do:

You are invited to draw your everyday life as a river and to imagine each bend (a curved part of the river) as a significant moment, person, experience that are enjoyable and had an impact on your wellbeing. Please don't worry about your drawing skills as this is an activity to help gain insight rather than your skills as an artist!

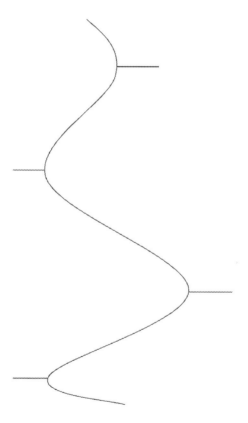

Figure 14.1 Rivers of wellbeing

life as a doctoral scholar, pinpoint potential stressors, and devise strategies to confront these challenges while embarking on the journey of cultivating self-care habits.

As previously mentioned, visual methods can be valuable and engaging self-reflection tools. It not only serves as a research technique but also encourages self-reflection. An example of such a technique is the "Rivers of Experience"

156 *Dangeni*

(Iantaffi, 2011), which involves drawing a river and associating each bend with significant factors at various stages of life and the academic journey (Figure 14.1). This could encompass aspects like the things that bring the most joy in everyday life, potential stressors and challenges in managing time and tasks, and the pivotal factors contributing to a content and stress-free lifestyle. This technique proves beneficial not just because it captures essential elements but also because the act of drawing and reflecting offers a meaningful space and experience. I would like to encourage you to give it a go by drawing your "River of Wellbeing", jotting down the enjoyable moments and things in everyday life, and reflecting on how you can create time and space to make these enjoyable moments happen continually, as part of your life routine.

Another technique is maintaining solicited diaries, i.e., diaries that are intentionally created for the purpose of research, reporting experiences and interpretations of events related to a particular research topic (Cao & Henderson, 2021; Hyers, 2018). One way of using it for self-reflections is to record 'what I enjoyed the most today/in this week', etc. This not only carves out dedicated time for self-reflection on self-care practices and wellbeing but can also become a habit that serves as a valuable outlet for everyday life. Diaries can take various forms, such as audio, photo, and video diaries, just tailor it to your preference and conducive to fostering reflection. Their feasibility, flexibility, and therapeutic power make them an accessible tool for self-care reflection.

References

Appel, M. L., & Dahlgren, L. G. (2003). Swedish doctoral students' experiences on their journey towards a PhD: Obstacles and opportunities inside and outside the academic building. *Scandinavian Journal of Educational Research, 47*(1), 89–110. https://doi.org/10.1080/00313830308608

Ayres, Z. J. (2022). Self-care: Without you there is no PhD. In Z. J. Ayres (Ed.), *Managing your mental health during your PhD: A survival guide* (pp. 41–60). Springer International Publishing. https://doi.org/10.1007/978-3-031-14194-2_4

Begun, A. L., & Carter, J. R. (2017). Career implications of doctoral social work student debt load. *Journal of Social Work Education, 53*(2), 161–173. https://doi.org/10.1080/10437797.2016.1243500

Bell, S. E. (2010). Visual methods for collecting and analysing data. In I. Bourgeault, R. Dingwall, & R. De Vries (Eds.), *The SAGE handbook of qualitative methods in health research* (pp. 513–535). SAGE Publications Ltd. https://doi.org/10.4135/9781446268247.n27

Bhat, Y. I. (2016). Social intelligence, study habits and academic achievements of college students of District Pulwama. *Research on Humanities and Social Sciences, 6* (7), 35–41. https://core.ac.uk/download/pdf/234675009.pdf

Buizza, C., Bazzoli, L., & Ghilardi, A. (2022). Changes in college students mental health and lifestyle during the COVID-19 pandemic: A systematic review of longitudinal studies. *Adolescent Research Review, 7*(4), 537–550. https://doi.org/10.1007/s40894-022-00192-7

Butler-Kisber, L. (2018). *Qualitative inquiry: Thematic, narrative and arts-based perspectives* (Second edition). SAGE.

Cambridge Dictionary (n.d.). Habit. In *Dictionary Cambridge.org.* Retrieved September 1, 2023, from https://dictionary.cambridge.org/dictionary/english/habit

Self-care: A Guilty Pleasure or Required Academic Work? 157

Cao, X., & Henderson, E. F. (2021). *Exploring diary methods in higher education research: Opportunities, choices and challenges.* Routledge.

Casey, C., Harvey, O., Taylor, J., Knight, F., & Trenoweth, S. (2022). Exploring the wellbeing and resilience of postgraduate researchers. *Journal of Further and Higher Education, 46*(6), 850–867. https://doi.org/10.1080/0309877X.2021.2018413

Dangeni, Lazarte, E. D., & MacDiarmid, C. (2021). Audio diaries: A creative research method for higher education studies in the digital age. In Cao, X & E. F. Henderson (Eds.) *Exploring diary methods in higher education research* (pp. 44–57). Routledge.

Dey, D. C. (2014). Effect of study habit on academic achievement. *Research in Humanities and Social Sciences, 2*(5), 101–105. https://www.raijmr.com/ijrhs/wp-content/uploads/2018/03/IJRHS_2014_vol02_issue_05_18.pdf

Elliot, D. L., Baumfield, V., & Reid, K. (2016a). Searching for 'a third space': A creative pathway towards international PhD students' academic acculturation. *Higher Education Research & Development, 35*(6), 1180–1195. https://doi.org/10.1080/07294360.2016.1144575

Elliot, D. L., Baumfield, V., Reid, K., & Makara, K. A. (2016b). Hidden treasure: Successful international doctoral students who found and harnessed the hidden curriculum. *Oxford Review of Education, 42*(6), 733–748. https://doi.org/10.1080/03054985.2016.1229664

Hazell, C. M., Chapman, L., Valeix, S. F., Roberts, P., Niven, J. E., & Berry, C. (2020). Understanding the mental health of doctoral researchers: A mixed methods systematic review with meta-analysis and meta-synthesis. *Systematic Reviews, 9*(1), 197. https://doi.org/10.1186/s13643-020-01443-1

Hyers, L. (2018). *Diary methods: Understanding qualitative research.* Oxford University Press.

Lau, R. W. K., & Pretorius, L. (2019). Intrapersonal wellbeing and the academic mental health crisis. In L. Pretorius, L. Macaulay, & B. Cahusac de Caux (Eds.), *Wellbeing in doctoral education: Insights and guidance from the student experience* (pp. 37–45). Springer Nature. https://doi.org/10.1007/978-981-13-9302-0_5

Leask, B. (2009). Using formal and informal curricula to improve interactions between home and international students. *Journal of Studies in International Education, 13*(2), 205–221. https://doi.org/10.1177/1028315308329786

Mackie, S. A., & Bates, G. W. (2019). Contribution of the doctoral education environment to PhD candidates' mental health problems: A scoping review. *Higher Education Research & Development, 38*(3), 565–578. https://doi.org/10.1080/07294360.2018.1556620

Mittelmeier, J. (2023, March 31). The glorification of overwork in academia and its impacts on our collective wellbeing by Jenna Mittelmeier. *Voices of Academia.* https://voicesofacademia.com/2023/03/31/the-glorification-of-overwork-in-academia-and-its-impacts-on-our-collective-wellbeing-by-jenna-mittelmeier/

Moses, J., Bradley, G. L., & O'Callaghan, F. V. (2016). When college students look after themselves: Self-care practices and well-being. *Journal of Student Affairs Research and Practice, 53*(3), 346–359. https://doi.org/10.1080/19496591.2016.1157488

Petre, M. (2010). *The unwritten rules of PhD research.* McGraw-Hill Education (UK).

Phillips, E., & Johnson, C. (2022). *How to get a PhD: A handbook for students and their supervisors 7e.* McGraw-Hill Education (UK).

Sakurai, Y., & Mason, S. (2022). Foreign early career academics' well-being profiles at workplaces in Japan: A person-oriented approach. *Higher Education.* https://doi.org/10.1007/s10734-022-00978-7

Shaw, C., & Ward, L. (2014, March 6). Dark thoughts: Why mental illness is on the rise in academia. *The Guardian.* https://www.theguardian.com/higher-education-network/2014/mar/06/mental-health-academics-growing-problem-pressure-university

Siddiquee, A., Sixsmith, J., Lawthom, R., & Haworth, J. (2016). Paid work, life-work and leisure: A study of wellbeing in the context of academic lives in higher education. *Leisure Studies*, *35*(1), 36–45. https://doi.org/10.1080/02614367.2014.967711

Urbina-Garcia, A. (2020). What do we know about university academics' mental health? A systematic literature review. *Stress and Health*, *36*(5), 563–585. https://doi.org/10.1002/smi.2956

Visit Glasgow's parks and gardens – People Make Glasgow. (n.d.). Visit Glasgow's Parks and Gardens – People Make Glasgow. Retrieved October 28, 2023, from https://peoplemakeglasgow.com/see-do/outdoor-activities/parks-gardens

Appendix
Titles in the Wellbeing and Self-care in Higher Education series

Wellbeing and Self-care in Higher Education:
Embracing Positive Solutions
Editor: Narelle Lemon

Healthy Relationships in Higher Education
Promoting Wellbeing Across Academia
Edited by Narelle Lemon

In this edited collection, authors navigate how they view relationships as a crucial part of their wellbeing and acts of self-care, exploring the "I", "We", and "Us" at the centre of self-care and wellbeing embodiment.

Creating a Place for Self-care and Wellbeing in Higher Education
Finding Meaning Across Academia
Edited by Narelle Lemon

In this edited collection, the authors navigate how they find meaning in their work in academia by sharing their own approaches to self-care and wellbeing.

Reflections on Valuing Wellbeing in Higher Education
Reforming our Acts of Self-care
Edited by Narelle Lemon

Designed to support readers working in higher education, this volume focuses on individual and collective practices of creativity, embodiment and movement as acts of self-care and wellbeing highlighting how connection to hand, body, voice and mind can be essential to this process.

Creative Expression and Wellbeing in Higher Education
Making and Movement as Mindful Moments of Self-care
Edited by Narelle Lemon

160   *Appendix*

This book focuses on the lived experiences of higher education professionals working in the face of stress, pressure and the threat of burnout and how acts of self-care and wellbeing can support, develop and maintain a sense of self.

Practising Compassion in Higher Education
Caring for Self and Others Through Challenging Times
Edited by Narelle Lemon, Heidi Harju-Luukkainen and Susanne Garvis

Presenting a collective international story, this book demonstrates the importance of compassion as an act of self-care in the face of change and disruption, providing guidance on how to cope under trying conditions in higher education settings.

Women Practicing Resilience, Self-care and Wellbeing in Academia
International Stories from Lived Experience
Edited by Ida Fatimawati Adi Badiozaman, Voon Mung Ling and Kiran Sandhu

Through a lens of self-care and wellbeing, this book shares stories of struggle and success from a diverse range of women in academia, illustrating the ways that higher education institutions can be more accommodating of the needs of women.

Writing Well and Being Well for Your PhD and Beyond
How to Cultivate a Strong and Sustainable Writing Practice for Life
Katherine Firth

Prioritizing wellbeing alongside academic development, this book provides practical advice to help students write well, and be well, during their PhD and throughout their career. Relevant at any stage of the writing process, this book will help doctoral students and early career researchers to produce great words that people want to read, examiners want to pass and editors want to publish.

Prioritising Wellbeing and Self-Care in Higher Education
How We Can Do Things Differently to Disrupt Silence
Edited by Narelle Lemon

This book illuminates international voices of those who feel empowered to do things differently in higher education, providing inspiration to those who are seeking guidance, reassurance, or a beacon of hope.

Sustaining Your Wellbeing in Higher Education
Values-based Self-Care for Work and Life
Jordan Cummings

Appendix 161

This book provides an evidence-based approach to sustainable self-care, anchoring these strategies in individual academics' core personal values. It teaches readers how to use their values to leverage self-care strategies into a workable, individualised, and effective map to wellness.

Exploring Time as a Resource for Wellness in Higher Education
Identity, Self-care and Wellbeing at Work
Edited by Sharon McDonough and Narelle Lemon

Bringing together international perspectives, this book demonstrates the importance of reframing time in higher education and how we can view it as a resource to support wellbeing and self-care. Whether it's making time, having time, or investing in time, this book explores strategies and reflections necessary to grow, maintain, and protect wellbeing.

Navigating Tensions and Transitions in Higher Education
Effective Skills for Maintaining Wellbeing and Self-care
Edited by Kay Hammond and Narelle Lemon

With a focus on skills development, this book provides guidance on how to navigate transitions between career stages in higher education and how to maintain wellbeing in the process. Written with all career stages in mind, this book will be an essential resource for new and experienced researchers alike.

Passion and Purpose in the Humanities
Exploring the Worlds of Early Career Researchers
Edited by Marcus Bussey, Camila Mozzini-Alister, Bingxin Wang and Samantha Willcocks

In the spirit of guiding emerging researchers in higher education, this book features twenty unique essays by emergent scholars who weave their personal lives into their research passions, offering a window into the experience of researchers in both professional and personal developments.

Supporting and Promoting Wellbeing in the Higher Education Sector
Practices in Action
Edited by Angela R. Dobele and Lisa Farrell

This book examines academic wellbeing from both institutional and individual perspectives, highlighting innovative approaches to support and promote the psychological health of faculty in an increasingly volatile higher education landscape. Featuring evidence-based practices and firsthand accounts, the book equips readers

162   *Appendix*

with practical ideas and strategies they can implement to become wellbeing champions within their own workplaces.

Understanding Wellbeing in Higher Education of the Global South
Contextually Sensitive and Culturally Responsive Perspectives
Edited by Youmen Chaaban, Abdellatif Sellami and Igor Michaleczek

This volume presents an alternative conceptualization of wellbeing in higher education, grounded in the socio-cultural context of the Global South. By delineating a contextually-sensitive and culturally-responsive perspective, the edited book challenges dominant Western notions of wellbeing and invites readers to explore the complexity and multi-dimensionality of this construct across diverse educational settings.

For more information about this series, please visit: www.routledge.com/Wellbeing-and-Self-care-in-Higher-Education/book-series/WSCHE

Index

Note: **Bold** page numbers refer to tables; *italic* page numbers refer to figures and page numbers followed by "n" denote endnotes.

Absent Body, The (Leder) 36
absented body 35–36
academic identity 4, 35, 110
academic time: conceptions of 16–17; notions of 4; as practice 19; practices 3
academic work 23; body awareness 36; care 6; individual understandings 21; individual wellbeing 8; lack of time 3; nature 7, 62; predictors 93; scheduled time 3; self-care 8; stress and pressure 62; women 34
accommodation 28, 29, 73, 103, 134, 153
acculturation 28, 30; acculturation stress 141
Action short of Strike (ASOS) 132–133
administrative duties 94, 125
ageing 5, 35–36, 38, 40, 119, 120
ageistic attitudes 35
Akama, Y. 124
Allison, S.T. 79
Ammigan, R. 30
analysis of variance (ANOVA) 97n2
Anderson, H.L. 146
annoyance 80, 83
anxiety 7, 28, 50, 80, 82, 84, 85, 119, 121, 125, 130, 134, 135, 153
artist date 146
Artist's Way program 146
assimilation 28
audio diaries 150, 152

Bailey, C. 121
Bailey, W. 28
balance: benefits 133; strategies 73, **74**; work-family life 91, 95; work-life 23, 35, 72, 75, 80, *89*

Bennett, A. 2, 3, 110
Bergson, H. 28
Bilby, C. 8
Billot, J. 34
Black community 129
body-based disciplines 37
Borromean rings theorem *37, 38*
boundaries 119, 124, 125; daily practice 146–147; personal 142; professional *vs.* personal life 91; relation to care 143–144; self-care 139; time management 51–52; work *vs.* private life 89
Bourdieu, P. 16
brain dump 146
Braxton, D. 7, 69
Brill, J. 146
Browning, L. 17
Bruno, N. 37
Bryan-Wilson, J. 123
Burch, T. 21, 22
Burke, K. 84
Burke, P.J. 2, 3, 110
Butler, J. 34, 35, 40

Callender, J. 29
Cameron, J. 9, 146
Campbell, J. 78, 84, 85
capitalism 139, 141
casualisation 132
Caulley, D.N. 78
Cavanagh, S.R. 63
Chamberlen, A. 120
changes: academic workload 95; advisors 143; culturally-based 28; health behaviour 36; higher education 62; life

164 *Index*

stages 144; motivations 39; pandemic and societal 77; people act 121; personal objectives 26; physical and cognitive 52; short/long-term 122; stock and integrate 20; structural 5, 54, 131; systemic 8; time allocation patterns 90–91; transnational cultural 26
childhood memories 31, 107
chronic disease self-management 36
Cloud, H.: *When to Say YES and When to Say NO, to Take Control of Your Life* 146
cognitive dissonance 48
collage reflection activity 85–86
Colley, H. 27
colonialism 2, 140
communication 3, 27, 28, 30, 50, 71, 72
communities of practice 28
community circles 144–146
constructive disruption: attachment 32; definition 25; international transitions 32; language 5; literature review 27–29; open-minded approach 32; personal and emotional adjustment 32; psychological and academic adaptation 32; reflection 29–31; social adjustment 32; visual narrative 26–27
consumerist approach 28
contemplative practices: connected literature 77–78; generative activities 85–86; *hero's journey* 78–85, *79*; multimodal literacies 77; self-care 77; visual narrative 79–80
contractual overworking staff *129,* 130, 132–133
corpse pose *see* Savasana
COVID-19 pandemic 6, 51, 62, 90, 91
Craft in Common project 120
The Creative Act: A Way of Being (Rubin) 83
creative analysis 78
Crenshaw, K. 139
CrimeWatch 117
criminal justice systems: complicated relationships 123; distorted working practices 8; elements 117; making time inside and out 122–123; prisons 120–122; visual narrative 118–120
cultural references 31
culture 5, 6, 8, 28, 31–32, 43, 53, 60, 65, 107, 109, 110, 128–135, 141, 143

daily boundary practice 146
Damasio, A.R. 36

descriptive statistics 93
Desikachar, T.K.V. 18
desistance 121
dialogical writing 103–104
digital platforms 110, 111
discounting double discrimination 139
discrimination 28, 49, 139
disruptions 25, 27–29, 32, 91, 121, 133, 153; *see also* constructive disruption
dissociative identity disorder (DID) 134
diversity 4, 28, 32, 53, 75, 131
doctoral students, color experiences 141–143
Dollarhide, C.T. 143
duo-ethnography 103–104, 110
Dutro, E. 77
Dweck, C.S. 22

Earle, R. 120
early career academics (ECAs) 149, 150
early career researchers (ECRs) 4, 16, 20, 150
Ecclestone, K. 27
Edber, H. 143
embodiment prompts 39–43
emotional experiences 63
English Education (Melanie) 60
enthusiasm 62, 103, 128
entrepreneurial self 21
Essentialism (McKeown) 51
Eteläpelto, A. 27
ethical approval 96
excitement 103, 105, 119, 121, 128, 135, 142
exhaustion 8, 103, 122
existential self-care 51

fatigue 40, 41, 82–83
feminism 142
fire: definition 68; experience burnout 68; goals 69; intentional strategies 68; literature 71–73; postpartum depression 70; self-care *69*
focus and balance strategies 73–74, **74**
Fortin, S. 37
found poetry reflection activity 86

gender stereotypes 141
Godard, H. 37
Goethals, G.R. 79
Goffman, E. 123
Good Lives Model 121
Gramsci, A. 36
Gretzky, M. 144
growth mindset 22–23

Index 165

habits 6, 7, 9, 31, 71, 104–109, 131, 149–154
Hattie, J. 22
healthy workplaces 35
Helin, J. 103
Hemmings, J. 123
Henderson, T.L. 71, 75
hero's journey (Campbell): adventure 80–81; creativity 81; home time 85; lightning 81; moments in time 82–83; outlook time thief 84; stages 78–79, *79*; story time 84–85; transformation setting 79; virtual conference 80
higher education (HE): academic research 128; African American women 75; changing university priorities 65; disruption (*see* constructive disruption); dysfunctional working practices 117–118; elitist-exclusionary origin 139; history 140; identity 4–6; industrialised and neoliberal approaches 9; injustice and oppression 1; intensification and care 6–7; passion 128; population 25; professors/teachers 47; self time investing 8–9; time conceptions 2–4; visual narratives 2; women faculty 77
Higher Education Statistics Agency (HESA) 27
Himelein, M.J. 146
homesickness 106
Hooks, B. 36, 140, 142, 144
Huopalainen, A.S. 73

identity: academic 110; agency 27; desistance 121; formation 4–5; person's behavior 28; professional 43, 48–50, 54; racial/ethnic 143; RCT theoretical orientation 147; self 119, 124; self-doubt 151; time 4–6
imagined career 19–20
imposter syndrome 71, 151–152
inclusiveness 75
industrialism 2
instrumental time 3
intensification 4, 6–7
intensified roles 96
interdisciplinary educator 40
internal authority 37
International doctoral researcher 151–152
international mobility 25, 30–31
intersectionality 9, 71, 74, 139–140, 142, 144
interstate dialogues: academic life 110–111; anticipation and enthusiasm

103; collaborative shifts 109–110; conversation live 103; daily routine 104–105; marital and familial bonds 102; new habits and routines 106–108; new job and place 105–106; poetic response, Instagram post *107*; rhythm 108–109; unfolding research and writing journey 103–104; vulnerability 102–103
invisible disabilities 134
isolation 7, 9, 21, 22, 28, 71, 75, 140, 142, 144, 146, 147, 149

James, E. 121
job crafting 5, *46*, 52, 54
job satisfaction: implications 90; outcome variable 100; paid and unpaid workload 89; during pandemic *89*; passions 132; subjective wellbeing 90; time allocation 6
job security 52, 54, 141
Jones, H. 27
Journal of Virginia Science Education (Angela) 60
Ju, J. 140, 143

kinaesthetic sense development 37

language processing, slower rate of 28
Lash. S. 3
Leavy, P. 78
Leder, D.: *Absent Body, The* 36
Lee, P.-L. 141
Lemon, N. 2, 4, 6, 8, 77; Navigating Academia's Labyrinth: Time, Identity and Wellbeing 4
Lenior, G.C. 141
Lerner, J. 144
Light, A. 124
Loomes, S.L. 29
Lorde, A. 62
Lovely Ladies Days 65

Maddox, C.B. 18
Mäntylä, H. 3, 17, 18
marginalization 142
market-oriented techniques 17
Marques, S. 35
master task list 52–53
maternity 70, 72, 73, 131
mattering 49, 63
McDonough, S. 77
McGarvey, A. 28, 32
McNaughton, S.M. 34
Mee, M. 143

166   *Index*

Melzack, N. 8
mental health 8, 30, 49, 54, 63, 70–73, 75, 80, 120, 130, 149–152
mental health continuum model 50
mentors 31, 54, 75, 79, 82, 85, 144
mentorship 9, 71, 143, 144–143
Methodological Innovations 124
microaggressions 143, 143
migration 102
mind body 37, 38
mindful time management 5
Ministry of Health (MoH) 36
mixed-media, hand-crafted items *118,* 119
Mlambo, Y.A. 141, 142
mobility: academic staff 102; international 25, 30, 31; migration 102; social and psychological dimensions 102
Morning pages 146
motherhood 70, 75; academia roles 73; and graduate students 72–73
motivation 21, 39, 51, 84, 128, 135, 153
Müller, R. 21
Multimodal Reflective Memoir 85
multiple regression models 93, **94–95**
multistage cluster sampling 92
Munch, R. 141

Nagy, J. 21, 22
Navigating Academia's Labyrinth: Time, Identity and Wellbeing (Lemon) 4
neoliberalism 120, 122
neoliberal systems 3
non-hierarchical movement theories 37
non-productive time 3
non-work strategies 63

occupational satisfaction 94
Oddell, J. 2
O'Dwyer, S. 59, 65
off-campus 64–65
Olsen, A. 40, 41
on-campus 64
Osbaldiston, N. 3
outcome variable 100
overworking: contractual staff 132–133; culture and power dynamics 129–132; emotional and mental component 128; final thoughts 135; non-exhaustive examples *129*; perspective 134–135; postgraduate students and research 133–134; reflection questions **136**
Owens, A.R. 29

parenting 71, 72
Parker-Jenkins, M. 144, 143
participatory design 124
Pavani, F. 37
peer networks 143–146
pendulation 18
perseverance 5, 40, 41, 43
personal autonomy 119
personal development 31, 53
personal resilience 59
Pho, H. 32
physicality 82
Poehler, A. 66
positioning wellbeing 62–63
power dynamics 129–132
power imbalances 142
pracademics 21
precarity of performativity 35
predictor variables 100–101
prisons 17, 117, 120–122, 123, 124
professional identities 5, 47–50, 54, 110
pronunciation 30
psychological pharmaceutical interventions 36
Purgason, L.L. 143

qualitative research reports 78
Quebec educational system 5
Quinn, B.P. 18

race-based campus organizations 143
racial minorities 140
racism 142–144
Reaves, M. 7
Reclaiming Embodiment of my Academic Time through Yoga Practice (Walker) 4
reflexive methodology 5
relational cultural theory (RCT) 9, 140, 144
resilience 5, 29, 40, 41, 43, 59, 72, 102, 144
Rhoades, G. 141
rhythm 7, 65, 108–110, 120
River of Wellbeing *155,* 156
Rivers of Experience technique 156
roles: academics activities 3, 35; administrative 91–94; family/life 72; health behavioural change 36; intensified 96; motherhood in academia 73; multiple relationships 143; part-time 117; postgraduate 134; practicing self-care *69*; women faculty 77; work/ life 72
Rose, R. 85

Rubin, R.: *The Creative Act: A Way of Being* 83

Satama, S.T. 73
Savasana 20
Schartner, A. 32
self-acceptance 28
self-awareness 5, 28, 59
self-care *89*; academia 8–9; benefits 152–153; black feminist 49; boundaries 139; competency 59; contemplative practices 77; definition 29; disrupted habit during pandemic 153–154; existential 51; habits 149–151; HE (*see* higher education (HE)); hormonal cycles 51; informal practices and reflections 150; international doctoral researcher 151–152; pedagogical skills 50; personal and structural considerations 7; potential reflection tools 154–156; practices 5, 8; researcher 50; stressful situations 49–50; systemic discrimination and oppression 49; teacher educators 77; time management 8; toolkit 5; transformative power 9; *see also* wellbeing
self-compassion 5–6, 28
self-determining modes 39
self-discovery 25
self-equilibrium 28
self-esteem 48
selfhood in health 35–36
self-identity 48, 119, 124
self-love 28
self-management 49–51, 54
self-preservation 62
self-reflection 156
self-reflexive approach 38
self-regulation 28
self-searching 125
Seligman, M. 54n1, 140
sensationalised cases 117
Set Boundaries, Find Peace (Tawwab) 146
sexism 142, 144
sexual offenders 117
Shaffer, D.K. 18, 20
Shapiro, L. 36
Sharif, R. 28
Silverman, J. 143
Simon-Kerr, J.A. 36
Slaughter, S. 141
slower pace 6, 106
slowness 17, 122

slow science 17
social culturalist 36
social imagination 78
socialization 143
social justice 36
socio-cultural approach 28
somathodology 5, 38
somatic activity 39–40
somatics 36–38
space-time 3
Spearman, C. 93
Spearman correlation test 97n1
Spry, T. 77
stealing time 17
strategies: academic life 5; collective 53–54, **74**; decision-making 36; focus and balance 73, **74**; health care 36; importance 151; individual and collective 7; intentional 63, 68; mental burdens 150; non-work 63; off-campus 64; practical 1; self-care 72, 75; self-management 50; time management 3, 47, 48, 52–53
subjective wellbeing 90
substantive time 3
Suddaby, R. 121
Supratman, A.M. 28

Tawwab, N.G. 143, 144, 146; *Set Boundaries, Find Peace* 146
temporal prisons 17
Thelin, J.R. 140
Thomson, P. 20
time: academia 16–17, 19; adaptation and connection 110–111; allocation patterns 6–7, 90–91, 93; attuning 23; community 21–22, 23–24; conceptions 2–4; current moment 20–21; definition 17–17; ECR 16; freedom failure 22–23; identity 4–5; imagined career 19–20; individual output 21; making inside and out 122–123; non-productive 3; self-care and wellbeing 1; self investing in 8–9; sense of enjoyment 16; shifting narratives 18–22; spent as practice 22; wasted 18–19, 120; yoga mat *15*
timeless time 3, 19
time management 3, 5, 9, 47; collective strategies 53–54; individual strategies 52–53; job crafting 52; priority and boundary management 51–52
timescape 2, 3

168 *Index*

time screw 17
tokenism 140
token status 142
Townsend, J. S.: *When to Say YES and When to Say NO, to Take Control of Your Life* 146
transitions, identity and agency 27
transnational cultural change 26
Tucson Saguaros Mountains 138, *138*
Twitter 131

unfamiliar paradigms 28
United Nations Department of Economic and Social Affairs (UNDESA) 35
University and Colleges Union (UCU) 132
university family 77
university research professionals 47

viparita karani 18, 20
visiting 31, 61–62, 65
visualizing wellbeing 60–62

Walkington, L. 72
walkography 82, 85
wasted time 18–19
wellbeing *89*; academic work 6; and alignment *26*; creativity 120; faculty 59, 66; family members 102; individual and collective 1, 6; institutional context 66; institutional spaces 59; malignant 122; movements 123; off-campus 64–65; office respite *61*; on-campus 64; personal interactions 60; positioning 62–63; prioritising 150; respite as 63–65; subjective 90, 91; visualizing 60–62; *see also* self-care

Wellbeing and Self-Care in Higher Education: Embracing Positive Solutions 2
wellbeing science 60
wellness 34, 35, 62, 89, 91, 139
When to Say YES and When to Say NO, to Take Control of Your Life (Cloud and Townsend) 146
wholeness 143
withdrawal symptoms 135
Wolff, M. 78
women academics 71; administrative responsibilities 94; data 92; ethical approval 96; financial satisfaction 93, 95; funding 96; job satisfaction *89*, 89–90, 96; literature review 91–92; methodology 93; pandemic 90; professional and personal responsibilities 90; recommendations 96; results 93–96; time allocation patterns 90; transitioning 34; workload predictors 94; workplaces 34
work demands 65, 149
worker voice and equity 63
work-life balance 35, 75, 80, *89,* 149
work-life harmony 63
workload models 16–17, 19, 23, 35, 77, 93

xenophobia 141

Ylijoki, O.H. 3, 17, 19
yoga 4, 5; definition 17–19; early classes 21; experience 21; instructors 19; mat *15*; teacher training 21
Yoga Sutras of Patanjali 19

Printed in the United States
by Baker & Taylor Publisher Services